Jonathan Fruoco
Chaucer's Polyphony

Research in Medieval
and Early Modern Culture XXIX

Studies in Medieval
and Early Modern Culture LXXV

Jonathan Fruoco
Chaucer's Polyphony

The Modern in Medieval Poetry

ISBN 978-1-5015-2727-2
e-ISBN (PDF) 978-1-5015-1436-4
e-ISBN (EPUB) 978-1-5015-1404-3

Library of Congress Control Number: 2020940971

Bibliographic information published by the Deutsche Nationalbibliothek
The Deutsche Nationalbibliothek lists this publication in the Deutsche Nationalbibliografie;
detailed bibliographic data are available on the Internet at http://dnb.dnb.de.

© 2022 Walter de Gruyter GmbH, Berlin/Boston
This volume is text- and page-identical with the hardback published in 2020.
Cover image: traveler1116/DigitalVision Vectors/© Getty Images
Typesetting: Integra Software Services Pvt. Ltd.
Printing and binding: CPI books GmbH, Leck

www.degruyter.com

To Aurélie,
Allas, that I ne had Englyssh, ryme or prose, suffisant this flour to preyse aryght!

Preface

It is hard to believe I started working on this project so many years ago. I initially became interested in the polyphony of Geoffrey Chaucer's poetry back in 2010 when I thought that a PhD in medieval literature would be a good way to spend my time. I had no idea this particular subject would keep on haunting me even after I successfully defended my dissertation in 2014. What started as the simple academic exercise of a student in his early twenties turned into the main obsession of the young scholar in his early thirties, and I am now glad to see my polyphonic quest come to an end in the form of this *litel bok*.

Although this volume is based on my doctoral dissertation, it has been largely rewritten, corrected, and modified to take into account the many things I have had the chance to learn from the scholars I met over the years. I could not have written this book without their input and encouragement.

I would like to start by thanking the late Professor Mohamed Benrabah who inspired me and encouraged me to go into academia – most of the elements developed in the first chapter of this book are the result of his teaching. I would not be who I am today if he had not nurtured my interest in the evolution of ancient languages and I will forever be grateful to him and forever regret that he did not live to see this book published.

My understanding of the intricacies of language studies has been greatly refined by the help of Professor Noam Chomsky, whose assistance was of great value in the early stage of my dissertation. I must also thank Professor Tom Shippey for his support over the years, for his encouragement, and for having generously shared with me both his knowledge and copies of his work.

I also need to thank the New Chaucer Society, which has been and will continue to be my intellectual family: Professors Paul Strohm, Jane Chance, Neil Cartlidge, Ruth Evans, Candace Barrington, Yoshiyuki Nakao have all been friends and colleagues; they have welcomed the lone medievalist that I was into the Chaucer family and have helped me at one point or another. I will always be grateful to them.

Most of you know how difficult it is to write a doctoral dissertation. I would probably never have started mine without my supervisor, Professor Denis Bonnecase. When no one wanted to take in the only student interested in medieval English poetry at our university, Professor Bonnecase, who specializes in Romanticism, welcomed me into his research team. His trust and advice allowed me to find my way into academia.

Friends and family – too many to name – should also be thanked for their continuous support and encouragement.

This book would not exist without the wonderful work of the people at Medieval Institute Publications and De Gruyter. Shannon Cunningham had the curious idea, when we met in Kalamazoo in 2017, that I might write something of interest – I certainly hope I did and thank her for giving me this fantastic opportunity.

Last but not least, my thanks go to Ms. Aurélie Manzato for her unconditional love and support. Her curiosity and patience are to be praised: not only has she accompanied me to conferences around the world, but she listened to me talk about my work even when *I* did not know what I was talking about.

Jonathan Fruoco
Chambéry, France
May 2020

Contents

Preface —— VII

Notes on the Texts and Translations —— XI

Abbreviations of Chaucer's Works —— XIII

Introduction —— 1

Chapter 1
Polyphony and Multilingualism in Medieval England —— 19
    England in the First Days of Old English —— 24
    Norman Invasion, Multilingualism, and Chaucer's English —— 27

Chapter 2
***Fin'amor, Stil Novo*: Chaucer's Early Influences —— 37**
    Chrétien de Troyes and the Novelistic Genre —— 38
    From Chrétien to the *Roman de la Rose* —— 45
    Dolce Stil Novo —— 55
    Chaucer's First Influences —— 61

Chapter 3
Narrative Evolution and New Discursive Strategies —— 65
    The Book of the Duchess —— 66
    The House of Fame —— 74
    From *Anelida* and *Arcite* to *The Parliament of Fowls* —— 88

Chapter 4
***Troilus and Criseyde* and the Ambiguity of Double Enunciation —— 95**
    Reprocessing Boccaccio's *Filostrato* —— 96
    Double Enunciation: Introducing Dante in *Il Filostrato* —— 101
    Dialogism and Mediation —— 112
    Resisting Closure and Refusing Judgment —— 119

Chapter 5
Hybridization and the Legend of Chaucer's Inventiveness —— 127
    Dream Vision and Narrative Poetry —— 130
    The Legend of Good Women and Chaucer's Exercise in Style —— 136
    Counterbalancing Pathos with Comedy —— 147

From Parody to Irony —— 154
Narrative Posture and Ironic Conclusion —— 160

Chapter 6
Extradiegetic Dialogue in *The Canterbury Tales* —— 167
General Prologue: Characterization, Drama, and the Theatrical —— 170
Dialogism in *The Canterbury Tales* and the Chaucer Pilgrim —— 177
Extradiegetic Dialogue —— 181

Conclusion —— 205

Bibliography —— 209
Archival Sources —— 209
Primary Sources —— 209
Secondary Sources —— 210

Index —— 221
Names and Works —— 221
Themes and Concepts —— 226

Notes on the Texts and Translations

The references to Chaucer's poetry all come from the *Riverside Chaucer*, edited by L.D. Benson and F.N. Robinson (1987). Likewise, the quotes from the *Divina Commedia* are taken from the edition introduced by Bianca Garavelli and annotated by Lodovico Magugliani (2008), while their translations in English come from Allen Mandelbaum's translation (1995).

The version of the *Aeneid* used is the one edited by Maurice Rat (1955) for the Latin text; the English translation comes from Frederick Ahl's edition (2007). The extracts from the *Decameron* come from Vittore Branca's 1998 edition.

The passages from the *Roman de la Rose* can be found in Armand Strubel's edition (1997), while the quotes from *Érec et Énide*, *Cligès*, *Le Chevalier au lion*, and *Le Chevalier de la charrette* are respectively taken from the editions of Jean-Marie Fritz (1992), Daniel Poirion (1994), Michel Rousse (1990), and Catherine Croizy-Naquet (2006).

Finally, one note about Bakhtin in English. I have, whenever possible, attempted to use the official English translation of his books—see for instance *Problems of Dostoevsky's Poetics* and *Rabelais and His World* (both published in 1984). It was, however, impossible to locate English versions of *Esthétique et théorie du roman* and *Esthétique de la création verbale*. In those cases, I used the French editions, quoted the text in French, and gave my own translation in the notes.

The source of all the other texts is clearly indicated in the "Primary Sources" section of the Bibliography. All the translations, unless otherwise mentioned, are the author's.

Abbreviations of Chaucer's Works

The abbreviations follow those used in *Studies in the Age of Chaucer*.

BD	*The Book of the Duchess*
CkT	*The Cook's Tale*
CT	*The Canterbury Tales*
GP	*The General Prologue*
HF	*The House of Fame*
LGW	*The Legend of Good Women*
Mel	*The Tale of Melibee*
MerT	*The Merchant's Tale*
MilT, MilP	*The Miller's Tale, The Miller's Prologue*
MLT	*The Man of Laws's Tale*
PardT, PardP	*The Pardoner's Tale, The Pardoner's Prologue*
PF	*The Parliament of Fowls*
TC	*Troilus and Criseyde*
Th	*The Tale of Sir Thopas*
WBT	*The Wife of Bath's Tale*

Introduction

Geoffrey Chaucer is in many ways the most modern of medieval poets. Remembered soon after his death as a great philosopher and craftsman of *fin'amor*, his importance in literary history became such that he began to be considered as the father of English literature. Indeed, his decision to start writing in his native language at a time when Latin and French dominated the intellectual, diplomatic, and religious spheres allowed Middle English to assert itself and absorb new ways of thinking, thus following a European dynamic and cultural tradition. If we were to embrace the Romantic terminology, then Chaucer could be defined as one of the *génies-mères*[1]—a title notably conferred by Chateaubriand on Dante—whose influence gave birth to the literary traditions of their respective countries. This notion allowed the Romantics to look back at the past and realize that the works of Homer, Rabelais, Chaucer, and Dante (to name just a few) contain the seeds from which grew the literature of the following centuries: just as Virgil lit Dante's way in the *Divina Commedia*, these *génies-mères* illuminate the path future generations have to tread. For as Chaucer himself reminded us in *The Parliament of Fowls*, "out of olde bokes, in good feyth, / Cometh al this newe science that men lere" (24–25).

It is however still very difficult to study Chaucer without losing sight of what he really represented to his contemporaries. The concepts of modern criticism, inherited from the conventions of the previous centuries, tend to assign the Chaucerian canon values and expectations that would have been completely foreign to the poet himself. Each period thus focuses on a different Chaucer: while some celebrated the greatness of his poetry of courtly love, others denounced the frivolity and ribaldry of his lines, remaining insensitive to the poet's humor. Just as Hamlet recommended that actors hold "the mirror up to Nature" (Act 3, Scene II), Chaucer seems to reflect the qualities of each reader and of their time, allowing us an almost constant rediscovery of his literary production. But in some cases, the past "threatens both to speak from the grave to complain of shaken bones and to shape the way the present conceives it."[2] The very idea of defining Chaucer with temporal markers such as the Middle Ages and the Renaissance becomes problematic when one needs to connect the poet with a larger European tradition. E.R. Curtius proposed, for instance, to set our literary and cultural history within the frame of a continuous present, embracing

---

1 See Chateaubriand, *Essai sur la littérature anglaise*.
2 McMullan and Matthews, *Reading the Medieval*, 2.

a period of twenty-six centuries, from Homer to Goethe.[3] G.M. Trevelyan even suggested the Middle Ages only ended during the seventeenth century, with the beginning of the Industrial Revolution, which had a bigger impact on our world than the Renaissance.[4] In effect, those concepts are but a retrospective invention, "one that has less to do with the particular qualities of the period than with the agenda of those who seek to define it."[5] C.S. Lewis likewise noted that we should beware of a generalized use of the term "Renaissance" in literary criticism, a word we tend to invoke in order to create a sense of unity in a particularly eventful and heterogeneous period of our history:

> Thus the "imaginary entity" creeps in. Renaissance becomes the name for some character or quality supposed to be immanent in all the events, and collects very serious emotional overtones in the process. Then, as every attempt to define this mysterious character or quality turns out to cover all sorts of things that were there before the chosen period, a curious procedure is adopted. Instead of admitting that our definition has broken down, we adopt the desperate expedient of saying that "the Renaissance" must have begun earlier than we had thought.[6]

Several medieval authors and thinkers such as Chaucer, Dante, and even Saint Francis of Assisi have thus been granted the title of Renaissance men. In English literary and historical studies, we are in effect faced with a very permeable border between the Middle Ages and the Renaissance—or the Early Modern, depending on the "disciplinary or theoretical affiliations of the writer."[7]

A concept with such fluctuating meanings cannot possibly be of any value in a literary analysis. Jacques Le Goff has argued for the unimportance of the Renaissance in any overarching framework of periodisation: "In History there is no such thing as rebirth. There is only change, in this case camouflaged as a return to antiquity."[8] The Renaissance is therefore nothing but a superficial interlude, an interrelated concept whose connection with the medieval is that each period is the product of the other.[9]

Chaucer was accordingly not trying to be "medieval"[10] and he certainly had no idea what a "Renaissance man" could possibly be; he was just being "modern"

---

3 Curtius, *European Literature and the Latin Middle Ages*, 12.
4 See Trevelyan, *English Social History*.
5 Williams, "Friar Bacon and Friar Bungay," 31.
6 Lewis, *Oxford History of English Literature*, 55.
7 McMullan and Matthews, *Reading the Medieval*, 3.
8 Le Goff, *The Medieval Imagination*, 19.
9 McMullan and Matthews, *Reading the Medieval*, 3.
10 The term "Middle Ages" actually appeared for the first time in Latin in 1469 as *media tempestas*; medieval writers had, as a result, no idea they were medieval.

in his own time. That is precisely why *Chaucer's Polyphony* will try, as much as possible, to escape historical categorizations: the Renaissance will be understood as a revival of knowledge based on classical writings, just as Humanism will be perceived as the critical study accompanying the teaching of Greek and Latin writings. Nothing more. The same is true for the notion of modernity that stands so prominently in the book's title: it will first and foremost be used to create a bridge between Chaucer's own time and ours: he was innovating without escaping the fourteenth century, but the specificity of his poetry allows him to reflect—as mentioned above—the idiosyncrasies of the time of each new generation of reader.

The image of Chaucer seldom ceased to evolve throughout the centuries. Some of his contemporaries[11] already had a great respect for his work, praising him as a man of letters, linguist, moralist, poet, and man of science. Henry Scogan, Thomas Usk, or John Lydgate even considered him as their master; the same is true for Thomas Hoccleve who wrote a portrait of Chaucer in 1412, now preserved in the British Library (MS Harley 4866), in which he laments that his loss deprived the country of a rhetoric as noble as that of Aristotle, Cicero, or Virgil.[12] But after having been praised for the quality of his rhetoric, Chaucer reached the sixteenth century in a much less conventional manner: first described as a radical, because of the erroneous attribution of anticlerical and Lollard texts to him, he was soon embraced by the Humanists, who thanked him for having enriched the English language with Latin words, and then was strongly criticized for the archaism of his Middle English. He became, in other words, one of the arguments in the controversy about the purification of English. However, this dynamic rapidly faded away and Chaucer progressively left the limelight to the benefit of a new generation of poets. Until Edmund Spenser, Chaucer's role in the history of English literature was still compared to Virgil's, but his influence lessened to the point that in 1560 he started to be compared to Ennius, the father of Latin literature whose writings only survived in fragments.

One of the turning points of Chaucerian criticism thus took place at the very end of the seventeenth century with the preface of John Dryden's *Fables, Ancient and Modern* (1700). In a few pages, Dryden paved the way for his successors in the next couple of centuries. If he nuances his judgment regarding Chaucer's versification—which he considers irregular—and his bawdiness, he nevertheless connects Chaucer with Giovanni Boccaccio, noting that they had a

---

11 Chaucer's audience was during his lifetime limited to a small group of friends and relatives. If he had been recognized by the court as a poet, it would certainly have been mentioned in the archives, and his *Life-Records* make no mention of it.
12 Brewer, "Images of Chaucer 1386–1900," 243–46.

similar style and a common ambition, and pointing out that they were both authors of "novels in prose."[13] Dryden did not mean by "novels" what we now call a novel, but rather what the French commonly term *nouvelle*, that is to say a short narrative. Nonetheless, as D.S. Brewer remarked, "it was a prophetic use of the word"[14] since Dryden was interested in the realism of Chaucer's descriptions, which made him feel like he was meeting his ancestors face-to-face. For Brewer, Dryden thus managed to create a link between the past and future of Chaucerian criticism:

> The eighteenth century saw the rise of the novel proper, with its claim to represent life with realism, its opportunities for vicarious experience, its unqualified demand for sympathy with people whom the novelist pretends are more or less ordinary.[15]

Stephanie Trigg has discussed Dryden's comments about Chaucer, and his impact on modern criticism. She has particularly described his imagined relationship with Chaucer as one with a "congenial soul" that still includes a sense of "historical distance."[16] In fact, when Dryden was writing, Chaucer was so obscure that his works were translated into Latin to make them accessible. Thus, in order "to explain his high regard for Chaucer, Dryden . . . stresses his modernity."[17] He wishes to assert Chaucer's importance to modern readers, which is in a way the purpose of this book.

The fact that it became common during the eighteenth century to consider Chaucer as an author of novels, precisely because of his realism, is not insignificant and reflects this constant need to redefine Chaucer for "modern" readers. But although Chaucer's realism is remarkable—we will discuss it further in Chapter 6—focusing solely on that aspect tends to make us forget that the vision of poetry during the Middle Ages was very different from ours. Even if Chaucer started, at the end of his career, to think of his poems as books[18]—he names *Troilus and Criseyde*, for instance, his "litel bok" (V. 1786)—and if he encourages the reader of the *Miller's Prologue* to turn the page "and chese another

---

13 Dryden, "Preface to Fables, Ancient and Modern," 2.
14 Brewer, "Images of Chaucer 1386–1900," 257.
15 Ibid.
16 Trigg, *Congenial Souls*, 150.
17 Butterfield, *The Familiar Enemy*, 31.
18 This evolution is linked to a sudden change in Chaucer's life: he began towards the end of the 1380s to think of himself as an "auctour" and no longer as a mere translator or "compilator." His *Canterbury Tales* were thus quickly perceived as an authentic book: "Its earliest manuscripts announce themselves as books, have the appearance of finished books, and modern editions, fortified with editorially added headnotes, endnotes, and titles, strike readers that way today." Strohm, *Chaucer's Tale*, 242.

tale" (3177), he was still primarily read aloud in public. Not taking into account this specificity blurs our vision of his poetry.[19]

Chaucer has always, as we have remarked, inspired new generations of readers to find their own answers and to take a fresh look at his creations. As we will see, the ever-modern dimension of his poetry that comes from its polyphony allowed a constant reinterpretation of Chaucer's writings, although as Dryden's remarks reveal, "this use of the past, and of Chaucer's role in promoting it, is caught between two contradictory views of Chaucer as at once modern and antique."[20] The poet has indeed notoriously been defined as the father of English poetry, an assertion that tends to condemn to oblivion several centuries of oral and written literature in English. J.R.R. Tolkien questioned that assertion and explained that

> [i]f you have ever heard that Chaucer was the "father of English poetry," forget it. English poetry has no recorded father, even as a written art, and the beginning lies beyond our view, in the mists of northern antiquity.[21]

If Chaucer were to be the father of English poetry, what could we say about the authors of *Beowulf*, *The Wanderer*, or *The Battle of Maldon*? That quest for a moment of origin, for a "usable past"[22] as Paul Strohm calls it, is very much a pipe dream. This idea that the past can speak directly to present experience is illusory, for both past and present "are constructed positions."[23]

In *Chaucer's Polyphony*, I consequently have no intention of considering Chaucer as the father of English poetry, and even less as the "firste fyndere of our faire langage," as Hoccleve put it.[24] As I explain in the Preface, this book started as a doctoral dissertation written in French and in France, in an academic environment that greatly ignored Chaucer and medieval English literature as a whole. To exist as a Chaucerian in France, I needed to prove that Chaucer could be reconnected with "modern stuff," and that he was not "obsolete," as a colleague once remarked.

---

19 The word "audience" will subsequently be used throughout this monograph to describe the contemporary readers and listeners of Chaucer's poetry. The term "readers" would strongly limit our reaction to his poetry to the last centuries and would exclude that of his contemporaries who did not so much read Chaucer as listen to oral readings.
20 Butterfield, *The Familiar Enemy*, 32.
21 Tolkien, *The Fall of Arthur*, 225–26.
22 Strohm, *Theory and the Premodern Text*, 77.
23 Butterfield, *The Familiar Enemy*, 32.
24 Blyth, *Thomas Hoccleve: The Regiment of Princes*, 4978. See also Cannon, "The Myth of Origin and the Making of Chaucer's English."

Polyphony allowed me to build a bridge and justified my initial research, but its importance in Chaucerian studies is greater than my own struggle with unsupportive French academic circles. Dialogism/polyphony—I will come back to the interchangeability of these terms—is a remarkable way to get to the heart of Chaucer's poetry, and see that the poet's approach to language, his linguistic sensibility (inherited from a larger European tradition[25]), influenced his narrative choices (even when we least expect it, as in the *Legend of Good Women*), his aestheticism, enunciation, and his philosophical perspective. As John Ganim points out about Bakhtin, the irony is that "his most helpful contribution may not be to help us reinterpret Chaucer, but to reorient the chief issues of Chaucer criticism. He can help us rewrite some of its traditional questions by replacing their controlling metaphors."[26]

With this book, I hope to fill a gap in Chaucerian studies. Although generations of critics have looked at the Bakhtinian quality of Chaucer's work, they have usually focused on the *Canterbury Tales*, or on the notion of Bakhtin and folklore. Separating these two aspects is in my opinion a mistake since the carnivalesque in Chaucer is closely related to the dialogism of his poetry. More to the point, what I hope to achieve here is to broaden our conception of polyphony, which is usually limited to a Bakhtinian reading. For much remains to be said about the impact of several aspects of dialogism, such as polyvocality, double enunciation, interlocutive, intralocutive, and interdiscursive forms of dialogism on Chaucer's narrative style and enunciative choices. Narratological and linguistic frameworks, supported by language sciences, will allow us to go further than Bakhtin ever went and offer a systematic study of Chaucer's polyphonic practice and of its sociolinguistic and philological origins.

My intention is, in other words, to leave aside any considerations of Old Chaucer as a father figure, and instead to show how he contributed to the birth of English polyphonic prose. Despite the great effort made by Chaucerian criticism to free itself from the hegemony of the novel, I will use the theory of the novel because it gives us the best analytical tools to provide a formal description of Chaucer's polyphonic practice. As Curtius remarked, "[w]e have modernized the railroads, but not our system of transmitting tradition,"[27] which implies that the characteristics specific to the "modern" novel are inherited from a much more ancient form of literature.

---

25 See Marion Turner's *Chaucer: A European Life*.
26 Ganim, *Chaucerian Theatricality*, 20.
27 Curtius, *European Literature and the Latin Middle Ages*, 16.

Bakhtin managed to identify embryonic traces of the novel and of its bivocal prose in various genres from antiquity: satires (those of Horace for instance), biographies, autobiographies (*The Apology of Socrates* . . .), diatribes, epistolary productions (*Letters to Atticus* . . .), and so on are all literary genres that contributed to the creation of the novel as we have come to think of it since the seventeenth century. These are but the embryos of a novelistic orchestration of meaning through multilingualism.[28] Medieval literature and its narrative or lyrical variants represent the first phase of development of these embryos. And even though Bakhtin rarely discussed the Middle Ages, his theories are still of great value for medievalists for his terminology is much more flexible than we might think. Bakhtin's silence about the Middle Ages allows us to apply and develop his theories in ways that are suitable to the texts we study, and approach them on their own terms. As we will see, polyphony is at the heart of this novelistic orchestration of meaning through multilingualism because, as Thomas Farrell remarked,

> The function of the novel (and of novelistic discourse generally) is to defrock the pretensions of sacredness attributed to the past by those currently in power . . . the novel now comes into focus as a rejection of established social hierarchies maintained by the authority of the monologic voice or the voice uncontested by dialogue.[29]

Discussing polyphonic literature in medieval times implies, however, an understanding of three things: the importance of scholastic debate, its relationship with music,[30] and the openness of polyphonic literature.

The first half of the thirteenth century represents in many ways the golden age of medieval civilization, and it is this particular period that witnessed the institutionalization of disputation in urban universities, and the growth of scholastic culture. The functions of theologians could be subdivided into reading (*lectio*), disputing (*disputatio*), and preaching (*praedicatio*), but while *lectio* was more factual, *disputatio* represented the pursuit of truth, and according to Stephen Langton (1187–1216), one of the masters at Paris, it allowed for a freer rhetorical approach.[31] Disputation allowed multiple interpretations and

---

28 Bakhtin, *Esthétique et théorie du roman*, 187.
29 Farrell, *Bakhtin and Medieval Voices*, 5.
30 A linguistic definition of dialogism and its connection with polyphony will be given in Chapter 1.
31 His commentary on Hosea 2:16 is notably interesting as Langton explains that in *disputatio* one may discuss the term "omnipotentes" adjectivally or substantively, but not during factual reading, for "Ex hoc habemus ex solis vocibus inordinate prolatis heresim posse incurri." Paris, Bibliothèque Mazarine, MS Mazarine 177, fol. 92d.

discussions about subjects that would have traditionally been closed to debate. Its aim was not sacrilegious, it was to pursue knowledge through what Alex Novikoff describes as an "exercise in logic and hermeneutics."[32] The fact that disputing became so central in universities, which gathered students, teachers, and mendicant preachers, allowed it to cross the threshold between monastic and scholastic learning. This cultural dissemination of the techniques of debate and argumentation "reached audiences not directly trained in the schools and universities"[33] and, in the case of quodlibetical disputations, offered drama and performance that attracted the public. It staged exchanges and gave audiences a show that disseminated intellectual ideas in the public sphere and in the arts. This kind of performance reflected the society in which it took place and became a unique medium allowing for debate and polemics.[34]

It is of course difficult not to notice a certain similarity between the performative aspect of quodlibetical disputations and contrapuntal polyphony. Polyphonic singing did not await the development of scholastic learning to appear, but its conceptual definition was still rather weak: the *Musica enchiriadis* is probably the first treatise to describe *organum*, the earliest form of polyphonic music, and might have been written at the end of the ninth century. It describes the *vox principalis* as being placed above the *vox organalis*, both moving in harmony with the chant at the interval of a fourth, a fifth, or an octave. We are still far from Guillaume de Machaut, the appearance of *consonantia*, and of part writing that allowed the independence of each voice in vocal counterpoint. One must recognize here the importance of Parisian scholasticism to the evolution of polyphony. As Richard Taruskin remarked,

> the burgeoning of polyphonic composition followed the exact same trajectory [as scholastic education] . . . it reached its first great, transfiguring culmination in the cathedral schools of Paris, and in a new form it radiated from the cosmopolitan centre throughout Western Christendom, receiving a special ancillary cultivation in the universities.[35]

The evolution of polyphony was thus in accord with the intellectual environment of the time. The practice and performance of disputation in universities and in public started to affect the arts. In fact, "counterpoint, like *disputatio*, is

---

32 Novikoff, *The Medieval Culture of Disputation*, 135.
33 Ibid., 134.
34 See Symes, *A Common Stage*, chapter 3. One may also find information about the dissemination of quodlibetical disputations in the theater in Bloemendal, Eversmann, and Strietman, *Drama, Performance and Debate*.
35 Taruskin, *Music from the Earliest Notation to the Sixteenth Century*, 149. For more information about the importance of universities in early polyphonic music, see Gushee, "The Polyphonic Music of the Medieval Monastery, Cathedral and University," 143–69.

a cultural expression of dialectic and rhetoric. Broadly speaking, the hermeneutic principles that Abelard applied to theology and that Gratian applied to law, polyphony applied to music."[36] The motet was for instance a dialogue of voices showing a remarkable capacity to engage in irony and polemics. Some of Philip the Chancellor's motets[37] thus show a close resemblance with scholastic disputation as they offered praise and criticism of the clergy. His motets

> adopt opposite stances in each of the upper voices, with the motetus dispensing an opinion on one side of the disputation, and the triplum taking the other. In each of these cases the disagreement between the texts is borne out ingeniously by their musical settings as double motets: each position is disclaimed simultaneously with the other, resulting in a verbal discord that, ironically, is offset by the harmonious musical setting that combines them.[38]

Philip is in other words the best example of how scholastic learning reached the cultural world as a whole. Vernacular and Latin debate poems were quite popular at the time, as seen in the production of *jeux-partis*,[39] which further helped the dissemination of scholastic learning into a wider sphere, notably in northern France, and thus probably in England.

There is a great variety of texts and commentaries in both Latin and the vernacular that provided a context to the idea of resistance to closure, as Rosemarie McGerr so eloquently explained. Refusing to offer a definite conclusion is one way to escape the absolute of a monologic vision. For that openness involves "a more direct challenge to traditions of resolution and reflects an aesthetic that privileges . . . the growth and multiplication of the possible meanings of a given text."[40] According to Umberto Eco, this is defined in terms of authorial intentions since the author willingly introduces ambiguity in his text, and "forms of organized disorder into a system to increase its capacity to convey information."[41] An open work offers, by definition, multiple perspectives and conclusions, instead of imposing a single point of view; it is a deliberate avoidance of resolution that fractures "the aesthetic in order to enhance the imaginative structure of

---

36 Novikoff, *The Medieval Culture of Disputation*, 148.
37 See Philip the Chancellor, *Motets and Prosulas*, 35–37, 142–45, 161–67.
38 Ibid., xix.
39 A *jeu-parti*, a sung debate in vernacular with several singers arguing for or against a specific question—often love—could have functioned "as a vernacular version of the academic sentences, which students learned and memorized while they prepared to argue in their own disputation; a new generation of *trouvères* could have similarly honed their craft through study of the manuscripts like the *Chansonnier d'Arras*." Saltzstein, "Cleric-Trouvères and the *Jeux-Partis* of Medieval Arras," 151.
40 McGerr, *Chaucer's Open Books*, 6.
41 Eco, *The Open Work*, 60.

reference."⁴² The open work is thus a good example of how a polyphonic poetics contributed to the embryonic growth of the novel. It is one expression "of a culture whose innumerable demands can be satisfied in many different ways—for instance, by using traditional structures in a more modern fashion."⁴³ This modern type of fiction can even be challenging to an audience because of its ambiguity, for it does not offer the easy satisfactions of traditional closed literature. This use of fiction to explore fiction, as Frank Kermode would put it, encourages a reassessment of how we perceive art.⁴⁴

Openness in literature thus increases ambiguity and presents the audience with various meanings that will inevitably divide them. Yoshiyuki Nakao remarks that the

> speaker observes and cognises a phenomenon and expresses it in words. Through this act the hearer understands the speaker's cognition in one way or another, and then proceeds to an interpretation of it. In the reading process, ambiguity arises when the readers are divided in their interpretation.⁴⁵

The author's initial intention to produce a variety of meanings implies that the ultimate meaning of an utterance may very well be what the audience reads into it. If the relationship "between the elements involved in the making of a text is absolutely fixed with no alternatives, its meaning is likely to be definitive, with no instance/occurrence of ambiguity,"⁴⁶ which therefore means that the text itself is monologic. On the other hand, if the "relationship between the above elements becomes a matter of degrees to a reader or between readers, the rise of ambiguity is likely to be inevitable."⁴⁷ Polysemy and resistance to closure are, in other words, some of the main devices producing a dialogical cycle contributing to the evolution and development of polyphony in the embryonic forms of the novel. The novel then managed to integrate those elements and allowed them to develop at each stage of evolution of European literature. Bakhtin explains that this particular genre "lives in the present, but always remembers its past, its beginning. Genre is a representative of creative memory in the process of literary development. Precisely for this reason genre is capable of guaranteeing the *unity* and *uninterrupted* continuity of this development."⁴⁸

---

42 Adams, *Strains of Discord*, 62.
43 Eco, *The Open Work*, 115.
44 Kermode, *The Sense of an Ending*, 152.
45 Nakao, *The Structure of Chaucer's Ambiguity*, 14.
46 Ibid., 21.
47 Ibid.
48 Bakhtin, *Problems of Dostoevsky's Poetics*, 106.

Although the origins of the novel genre go back to the classics of antiquity, we will focus here more precisely on medieval vernacular literature and on its relation with Chaucer's poetry.

The influence of courtly love poetry and of the *Divina Commedia* on Chaucer has long been recognized and accepted. It earned him the description by Eustache Deschamps as the "Dieux en Albie"[49] of *fin'amor*, while his poetry was defined by Lydgate as "Dante in Inglissh."[50] However, Chaucer did not simply translate or adapt his sources. On the contrary, he transformed them and gave them a new dimension. Is it possible then to consider that the intertextuality of his poetical influences and the assimilation of their different voices allowed Chaucer to revolutionize his conception of literature, and thus sow the seeds in English of what Bakhtin would later define as literary polyphony?

That is the question at the heart of *Chaucer's Polyphony*. But looking for an answer means following Chaucer's career chronologically in order to witness the progressive development of the polyphonic phenomenon. For the latter develops over a long period of time; it proceeds by trial and error and appears above all diachronically. This constant experimentation is one of Chaucer's great strengths: he takes an evident pleasure in *writing*, in attempting new things, and in playing with literary conventions and with the expectations of his audience; that is precisely what makes him a timeless artist. If his work appears so modern to us, it is not only because of Chaucer's refining of contemporary narrative processes but because of the polyphonic dimension of his poetry.

A first chapter, entitled "Polyphony and Multilingualism in Medieval England" will allow us to look back at the linguistic history of the country Chaucer grew up in, and to realize how his sensitivity to languages was essential in the development of the polyphonic process. Indeed, if we acknowledge that a language is an organism evolving naturally, it is then possible to define a variety of environmental factors influencing it endogenously and exogenously. Thus, when different ethnolinguistic groups get closer to each other, whether because of the increase of social interaction or through colonization, language contact occurs. According to Uriel Weinreich, several languages are in contact when they are used alternately by the same speakers, a phenomenon that may generate a certain degree of bilingualism. Language contact allows, for instance, new linguistic forms to emerge, as Dante explains in relation to the vernacular: "[d]ico autem 'formam' et quantum ad rerum vocabula et quantum ad vocabulorum constructionem et

---

49 Paris, Bibliothèque Nationale de France, MS fr. 840, fol. 62. The ballade is also available in Chaucer, *Les Contes de Canterbury et autres œuvres*, 712–13.
50 Lydgate, *Lydgate's Fall of Princes*, I:9.

quantum ad constructionis prolationem."[51] But it also allows more ancient forms to disappear, be modified, or simplified. A distinction is, as a result, usually made between two types of linguistic changes with, on the one hand, fast-acting transformations that mainly modify the lexicon and the spelling and, on the other, long-term changes that focus on syntax and morphology.

In a multilingual society, it becomes necessary to attribute a function to languages, which inevitably implies thinking about their prestige. As the official language of religion and knowledge, Latin was crowned with a prestige that long assured its hegemony. Old English, on the other hand, inherited a completely different role in Anglo-Saxon society, since it remained present both as a vernacular, and as a literary and juridical language. Yet even though this sort of language planning allows us to have a glimpse of the political distribution of languages, one should not lose sight of their social distribution. The latter implies the existence of social stratifications, something that Bernard Barber defined as the product of social differentiation and social evaluation.[52] But this does not imply the existence of specific and fixed castes. As William Labov notes, it only means that "the normal workings of society have produced systematic differences between certain institutions or people, and that these differentiated forms have been ranked in status or prestige by general agreement."[53] In other words, it may be necessary in order to move up socially to adopt the most prestigious language and culture available, which generally leads to an extreme form of acculturation, namely cultural and linguistic assimilation.

These sociolinguistic concepts will allow us to understand that when Chaucer started writing in Middle English, he was already the heir of a culture that had been at the intersection of several civilizations and that had left deep marks on its language. This cultural diversity and multilingualism are perceived and absorbed by authors who, consciously or not, then transcribe in their writings a stratification revealing literature's steps on the path to literary polyphony.

A second chapter, "*Fin'amor, Stil Novo*: Chaucer's Early Influences," will then give us the opportunity to focus on Chaucer's influences, namely French and Italian courtly love poetry. Despite a certain sensitivity to polyvocality, absorbed from his linguistic environment, it is ultimately with the assimilation of *fin'amor* and of the Italian *Dolce Stil Novo* that Chaucer managed to give his poetry an increasingly polyphonic dimension.

---

51 "I say 'form' with respect to lexicon, syntax and morphology." Dante, *De vulgari eloquentia*, 14.
52 Barber, *Social Stratification*, 1–3.
53 Labov, *Sociolinguistic Patterns*, 44.

Indeed, according to Philippe Walter, "[c]'est à partir de Chrétien [de Troyes] que commence (et peut-être finit) tout voyage littéraire dans le Moyen Age,"[54] and it now seems obvious that Chaucer followed his illustrious predecessor on this novelistic journey, long before he would himself take the road to Canterbury. The twelfth-century cultural renaissance effectively saw the appearance of a brand-new vision of literature. The French troubadours and *trouvères* distanced themselves from ancient and medieval Latin[55] and drew from courtly life a new poetry bringing together amorous feelings and chivalry, while clerics worked on the elaboration of Arthurian novels and *chansons de geste*. But a few years after Chrétien had given birth to a novelistic language, Guillaume de Lorris set aside the chivalric dimension of the Old French narratives and highlighted the treatment of feelings through allegory in *Le Roman de la Rose*. Guillaume's use of allegory allowed him to diversify his characters, abandoning the traditional hero in favor of several personifications representing the different facets of the human mind. The ingenuity of this narrative process transformed the author's presence within the story for the poet became at once narrator, dreamer, and an allegorical representation of young lovers. The strength of the authorial voice is accordingly reduced, leaving in its stead a dialogical logic in which the narrator is no longer master but witness. Jean de Meun concluded *Le Roman de la Rose* a few years after Guillaume's death but could not preserve his predecessor's narrative structure. If the dialogism of his continuation was reduced by the disappearance of Guillaume's narrative strategy, Jean nonetheless introduced in the poem elements specific to the bourgeois tradition,[56] defined by carnivalesque laughter and opposing to the rigidity of courtly aristocracy a popular polyvocality.

The *Roman de la Rose* thus became a fertile work that influenced the development of European literature for centuries. The Italian Trecento saw, as a result, the birth of a poetical style inherited from French poetry. Yet whereas troubadours and *trouvères* had turned amorous passion into an object of veneration, the partisans of *Dolce Stil Novo*—most notably under the guidance of Brunetto

---

54 "any literary journey into the Middle Ages begins (and perhaps ends) with Chrétien [de Troyes]." Walter, *Chrétien de Troyes*, 4.
55 Troubadour poetics emphasized two major innovations since it introduced the rhyme, i.e., the syllabic rhythm of the line (as opposed to the vocalic rhythm based on the quantity of long and short vowels), as well as strophic forms. See Zumthor, *Langue et techniques poétiques à l'époque romane*.
56 The bourgeois tradition (in the medieval sense of the word, not to be confused with the Marxist theory) is defined by an attachment to the marketplace, where different voices mingle and cross, while the members of the aristocracy are, by opposition, marked by a conventionalism alien to popular life.

Latini—transformed that same passion into an instrument of transcendence leading to spiritual renewal. Dante probably expressed better than anyone else, with the figure of Beatrice, that transition between an allegory of condemnable love (dominating the senses, as seen in his *Vita Nuova* and in the fifth Canto of the *Inferno*), and a transcending passion leading to illumination.

Before Chaucer even visited Italy, he showed a capacity to play with his sources and to compile them in such a way that their intertextuality produced new shades of meaning. A third chapter on "Narrative Evolution and New Discursive Strategies" will allow us to see the direct consequences on Chaucer's poetry of what was established in Chapter 2, namely how he managed to articulate the narrative processes inherited first from *fin'amor* and then from Italian poetry.

Chaucer indeed rapidly distinguished himself from Guillaume de Machaut or Jean Froissart and presented a first alternative to the conventions of *fin'amor* in *The Book of the Duchess*. But then he visited Italy, in 1373, and discovered a country deeply divided politically, linguistically, economically, and socially. This divide was such that it profoundly influenced the poetry of men like Boccaccio, Dante, or Petrarch. Consciously or not, they had interiorized that cleavage and expressed it in their respective poetical productions. As a result, when he experienced and assimilated Italian poetry, Chaucer, who had already been marked by English multilingualism and multiculturalism, managed to transcribe that dissolution of unity into an increasingly polyphonic literature, connecting *fin'amor* narrative structure, Italian plurality, and English polyvocality. *The House of Fame* therefore shows Chaucer innovating and experimenting with narrative. He turns his persona, here aptly named Geoffrey, into an artifice that, by liberating the potential of dialogism, allows him to take up and challenge some of the notions developed by Dante in the *Commedia*. In questioning for instance Dante's assumptions about the authority of literature, Chaucer attempts to demonstrate in a Neoplatonist way that there is no absolute version of truth, but rather that in "looking for significant likenesses and comparisons" one may stumble upon a "*working* discovery of the best or near best approximation of form (or truth)."[57] Thus, whereas Dante authenticated his poem by placing himself under the aegis of God, Chaucer acknowledged, notably by means of a bivocal narration, the artificial aspect of *The House of Fame*, and repeatedly drew attention to the frailty of a story based upon an instrument as fallible as the human mind.

If Chaucer had already shown a certain artistic maturity in *The House of Fame*, he was still looking for a way to harmonize the French and Italian voices

---

57 Hill, *Chaucer's Neoplatonism*, 10.

he had heard. *The Parliament of Fowls* was accordingly a new major step forward in his career since he effectively managed to combine the aristocratic courtly tradition with carnivalesque laughter and the richness of Trecento poetry (in this case, Boccaccio's *Teseida*). To that end, he reduced his narrator to the rank of passive witness, thus refusing to affirm authorial intent, and embedded him in an intertextuality connecting Boccaccio with Alain de Lille, before plunging him into a formidable parliamentary cacophony transcribing popular polyphony and polyvocality. Chaucer's balancing of aristocratic and bourgeois values allowed him to put forward a new vision of his poetical art, progressively liberated from the conventions of *fin'amor* and increasingly reflecting a plural world still in the making.

But it is really with *Troilus and Criseyde* that he reached new artistic heights. A fourth chapter dedicated to the "Ambiguity of Double Enunciation" of that poem will make us understand how reading Boccaccio's *Filostrato* allowed Chaucer to abandon, for the first time, the courtly love allegories which had provided him with a narrative frame for so long, to the benefit of a pseudo-historical mode of representation. Boccaccio's use of that narrative process a few decades earlier represented a first step towards a new artistic and aesthetic sensibility specific to the Renaissance. Chaucer, however, chose a different approach: instead of following Boccaccio all the way, he adopted that new frame and went back to the very origins of the novel genre, notably through a presentation of *fin'amor* in line with the doctrine developed by Chrétien de Troyes or Guillaume de Lorris. He was, as a result, able to develop a conception of love that revealed the positive and negative effects of literature. After having defended the idea that History is a juxtaposition of often contradictory points of view in *Fame*, Chaucer accordingly transformed *Troilus and Criseyde* into a reading experience. His narrator becomes the central node of a double enunciation, a witness and historian offering us an apparently objective vision of the romance between Troilus and Criseyde, punctuated with personal remarks about the fate of the characters. Whereas Dante sought to join an objective narrative with a subjective commentary, to mix fiction and History, while attempting to preserve his role as guide, Chaucer suggested, by means of the destruction of the narrative's authentication, that the integrity of a story is inevitably altered by the will of its narrator. In doing so, he presented a surprisingly modern vision of the genre in which the characters no longer rely on the exclusive will of the author, and in which no single voice dominates the debate. Despite the narrator's desire to influence the development of his story, the dialogic relationship that he sustains with his narrative prevents any form of monological control. The narrator in *Troilus and Criseyde* thus wished he could alter the integrity of his story, because of his refusal to witness Criseyde's betrayal, but was unable in the end to prevent the inevitable.

Troilus and Criseyde consequently represented a transition between two different stages in Chaucer's career. A fifth chapter, entitled "Hybridization and the Legend of Chaucer's Inventiveness" will be the occasion to see that the reception and assimilation of his literary influences had reached a stage that forced Chaucer to move beyond the limits of the genre that had formed him in order to continue to innovate. With *The Legend of Good Women* Chaucer turned a page: leaving behind him the lyricism and codes of *fin'amor*, he engaged in the composition of a collection of short narratives in which he could both give free rein to the plurality he embodied, and continue to defend a particular vision of literature.

Nonetheless, if Chaucer had managed, until that point, to develop the polyphony of his poetical universe by playing with intertextuality and harmonizing the voices of his literary influences, the very nature of *LGW* forced him to change his strategy. In order to justify the transformation of his poetry and the innovation it would introduce, Chaucer presents his legends, in the Prologue, as a penance imposed by the God of Love. He is to write a collection of stories about virtuous women, which gives him a good opportunity to introduce the theme of this new work while justifying its unorthodox nature. But to accomplish this task, Chaucer needed to put himself forward as a poet, and no longer as a passive narrative persona. He thus manages to produce polyvocality by way of hybridization: moving from pathos to comedy, from irony to parody, he shows the various dimensions of passionate love once it is freed from the conventionalism of the courtly love code. His aspiration to present the difference that exists between the world of literature and the real experience of love could thus be attained by this dialogue between effects and genres. Each legend is therefore endowed with its own voice, which allows Chaucer to offer a unique vision of love and of its place in the world.

Yet despite the importance given to hybridization in *LGW*, Chaucer's presence throughout the collection of legends foreshadows the return of his persona in the *Canterbury Tales*. The author of the Prologue is indeed presented as a man faithful to Love and ready to make amends. He accordingly starts writing his hagiographies, but progressively moves away from the terms of his penance. The partisan of courtly love from the Prologue, who encouraged his audience to beware of appearances, and who reminded women that he is the only man they can trust, does not hesitate to mock or attack some of the good women he is supposed to praise. He also remarks in several instances that he is getting bored—a weariness that critics have often taken literally—which will lead him to reproduce the pattern he has been describing in each legend.

For how could a poet who has long been resisting closure conclude a collection of narratives emphasizing the contrast between reality and conventions if not by becoming himself the avatar of the unfaithful lover?

Chaucer teaches his audience in *LGW* that appearances can be misleading, and he accordingly illustrates that statement by betraying his audience: he abandons us with an unfinished collection and narrative. He first makes us believe in the Prologue that he is composing a courtly love poem, then moves away from the codes of *fin'amor*, and after having guided us into a brutal and violent world, he leaves us there. That ultimate narrative twist, which allows Chaucer to flee at the same time as Hypermnestra's husband, leaves us, the audience, with a woman condemned to death on her wedding night by her father's madness and her husband's cowardice. In other words, if Chaucer's persona never enters into a dialogic relationship with the elements of the collection, the author himself avoids monologism through a hybridization highlighting the ambiguity of his poem and allowing him to affirm his authority as an author without suppressing the work's polyphony.

It is, as a result, not surprising to see the Chaucerian persona appear as soon as the first lines of the *Canterbury Tales*. And Chaucer tries once more to innovate by pushing the hybridization of *LGW* a step further: the tales told by the pilgrims, among whom is Chaucer himself, will now embody this notion of hybridization. We will see in a final chapter entitled "Extradiegetic Dialogue in *The Canterbury Tales*" that each tale is part of a cacophonic background. For when the pilgrims interrupt, answer each other, and argue, Chaucer opposes different visions of literature thanks to an extradiegetic dialogue between literary genres. In other words, whereas his narrative strategy once consisted in establishing dialogism between the narrator's voice and his characters' (thus in the diegesis), he now develops the polyphony of his work by creating a dialogue escaping the limits of the narrative, that is to say a dialogue between the genres associated with the tales. *The Canterbury Tales* is consequently a resolutely modern work since it gives dialogue the chance to happen both inside and outside of the narration.

Conceived as a guide allowing us to follow Geoffrey Chaucer throughout his process of elaborating polyphony, this book is both an attempt to find a new approach to his poetry, and a reminder of Chaucer's importance in the history of English literature as a whole. More importantly, it intends to show that Chaucer belonged to a vast European cultural tradition; the major works mentioned and analyzed here thus deserve that we cross the linguistic barriers separating them from our own time in order to see that they keep on illuminating our intellectual journey.

Chapter 1
Polyphony and Multilingualism in Medieval England

A few words have been said in the Introduction about polyphonic music and its connection with *disputatio*, but it still remains to be seen how this concept is related to language sciences. I will accordingly need to leave Chaucer for a while, so bear with me: it is only to define the concepts necessary to my thesis and to paint the linguistic picture of the elements that generated and nourished his polyphonic practice.

We owe the description of enunciative heterogeneity phenomena as "polyphony" to Mikhail Bakhtin, who describes them either as dialogism—he coined the words *dialogichnost'* (dialogism) and *dialogizatzija* (dialogization)[1]—or polyphony. Bakhtin's theories are above all associated linguistically with dialogism, a term he uses in most of his production from 1929 to 1970. The word "polyphony" only appears however in his 1929 book on Dostoevsky's novels, and even then, Bakhtin is borrowing it from a study written by V.L. Komarovich in 1924 on Dostoevsky's *A Raw Youth*. He uses this concept because it allows him to develop an analogy with polyphonic music and the contrapuntal voices in a fugue.

Polyphony is thus originally a metaphor, but it eventually became a powerful image for Bakhtin, representing the artistic use of the dialogic possibilities of discourse. It is the novelistic exploitation of what he perceived as the inherent dialogism of daily speech. Bakhtin does not strictly speaking define dialogism anywhere, but for him verbal interaction remains the main purpose of language use and it appears in dialogues. Dialogism is, in other words, the principle at the heart of language use; it is the orientation of discourse towards other discourses, which can be classified as being either interdiscursive, interlocutive, or intralocutive.[2] The interdiscursive form of dialogism is basically the speaker's encounter with the discourses held by others: in his understanding of a discursive object, the speaker engages with the speech previously uttered by others about this very object; he opens a dialogue with this speech. The interlocutive line however is more direct since the speaker directly addresses an interlocutor and anticipates being answered. The intralocutive form of dialogism, also called autodialogism by Jacqueline Authier-Revuz,[3] concerns the dialogic relation between

---

1 Bres and Mellet, "Une approche dialogique des faits grammaticaux," 4.
2 See Bakhtin, *Problems of Dostoevsky's Poetics*.
3 Authier-Revuz, *Ces mots qui ne vont pas de soi*.

the speaking subject and his own enunciation. Discourse is structurally determined, according to Bakhtin, by the interdiscursive and interlocutive lines.[4]

In his writings, Bakhtin notes that every ideology, whether religion-based, scientific, or literary, is fundamentally grounded in a semiotic structure. Linguistics can be considered as a global science encompassing a vast network of subjects and substructures and whose purpose is essentially sociological. The reactions of each organism or sub-structure, although subjective and individual, thus acquire a semiotic dimension when they become the signs of a linguistic matrix and in joining the vast system that is language itself.[5] Language is, therefore, dialogical since it involves a *social* relation between these various organisms. Bakhtin's central concern throughout his career was accordingly the relationship between the "I" and the "other," each needing the other for completion. He notably frames his thinking in *Towards a Philosophy of the Act* through a set of oppositions, the most important being that between a given and a posited mode of reality. The former is characterized by its closure and its self-sufficiency whereas the latter is open and still in development.

Bakhtin has, of course, specific ideas about how these oppositions are distributed in the world, but what is of particular interest to us is the fact that "the human subject displays both given and posited modes in his or her situation in being."[6] In other words, our perception is by nature axiological and depends upon what we think our relationship with the other should be: "I perceive myself as incomplete and developing, but other people perceive me as completed and whole. Likewise, in my nature as agent I am active and posited, whereas in my capacity as object I am passive and given."[7] The human act thus becomes the plane upon which this duality can reach a certain unity and can define itself. It is accordingly in the very nature of language to communicate with the "other."

And Chaucer's own linguistic performances were nothing if not turned towards the other—the man in the marketplace, the outcast, the stranger. The dialogic approach of Chaucer's poetry is, in this respect, as much the result of the inherently sociological dimension of language as it is of England's multilingualism. For a culture is nothing but an open-ended "creative dialogue of subcultures, of insiders and outsiders, of diverse factions."[8] As James Clifford observed,

> [f]or Bakhtin, the polyphonic novel is not a tour de force of cultural or historical totalization (as reality critics like Lukacs and Auerbach have argued), but rather a carnivalesque arena

---

4 Perrin, "La notion de polyphonie en linguistique et dans le champ des sciences du langage," 266.
5 Bakhtin, *Esthétique et théorie du roman*, 12.
6 Coates, *Christianity in Bakhtin*, 27.
7 Ibid.
8 Clifford, "On Ethnographic Authority," 136.

of diversity. Bakhtin discovers a utopian textual space where discursive complexity, the dialogical interplay of voices, can be accommodated.[9]

During his career, Bakhtin started to consider Fyodor Dostoevsky as the creator of what he calls the "polyphonic novel," that is to say a novel essentially based on dialogue. According to him, the novelist expresses himself not through a specific character, but through the global structure of his work. Michel Aucouturier remarks that "[l]oin de faire du personnage un 'il' enfermé dans un réseau de déterminations (la nature humaine, le type social, le caractère psychologique), il en fait un 'tu,' une liberté."[10] Dostoevsky thus provokes his characters: he questions them and forces them to react. Yet, Bakhtin shows that this game of listening to discourse relies on the language used by the author, on this exchange between two voices, two intentions that cross, mingle, oppose, complement, and contradict each other. He believed that Dostoevskian philosophy was based on this exchange and that it was not locked within a single consciousness, easily represented by a monologue. It is, on the contrary, in perpetual motion; it comes and goes in our minds as an uninterrupted dialogue. In other words, Bakhtin uses the term "novel" in two senses: the historical genre, and the linguistic qualities tied to it.[11] Or as Michael McKeon would put it, "the relatively determinate literary form" and the "generalized aura and ethos of that form."[12] It is thus novelness "not the novel, not Rabelais, not even Dostoevsky—that is the name of [Bakhtin's] real hero."[13]

Bakhtin's assertions on the polyphonic tradition deserve, however, to be nuanced. Indeed, the Russian critic was then working with rather lacunar and dated documentation about the Middle Ages. And even though he does connect Dostoevsky with a larger literary tradition, he seems to completely ignore the fact that the very essence of polyphony had been in development since antiquity—one may find traces of it in Socratic dialogue and in Menippean satire. And although Bakhtin's name is at the center of dialogic studies, quite a few linguists have tried to question his terminology. Julia Kristeva, Tzvetan Todorov,

---

[9] Clifford, "On Ethnographic Authority," 137.
[10] "far from turning the character into a 'he' enclosed in a network of determinations (human nature, social type, psychological character), he makes him a 'you,' a freedom." Bakhtin, *Esthétique et théorie du roman*, 14.
[11] Sadlek, "Bakhtin, the Novel, and Chaucer's *Troilus and Criseyde*," 89.
[12] McKeon, *The Origins of the English Novel*, 13.
[13] Holquist, *Dialogism: Bakhtin and His World*, 72.

and Authier-Revuz have,[14] for instance, tried to understand how discourse represents itself in the very process of being enunciated as an association of other discourses and heterogeneous languages. Gérard Genette's writing[15] on the point of view inspired Oswald Ducrot's own work[16] on dialogism, which allowed the introduction of polyphony in the field of semantics on account of a theory based on an enunciative conception of meaning—a tradition going back to Charles Bally's work. Indeed, Bally noticed well before Émile Benveniste and John L. Austin[17] that language use allows the staging of language's own enunciation. According to him, sentences not only contain a *dictum* expressing a content, but also a *modus* whose purpose is the conventional staging of the *dictum* itself. Bally tries to show how enunciation is also an object of meaning, that meaning describes the world and shows the enunciation, presents a reflexive image of it.[18] Ducrot later specified that the object of what he names "integrated pragmatics" is not "ce que l'on fait en parlant mais . . . ce que la parole, d'après l'énoncé lui-même, est censée faire."[19] Ducrot and Bally are therefore of great importance if one wishes to understand the linguistic intricacies of Chaucer's dialogism.[20] Relying solely on Bakhtin would greatly limit our comprehension of the concept and deprive us of the tools necessary to the definition of Chaucerian polyphony.

Russian formalists defined poetical language in opposition with practical language and considered prosaic forms as being motivated by the implementation of a certain number of narrative processes. Language was accordingly reduced to the role of a medium whose sole purpose was to transmit information, and which had to be approached differently according to the literary genre. But Bakhtin refused to establish a distinction between a poetics of language adapted to poetry and another to prose, and although he noticed the difference between the forms, he linked them together as language acts. In subordinating language to abstract forms, Saussurians had notably lost sight of its living aspect. Bakhtin, on the other hand, indicated that without the *parole* animating it,

---

14 Kristeva, "Le mot, le dialogue et le roman," 82–112; Todorov, *Mikhaïl Bakhtine, le principe dialogique*; Authier-Revuz, "Hétérogénéité montrée et hétérogénéité constitutive: éléments pour une approche de l'autre dans le discours," 91–151; Authier-Revuz, *Ces mots qui ne vont pas de soi*.
15 See Genette, *Figures III*, and Genette, *Nouveau discours du récit*.
16 Ducrot, "La notion de sujet parlant," 65–93. Ducrot, "Esquisse d'une théorie polyphonique de l'énonciation," 171–233.
17 See Benveniste, *Problèmes de linguistique générale*. See Austin, *How to Do Things With Words*.
18 Bally, *Linguistique générale et linguistique française*, 35–36.
19 "what we do when we speak . . . but what speech, following the enunciation, is supposed to do." Ducrot, "Esquisse d'une théorie polyphonique de l'énonciation," 174.
20 See for instance Chapter 4 in which the connection between *dictum* and *modus* is central to the understanding of the double enunciation developed by Chaucer.

language is nothing and that without dialogue, *parole* becomes static and dies. It is this orchestration of the structures of dialogue that are at the heart of novelistic discourse, and which strongly contrast with a lyric poetic discourse that might be delivered by a single voice, whose authority cannot always be questioned.

The novel has, in fact, long been considered a secondary literary genre, unlike lyric poetry. It was appreciated as an instrument of communication until the Russian formalists remarked, during the 1920s, that "all the categories of traditional stylistics, and the very conception of poetic discourse that lies at their basis, are not applicable to novelistic discourse."[21] Indeed, for Bakhtin it was essential to see the novel as a unique and global object, simultaneously pluristylistic, multilingual, and polyvocal. He consequently defines the linguistic stratification of the novel in a concrete way: it may be generic (serial fictions or epistolary novels use different language features), professional (a lawyer will not use the same jargon as a medical doctor or a miller), but also social (which implies an understanding of the origin and education of a character), and temporal (there is linguistic and ideological diversity among different periods). It is accordingly this "social diversity of languages, sometimes of tongues and individual voices, a diversity literarily organized"[22] that constitutes the novel genre. The novel wields multilingualism and polyvocality as tools allowing the connection of its constitutive units.

Nonetheless, although the poetic genre embraces all of the linguistic system, it is in fact the linguistic and verbal unicity of the poet creator that will dominate—in the case of a monological work—whereas one of the founding principles of the novel genre is the social and vocal diversity of language. The discourse, strongly influenced by the social consciousness of the author, will intertwine with external ideas:

> he is twined, penetrated by general ideas, views, appreciations, definitions of others. Turned towards his object, he enters this environment of foreign words, agitated by dialogues, and tense with words, judgments, foreign accents; he sneaks through complex interactions, merges with the one, breaks off from the other, intersect with the third.[23]

This movement seems rare in poetry, however.[24] The lyric poetical style alienates, by definition, all foreign discourses for they are incompatible with the inherent domination of the poet creator. Yet, a poet living in a society marked by

---

21 Bakhtin, *Esthétique et théorie du roman*, 87.
22 Ibid.
23 Ibid., 100.
24 Rare but not inexistent. A look at the highly novelistic and dramatic poetry composed by Robert Browning is enough to see the polyphony of a poetic discourse.

multilingualism may be affected by it, and Bakhtin remarked that in order to integrate multilingualism into his work, the artist must transform the poet into a prose writer.[25] Chaucer himself started his career as a courtly love poet and composer of ballads, *rondeaux*, and *virelais* before turning to narrative poetry. And as we will see, the more he gave free range to the polyphonic art, the more the poet became prose writer, switching from lyric poetry to narrative poetry, and in some instances to prose. The lyric poet is not supposed to share his language form, which he painstakingly molded for his poetic work; it is interdependent and remains untouched by linguistic plurality.

That does not mean, however, that multilingualism does not affect poetic discourse. Multilingualism is the linguistic norm, and nothing can contain it completely. In other words, the poet artificially integrates multilingualism by translating all that is foreign to him into his own language. The diversity of multilingualism is feigned, whereas the prose writer completely reverses the situation by using a foreign language to represent his own *parole*: "he often measures his own world in accordance with others' linguistic range."[26] Chaucer rapidly became aware of the inherent limits of courtly love poetry's mode of representation and decided to present his own vision of the world, notably in *The Legend of Good Women* and *The Canterbury Tales*, by means of different voices, each belonging to a particular genre or vision of literature. And that would never have been possible if he had not been receptive to the linguistic and cultural richness of medieval England. As we will see in this chapter, centuries of Latin, Scandinavian, and French domination had greatly fertilized the country's linguistic soil, giving Chaucer a multilingual and polyvocal heritage unique in Europe. It is most certainly this inheritance, enriched a few years later by Italian poetry, which allowed him to represent a plural and polyphonic world with such vibrancy.

England in the First Days of Old English

Chaucer's English background and his European influences, from antiquity to the Latin Middle Ages and beyond, are well known.[27] But despite our knowledge of Chaucer's literary connections, it is essential to investigate the multifarious

---

25 Bakhtin, *Esthétique et théorie du roman*, 108.
26 Ibid., 109.
27 Some of the material and data given here were prevísouly published in Dean, *Critical Insights: Geoffrey Chaucer*, 216–30. I thank James M. Dean and Salem Press and Grey House Publishing for the authorization to reproduce parts of my work.

nature of Chaucer's language and how it might have affected his vision of poetry. Indeed, Chaucer's approach to literature reflected his approach to the world he lived in: he embraced a pluricultural and multilingual world and transposed this sensitivity into a rich polyphonic vernacular, something he accomplished with the abilities of a true sociolinguist. What will interest us in this chapter is not, therefore, the myth of Chaucer as the father of the English language. As Christopher Cannon explained,

> the significance of Chaucer's linguistic making cannot be addressed or solved by an "accurate" history of the language because it cannot be separated from the project of writing that history. The problem is epistemological not historical, a question finally of origination and how the history of a "beginning" may be written without determining it.[28]

Instead of focusing on the myth, we will therefore examine Chaucer's idiom and how centuries of language contact left traces in its linguistic DNA. That will allow us to see that Chaucer was dealing with a language whose very fabric was already marked by different voices—something that would inevitably influence the writing of a poet and linguist.

The history of the English language is not a peaceful one. It has been marked by centuries of invasions, wars, and massacres between different peoples, each defending its own language, culture, and faith. Thus, when the Anglo-Saxons first encountered the Celts, the Romans, and later on the Vikings and the Normans, the dialects they all spoke entered into contact with each other and evolved as any other living organisms would.

Britain had been inhabited by the Celts for centuries before its Romanization started in 55 BC. Linguistically speaking, this first conquest played an important role since it allowed Latin to be introduced in this part of Europe. The Celts did not, however, stop using their vernacular but they were forced to switch to Latin in order to communicate with their rulers, a diglossia that reinforced Latin's role as *lingua franca*. Yet, Latin's hegemony could not protect the language against pidginization: the Latin spoken by the legionaries was, in effect, a provincial variety, different from the standard Latin used in the streets of Rome. However, it is believed that the Celts never learned it, and although their own vernacular was displaced in the south of Britain, it remained firmly implanted in the north, where the resistance stopped the invaders near Hadrian's Wall. But while the Romans and the Celts were still fighting for the dominion of Britain, in the second half of the fifth century they were overrun by Germanic tribes.

---

[28] Cannon, "The Myth of Origin and the Making of Chaucer's English," 648.

Although in some ways this helped the Celts to free themselves from the Latin yoke, their arrival was not exactly a benediction. The disorganized Celtic resistance was in no position to match what Bede described as "an invincible army."[29] They were finally overwhelmed and had no choice but to accept the inevitable: those who gave up the fight were culturally and linguistically assimilated by the Anglo-Saxons while a substantial number of them fell back westwards behind the Cambrian Mountains, in Cornwall and even in Ireland and Armorica.[30] Nonetheless, this contact between the Anglo-Saxons and the Celts had fairly limited linguistic consequences. The Anglo-Saxon people brought with them their culture and Germanic dialects and obviously meant to keep them. As a result, even though the majority of the native inhabitants held to their idiom (already weakened by Roman domination), they could not match the strength of the Germanic presence.

The Viking raids on England began in 793 with the sack of Lindisfarne and Jarrow, continued throughout the ninth and tenth centuries, and would have long-term consequences on the evolution of the English language. In only a few decades, the Vikings had overrun most of the Anglo-Saxon kingdoms, but Alfred the Great's resistance forced the invaders to settle in the Danelaw (a region under Viking control in the northeast of England), which allowed Old English and Old Norse to enter into frequent contact. Until these invasions, Old English had been a highly inflected language. The meaning of a sentence was, thus, not determined by the order of the words (as it is in Modern English) but by their ending, defined by the words' grammatical function. But the processes of pidginization and creolization that began with the contact between Old English and Old Norse gradually levelled these inflections. Although the two languages were very similar, these complications clouded the meaning of some sentences. For instance, if an Anglo-Saxon were to sell one of his horses to a Scandinavian, he would say "Ic selle ðe ðat hors ðe draegeð minne waegn" (I will sell you the horse that pulls my cart). On the other hand, if the Scandinavian were to trade the same thing, he would say "Ek mun selja ther hrossit er dregr vagn mine." The content words are closely related: the Anglo-Saxon uses the words *hors* and *draegeð*, while the Scandinavian says *hros* and *dregr*. But, the rest of the sentence will eventually disturb the conversation since the Scandinavian does not understand Old English grammatical structure. Indeed, the Anglo-Saxon says *ðat hors* for "one horse," and *ða hors* for "two horses." In other words, the word *hors* does not change in the singular

---

29 Bede, *The Ecclesiastical History of the English People*, 27.
30 Leith, *A Social History of English*, 17.

and the plural since number is conveyed by the forms of the pronoun; in consequence, no one will really understand how many horses are for sale.[31] The language had therefore to be simplified.

This contact also resulted in the borrowing of large quantities of words, most of which are still present in Modern English and which coexist with Old English words. Such is the case with "shirt," from the Old English *scyrte*, and "skirt," from the Old Norse *skyrta*: both words have the same Germanic etymology and essentially mean the same thing but each represents a different dialect (MED, s.v. "skirt(e)"; OED, s.v. "skirt," noun). On one side of the Danelaw, speakers tended to say *skirte*, and on the other side of it *shirte*.

Norman Invasion, Multilingualism, and Chaucer's English

The Battle of Hastings and the Norman Invasion in 1066 brought another massive language shift and cultural revolution. William's takeover was particularly bloody, and interestingly enough, the new order and its violence were reflected in the first stage of the Old English lexical transformation. The *Peterborough Chronicle* thus gives us a general idea of what sort of words were then borrowed: except for new ranks (*cuntesse*, *duc*), we find concepts such as doing *iustice* (to hang someone), *castel*, *prisun*, or *crucethur* (a torture device).[32] These first loan words show, once more, the capacity of language to reflect a profound social and political transformation. But while contact with Old Norse helped to simplify Old English through the loss of some of its inflections, the French dialects[33] spoken by the invaders influenced English at a different level. Indeed, the Norman political shift was followed by such a massive transformation of the Old English lexicon that together with the already ongoing process of morphological synthesis, the language evolved into a new variety considered by linguists as a different idiom.[34]

In the decades following the Norman Invasion, Old English began to evolve at an extraordinary rate, losing in that process many of its most distinctive

---

31 McCrum, Cran, and McNeil, *The Story of English*, 70–71.
32 Barber, *The English Language*, 166.
33 There was a great variety of dialects in the French-speaking regions. Some of the people who accompanied William were Picard and supposedly spoke that dialect. But as Butterfield comments, one might add "that the designation '*picard*' should itself be taken broadly, since the linguistic (and cultural) borders between *picard*, *wallon*, *Hainault*, and *artois* (not to mention Anglo-French) are notably fluid." *The Familiar Enemy*, 60.
34 See Mossé and Jolivet, *Manuel de l'anglais du Moyen Âge*, 1:21.

characteristics. Nonetheless, even though inflections were gradually levelled, we cannot consider the Normans or the Vikings responsible for this morphological synthesis. Both Hastings and the Danelaw might be considered merely as accelerative factors of a natural phenomenon. This simplification of language is indeed very similar to what Dick Leith describes as a "gradual erosion."[35] In the centuries following the Norman Conquest, this erosion was concretely represented by the appearance of grammatical words (*to*, *by*, *for* . . .) whose purpose was to clarify syntactic relationships. By Chaucer's time, the conjugation of verbs was not completely fixed yet, often leading to the coexistence of ancient and modern grammatical forms. For instance, the past singular stem of certain verbs was different from its past plural (as seen in *was* and *were*). Chaucer thus used the singular "ran" as a plural ("and after hym they ran"; *CT*, VII. 3381), but then switched to its regular plural form "ronne" ("They ronne so hem thoughte hir herte breeke"; VII. 3388).

The contact between French and English did not produce, as one might have expected, a large-scale pidginization since the invaders were simply too few in number. Between 50,000 and 60,000 Normans settled in an England then inhabited by a million and a half people, leading to a reinforced multilingualism.[36] England was still, as a result, a multilingual society, even during the fourteenth century, and "[b]y Chaucer's time it is probable that almost everyone born in England, with the exception of some of those on the Celtic marches of Wales and Cornwall, grew up with English as their main and native language."[37] But even though English had become the main language used by most of the population, its essence was still marked by the contact with other cultures.

To illustrate this point, let us have a look at Table 1 below which presents the etymology of the content words used by Chaucer in the five first lines of the *General Prologue* of *The Canterbury Tales*. This table allows us to see more concretely how Old English evolved through more than nine centuries of language contact. There is no real difference between the number of French and Germanic words used by Chaucer. Yet, although 55 percent of the content words do come from Old English, the replacement of some of those words bears witness to the strength with which Latin and French influenced English culture. Some borrowings not only replaced already existing concepts but also became deeply rooted in Anglo-Saxon culture, with, for instance, the disappearance of the traditional names of the months. Chaucer's "Aprill," which was spelled with two *l*s because

---

35 Leith, *A Social History of English*, 100.
36 Crépin, "Le plurilinguisme de l'Angleterre médiévale," 30.
37 Shippey, "Bilingualism and Betrayal in Chaucer's Summoner's Tale," 126.

of the Old French *avrill*,[38] was accordingly used instead of the Old English *Eastermonað*, while "March" replaced *Hreðmonaþ*.

Table 1: Etymological analysis of the First Lines of the *General Prologue*.

	Old English	Middle English	Old French	Latin	Modern English
	Eastermonað	Aprill	avrill	Aprilis	April
	Hreðmonaþ	March	marz	Martius	March
	stingan	perced	percier	*pertusiare	pierce
	ædre	veyne	veine	vena	vein
	flogoða	licour	licour	liquorem	liquor
	ārfæstnes	vertu	vertu	virtutem	virtue
	tíeman	engendered	engendrer	ingenerare	engender
	mearu	tendre	tendre	tenerem	tender
	blowan	flour	flor	florem	flower
General Prologue					
	scūr	shoures	la verse	versare	shower
	swete	soote	dulce	dulcis	sweet
	drugað	droghte	secheresse	siccare	drought
	rot	roote	racine	radix	root
	swete	sweete	dulce	dulcis	sweet
	cropp	croppes	pousse	Pulsare	crop
	geong	yonge	jofne	Juvenis	young
	sunne	sonne	soleil(l)	sol	Sun
	bræð	breeth	sofle	sufflare	breath
	holt	holt	boscage	boscaticum	holt
	hæð	heeth	bruiere	brugaria	heath

---

38 See MED, s.v. "april," and Andrew, Ransom, et al., *A Variorum Edition of The Works of Geoffrey Chaucer*, 2:1–2.

As we can see, the Norman Invasion had left deep marks on the English linguistic context, especially in the upper reaches of society, where social rank and fluency in French were still strongly correlated. Although a situation of coexisting monoglots certainly lasted for some time once William the Conqueror was crowned, it gradually disappeared, leaving in its wake a much more enduring sense of linguistic stratification: "French outranked English. Latin, the international language of the Church, in some ways outranked even French. And on the Celtic marches English was allowed to outrank Welsh, and with many local adjustments Cornish, Irish and Scots Gaelic too."[39] Britain was therefore not just a trilingual country, despite the official distribution of languages. Richard Sharpe finds, for instance, no fewer than eleven distinct language groups addressed in different parts of Britain and Ireland in the charters from the eleventh and twelfth centuries:

> English is always mentioned in address clauses, though never in first place. After 1066 French is almost always included. We have seen "Welsh" appearing not only in Wales but also in Cornwall and Ireland. Flemish is found occasionally in Wales, Ireland, Scotland, and, exceptionally, in England. Breton, Cornish, Danish, Gaelic, and Irish appear in particular areas where speakers of these languages were present.[40]

A shared language could thus easily be seen crossing between a wide range of cultural perspectives:

> from French-to-French (Machaut and Paien); English-to-English—in French (Froissart and Gower); Anglo/Savoyard French-to-English (Graunson and Chaucer), and English (in French)-to-English (in English) (Gower and Chaucer). There are probably more permutations to be invented even than these, but the real argument is that their very plurality undermines the attempt to categorize.[41]

But let us take a look at the situation "on the ground," far from the "deadening atmosphere" of the Anglo-French polarity.[42] A brief detour by way of Thomas Cantilupe's beatification commission, which was held in 1320 in Hereford, near the Welsh border, will help us to better visualize how thorough England's multilingualism was and how the English people reacted to the situation. Michael Richter notes that the detailed records of Cantilupe's beatification commission show that 163 witnesses were questioned, most of whom code-switched and tried to speak in the most prestigious language they knew. Table 2 below thus gives a unique glimpse of the linguistic hierarchy in medieval England: among

---

39 Shippey, "Bilingualism and Betrayal in Chaucer's Summoner's Tale," 128.
40 Sharpe, "Addressing Different Language Groups," 23.
41 Butterfield, *The Familiar Enemy*, 265.
42 Ibid., 56–57.

the thirty-one clerics, none spoke English or Welsh, sixteen used pure Latin, twelve French, and three used a mixture of French and Latin.

The situation is even more interesting for commoners: 132 people addressed the commission, one hundred of whom spoke in English, twenty-one in French, ten in a mixture of French and Latin, and only one in Welsh.[43] Bear in mind that this happened in Hereford, only a few miles away from Wales! In other words, 75 percent of commoners used English, which proves that the vernacular was still quite important for many people, but 23 percent of them tried to impress the commission with the highest-ranked idiom they could possibly speak. Besides, we know that out of the 64 percent of commoners living in rural areas, only 9.4 percent used French while out of the 35.6 percent living in cities, almost 49 percent spoke either French or a mixture of French and Latin. For Herbert Schendl, the long-attested history of this multilingual discourse strategy "provides strong evidence that code-switching was an acceptable and accepted mode of discourse in Britain for many centuries, which was neither stigmatized nor unusual, but a natural reflection of a multilingual society."[44] There was consequently a major difference between the provinces and the cities, a difference that was not only geographical or political but also ideological. In the provinces, people were traditionally more conservative than in urban areas, where both languages and cultures were subjected to a strong homogenization.

Table 2: Language Distribution During Thomas Cantilupe's Beatification Commission.

	Commoners	Clerics
Latin	0	16
French	21	12
French-Latin	10	3
English	100	0
Welsh	1	0
Total	132	31

If J.R.R. Tolkien was correct in his 1934 lecture to the Philological Society, then Chaucer was not only a gifted poet but also a remarkable philologist, thinking

---

43 Richter, *Sprache und Gesellschaft im Mittelalter*, 188–90.
44 Schendl, "Code-Switching in Late Medieval Macaronic Sermons," 154.

like a linguist of the nineteenth and twentieth centuries. Chaucer is the ultimate "tourist/anthropologist/historian voyaging through strange scenes in far off locations, seeking to make intelligible what he sees and hears."[45] In this respect, Chaucer was probably more conscious than anyone else of the sociolinguistic situation in England. Indeed, Middle English was more than just Chaucer's language and was spoken in a variety of dialects, identified during the fourteenth century as Northern, Midlands, and Southern, and nowadays as the Northern, West Midland, East Midland, Southern, and Kentish dialects. Each of these idioms had characteristics of its own: for instance, while the author of the epic romance *Sir Gawain and the Green Knight* wrote in the West Midland dialect, Chaucer wrote in the Southern dialect, more precisely the one spoken in London and which would later become the standard variety of English. And although Chaucer spoke "the king's English," he was perfectly aware of the coexistence of these varieties of English and knew how to reproduce and use them.

The Reeve's Tale is thus a wonderful example of Chaucer's abilities as a sociolinguist. The clerks in this tale are from Strother in the north of the country and accordingly speak in the Northern dialect. But Chaucer does not merely imitate comical accents or local grammatical forms; he reproduces with great care their idiom and makes his characters utter words his own audience would have found difficult, such as the deponent form "Hym boes" (I. 4027); "heythen" (I. 4033); or "ymel" (I. 4171). As Jonathan Hsy explains, a polyglot poet such as Chaucer code-switches "not only for pragmatic purposes but also for deliberately artistic ends."[46] In the case of *The Reeve's Tale*, Chaucer clearly switches from one variety of Middle English to another to "develop distinct expressive registers" and "evoke a vivid sense of place"[47] that creates a greater contrast between the clerks and their victims.

The Summoner's Tale is equally interesting, for it illustrates this multilingualism and the sense of social snobbery made obvious by the details of Cantilupe's beatification commission. Indeed, in that tale, the friar often uses Latin, which seems normal for a cleric, but also tends to code-switch, especially when he is addressing Thomas ("O Thomas, je vous dy, Thomas, Thomas!"; III. 1832) and his wife ("'Now dame,' quod he, 'now je vous dy sanz doute'"; III. 1838). Here, the Friar obviously uses fragments of French in order to reveal his social rank and to impress Thomas's wife. Indeed, "one can say that code-switching can constitute a particular mode of bilingual discourse used to express dual or multiple group

---

45 Butterfield, *The Familiar Enemy*, 208.
46 Hsy, *Trading Tongues*, 5–6.
47 Ibid.

membership or to establish in-group feeling in certain communicative situations."[48] Yet when the friar asks Thomas about the whereabouts of his spouse, he shows little desire to react to this linguistic competition and answers in provincial Middle English: "Yond in the yerd I trowe that she be, . . . and she wol come anon" (III. 1798–99). When his wife finally joins them, she starts reacting to the friar's linguistic prowess and flirtatious words in the same provincial Middle English, but this time enriched by French words ("desire," "disport," "plese," 1826, 1830, 1831). If code-switching has a clear function, it has been remarked that "individual switches, especially intrasentential ones, in contrast, frequently have no discernible particular function, even though they may serve certain stylistic purposes."[49] In that case, as Shippey remarks,

> her by-play with the friar is meant to show an urge towards social climbing, a readiness to side with, and flirt with, what she takes to be the upper classes. She uses the French vocabulary of romantic involvement not because she needs it or has no other words available, but to indicate, or to pretend, that she is, or was, or one day will be, something better than a farmer's wife in a barnyard.[50]

Chaucer was, in other words, quite aware of the importance of multilingualism in England, of the prestige associated with French and Latin, and of the communicative importance of code-switching. Like a true sociolinguist, he shows how language could be manipulated to enhance one's social rank. After all, even the Pardoner, in a reference to mixed sermons—that is to say, sermons in different languages directed to a multilingual audience—recognizes that

> in Latyn I speke a wordes few,
> To saffron with my predicacioun,
> And for to stire hem to devocioun.
>   (VI. 344–46)

In order to show the linguistic consequences of the Norman Invasion, Manfred Scheler compared the etymology of the words listed in the *Shorter English Dictionary*, or SED (80,096 headwords of all stylistic levels), the *Advanced Learner's Dictionary*, ALD (27,241 headwords, representing various stylistic levels), and finally the *General Service List*, GSL, which only lists the most common words (3,984 headwords). He thus established a certain number of categories based on his etymological study, here limited to five sources of

---

48 Schendl, "Code-Switching in Late Medieval Macaronic Sermons," 160.
49 Ibid.
50 Shippey, "Bilingualism and Betrayal in Chaucer's Summoner's Tale," 137.

lexical influences: *Inselgermanisch* (the Germanic part of the English lexicon), French, Latin, Celtic languages, and various other sources.[51] Figure 1 illustrates once again the richness and diversity of the English lexicon, even six centuries after Chaucer's death. As we have seen, Chaucer's vocabulary had already ceased to be purely Germanic and had integrated elements from different cultures and languages. Scheler's analysis confirms that in the most general vocabulary, *Inselgermanisch* is less represented than French (22.2 percent in the *Shorter English Dictionary* and 27.43 percent in the *Advanced Learner's Dictionary*). Even if this Germanic origin seems more important for the most frequent words (47.08 percent), it remains slightly less so than the languages of Latin origin: French (38 percent) and Latin (9.59 percent) amount together to 47.59 percent. Likewise, more than half of the words present in the entire lexicon come from French or Latin (56.66 percent in the SED). It is also particularly interesting to note that the Celtic languages, which have been used in Britain longer than Anglo-Saxon dialects, left almost no mark on Modern English. By contrast, Latin's percentage reflects a strong cultural borrowing while the importance of French is due to a forced linguistic contact between a conqueror's superstratum and the conquered's substratum. It is, in this regard, a reflection of the far-reaching influence of French and Anglo-Norman culture and civilization on late medieval England.[52]

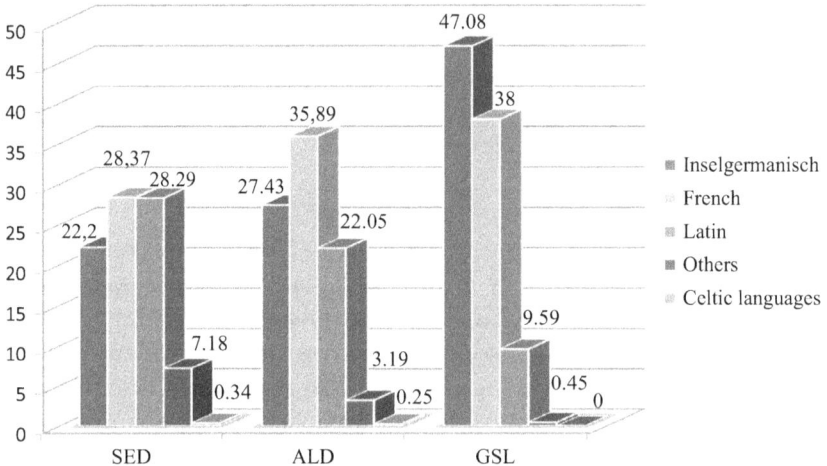

Figure 1: Scheler's analysis of Modern English Lexicon in the SED, ALD, and GSL.

---

51 Scheler, *Der englische Wortschatz*, 72.
52 Ibid., 55.

As we have seen, Chaucer's Middle English was more than just a Germanic language. It was the linguistic representation of Europe's incredible history and culture, for Europe was already a vast political and cultural entity. Indeed, as E.R. Curtius explains, "European literature is coextensive in time with European culture, therefore embraces a period of some twenty-six centuries (reckoning from Homer to Goethe)."[53] Chaucer was of course aware that he owed much of his inspiration and both his artistic and linguistic legitimacy to an international cultural tradition, for "it is only from the perspective of those post-Chaucerian centuries that the very subject of Chaucer as a European writer comes into focus as a subject at all: for Chaucer there was no question of being anything else."[54]

Chaucer's decision to write in Middle English was then very much, as Elizabeth Salter noted, "the triumph of internationalism"[55] since he was deeply nourished by the "international and courtly world" in which he "received his training and spent his mature life."[56] Chaucer was also the *grand translateur* described by Eustache Deschamps, inspired by the masters of vernacular literature to elevate his own limited and marginal idiom into a prestigious literary language. French troubadours and *trouvères* had, after all, been nourishing Europe since the twelfth century with masterpieces such as Chrétien de Troyes's Arthurian legends, the *Chanson de Roland* or the *Roman de la Rose*. And from the thirteenth century onwards, that creative momentum was transferred from France to Italy, establishing a bridge "fra il Medioevo (latino e francese) e la modernità, in una fecondazione che supera le barriere linguistiche, le dilanianti divisioni nazionali."[57] Dante Alighieri and other poets, such as Francesco da Barberino, author of *Documenti d'Amore*, were thus among the first to compose in an Italian vernacular, a decision that regenerated the whole European artistic tradition through successive waves of "Italianism"[58] which ended up crashing on the shores of Spain, France, Germany, and England. Charles V of France commissioned, for instance, several translations during the second half of the fourteenth century. Jacques Bauchant, who translated Elisabeth of Schönau's treatises, even went so far as to tell his king that "[l]e latin n'est si entendible ne si commun que

---

53 Curtius, *European Literature and the Latin Middle Ages*, 12.
54 Simpson, "Chaucer as a European Writer," 57.
55 Salter, "Chaucer and Internationalism," 79.
56 Ibid., 73.
57 "between the Middle Ages (Latin and French) and modernity, in a fertilization that overcomes linguistic barriers and wrenching national divisions." Boitani, *Letteratura europea e Medioevo volgare*, 15.
58 Curtius, *European Literature and the Latin Middle Ages*, 34.

le language maternel"⁵⁹ and that his translations would help "vostre peuple gouverner et entroduire en science et en bonns meurs par exemple de bonne et ordenee vie."⁶⁰ Such a statement would have been inconceivable a few decades earlier and shows the increasing prestige acquired by vernaculars.

But writing in a vernacular meant more than just language transfer. It encompassed "a vast array of acts of cultural transmission and negotiation, deviation and/or synthesis, confrontation and/or reconciliation."⁶¹ Chaucer's use of Middle English was, therefore, a creative act, part of a pan-European literary shift towards giving vernacular languages access to writing. His English "seems new because he so brilliantly stages the choices he makes between words: English emerges as a newly powerful vernacular because it is shown to be a matter of artful selection rather than familiar formulas."⁶² But Chaucer's Middle English also synthesized, as we have seen, centuries of language contact and of cultural transmission.

---

59 "Latin is not as understandable nor as common as the mother tongue." Paris, Bibliothèque Nationale de France, MS fr. 1792, fol. 2r.
60 "to govern your people and teach them science and good mores by the example of a good and organized life." Ibid., fol. 2v.
61 Minnis, *Translations of Authority in Medieval English Literature*, 16.
62 Butterfield, *The Familiar Enemy*, p. xxiii. See also Cannon, *The Making of Chaucer's English* and "What Chaucer's Language Is."

Chapter 2
Fin'amor, *Stil Novo*: Chaucer's Early Influences

In the previous chapter, I attempted to show how the linguistic situation in medieval England helps to explain Chaucer's polyphonic abilities. This linguistic approach gave us a general understanding of how dialogism functions, what might trigger it, and why Chaucer was so sensitive to this device. In this chapter, I continue to set the scene as I take a closer look, this time, at Chaucer's early literary influences, namely the poets of *fin'amor* and of the *Dolce Stil Novo*. This will allow us to discern the first signs of interdiscursive dialogue between Chaucer and the great European poets of his time.

Very few of the major Western literary productions that have entered our canon would have existed without the development of the courtly love tradition in Languedoc during the twelfth century. Even though our values and literary expectations have changed, there still remains a fundamental connection between the poetry of the troubadours, the *trouvères*, the Stilnovists, the art of the Trecento, and ourselves. There is thus a strong sense of continuity between the Middle Ages, the Renaissance, and our own time. For without Chrétien de Troyes, Guillaume de Lorris might never have written his famous romance, and it is fair to wonder if the works of Dante and Chaucer might have existed without the *Roman de la Rose*. In *The Allegory of Love*, Lewis remarks that the link between poetic art and love has become so obvious that we tend to forget that it is not a natural connection at all. The poetry of antiquity and the Latin Middle Ages proves that this link is not so self-evident:

> It seems—or it seemed to us till lately—a natural thing that love (under certain conditions) should be regarded as a noble and ennobling passion: it is only if we imagine ourselves trying to explain this doctrine to Aristotle, Virgil, St. Paul, or the author of *Beowulf*, that we become aware how far from natural it is.[1]

Courtly love, or *fin'amor* to give it a more accurate name, became the foundation of the European literature of the past eight centuries because it allowed the elevation of vernaculars to the level of Latin as written languages.

---
1 Lewis, *The Allegory of Love*, 3.

Chrétien de Troyes and the Novelistic Genre

Before European vernaculars were able to reach a written phase of development, French clerks, taking advantage of the evolution of education and of the prosperity of the kingdom, endeavored to improve the prestige of the French language,[2] thus establishing a precedent for their European colleagues. Although courtly love poetry was spreading, it was still transmitted orally and did not have the means to disrupt the hegemony of Latin, which explains why French had first to go through a translation of the classics. Works such as the *Énéas* (1160), the *Roman de Troie* (1165), or the *Roman de Brut* (1155) all adapt Latin texts. The production of these works is not, in fact, inconsequential and is certainly no coincidence. Whereas some would have translated theological treatises, the clerks chose a different approach. Their decision to translate stories narrating the fall of Troy, Aeneas's journey, and the conquest of Britain by his descendant, Brutus, gave them enough material to inspire the Arthurian legends glorifying the English royal line. Indeed, most of these works were composed at the court of Henry II (1133–1189), Count of Anjou, Duke of Normandy, and King of England from 1154 until his death.

Henry played an essential role in the development of courtly love poetry after marrying Eleanor of Aquitaine, whose marriage with Louis VII of France had just been annulled. Eleanor was herself the granddaughter of the first troubadour, William IX, and she contributed to the diffusion of the Occitan lyrical tradition in the Anglo-Norman environment by encouraging the composition and translation of texts updating Breton and ancient subjects. It is accordingly not surprising to see Bernard de Ventadour, one of the greatest troubadours of his time, staying in London between 1154 and 1173, or to learn that he wrote a song for Eleanor and Henry. Wace also dedicated his *Roman de Brut*, a translation of Geoffrey of Monmouth's *Historia Regum Britanniae*, to Eleanor and composed his *Roman de Rou* between 1160 and 1174, in which he tells Henry II the story of the Dukes of Normandy. John of Salisbury, Peter of Blois, and Gerald of Wales also figured among the artists who exercised their art at the court of Henry II.

The first clerk to transform the novelistic genre was, however, none other than Chrétien de Troyes. When he started composing his first poems, the literary genre that would gain respectability thanks to him had only existed for a couple of decades. Chrétien was rather unsatisfied with the inherent limits of the translation process and thus decided to burn the bridges connecting him to

---

2 Old French belongs to the *langues d'oïl* category, mainly spoken in the north of France.

the Latin world by creating an original fiction that would incorporate the distinctive features of *fin'amor* and of Breton culture. He accordingly decided, as Catherine Croizy-Naquet remarks,

> d'inventer un dispositif romanesque qui insère et s'approprie les sources, par bribes et par voies détournées, donnant le sentiment d'un canevas impressionniste que reflète la syntaxe, aux antipodes de la peinture expressionniste de ses rivaux en écriture.[3]

With *Érec et Énide* (1170), Chrétien draws a link—or as he calls it, a *conjointure*[4]—between a Romanesque age defined by his translations and what later became known as the Gothic age. The word "Romanesque" alone already implies polyvocality since the word is formed on the adjective *romanus*. *Romanice loqui* then defined the language of the Roman Empire, as opposed to the various dialects spoken by Germanic tribes. And so, with the natural evolution of Romance languages (the *langues d'oïl* and *d'oc* belong to this language family), people in the north of France started to realize that they were not actually speaking Latin, but a variety of it known as *romanz*. The Romanesque age and the novelistic genre that evolved from it bear this name because the first novels to be written were translations of Latin texts into Romance languages, mixing Latin authors, Breton sources, and *fin'amor*.

The richness of that intertextuality accordingly gave Chrétien a central position in the evolution of Western literature since he was at the crossroads of the *chanson de geste*, the ancient novel, the Breton tradition, and Tristan novels.[5] It is through the assimilation and transformation of narrative processes inherited from different sources that Chrétien managed to transform the novelistic genre: in *Érec et Énide*, for example, the many fight scenes and lists typical of the epic connect the poem with the *chanson de geste*. Yet Chrétien competed with the epic by giving the character of Arthur a superior status to that of the kings of the *geste*. Jean-Marie Fritz even reminds us that such hyperbole is especially apparent in connection with ancient subjects, which were so important to the literary

---

[3] "to invent a novelistic device that inserts and absorbs sources, by fragments and indirectly, giving the feeling of an impressionist canvas reflected by syntax, diametrically opposed to the expressionist painting of his writing rivals." Chrétien de Troyes, *Le Chevalier de la charrette*, 25.
[4] Line 14 of the prologue. Chrétien borrowed the word *conjointure* from Latin and medieval rhetoric to emphasize the originality of his art. It means the cohesion of a united work, based on different traditions and various structures. See the definition given by Sylvie Lefèvre in Chrétien de Troyes, *Œuvres complètes*, 1474.
[5] The Tristan novels do not strictly speaking belong to the *fin'amor* tradition since their characters are incapable of controlling the feelings artificially produced by a love philter.

development of Romance languages. By insisting on the generosity of Érec and Arthur, Chrétien turns them into "hyper-Alexandre."[6]

Breton subjects are likewise assimilated and reinterpreted to fit this new genre. For example, Chrétien mentions several times that he does not want to betray his *estoire* (see for instance 6725–35), with respect both to names (Érec is the Romance equivalent of the Armorican names Guerec and Weroc, but also of the Welsh Gereint) and themes. The hunt for the white deer that opens this poem thus comes from a Celtic myth in which its appearance heralds the passage into the other world. But despite the richness of its borrowings and its intertextuality, the main idea in *Érec et Énide* is not the clever combination of different sources but their transformation. In Chrétien, the hunt mentioned above loses its mythological meaning and gains a new one in the *fin'amor* tradition where it will now be associated with a kiss given by the king to the most beautiful lady of his court. The episode of the "Joie de la Cour" in which Érec faces a knight enslaved by his promise to a lady is another fine example of Chrétien's adaption. Indeed, the scene loses its magical and fantastic aspect, which is replaced by a perversion of the courtly relation, with a man enslaved against his will by a woman. In other words, Chrétien modernizes his sources to the point of elevating these episodes to the rank of topoi of the novelistic genre: "combien de chasses au blanc cerf, de morts ressuscités . . ., de combats contre les géants ou de vergers merveilleux ne retrouverons-nous pas dans les romans du siècle qui va suivre ?"[7]

The coherence of the novel as conceived by Chrétien, therefore, comes from the inventiveness with which the poet handles his various narrative strands and develops his main character. Chrétien actually manages, while bringing into play different poetical figures, to attract our attention to a central element protecting the unity of a novel in which *conjointure* and *disjointure* face off, namely love. But Chrétien does not merely transform his sources, for he is constantly trying to innovate and surprise by disrupting the expectations of his audience. His treatment of the ancient Greek novel is particularly instructive. Indeed, the foundations of the Greek novel are incredibly stable for they always rely on the same narrative strands, giving the poet simple themes that he can combine how he wishes. The plot is also relatively simple since it merges two temporal episodes: the meeting of young lovers and their wedding, which concludes the narrative. Between those time markers, however, the heroes will face

---

6 Chrétien de Troyes, *Érec et Énide*, 6.
7 "How many hunts for white deer, resurrected dead . . ., fights against giants or wonderful orchards are to be found in the novels of the following century?" Ibid., 8.

a number of trials, such as the abduction of the lady, the opposition of their families, not to mention the various rescues and threats to the chastity of the lovers.[8] The situation is usually made more difficult for the hero by the fact that his lady is seldom held captive nearby: he has to embark on a long journey, which will see him cross unknown countries with strange mores and customs. All these elements, inherited from the ancient epic, from tragedy, Hellenistic love poems, and even rhetoric, thus give the Greek novel a unique capacity to concentrate in a single point all the genres of ancient literature. Bakhtin writes on this very subject:

> tous les éléments appartenant à ces divers genres sont ici remaniés, unifiés, pour former une nouvelle et spécifique entité romanesque. Dans un chronotope tout à fait nouveau, un monde étranger dans le temps des aventures, les éléments des divers genres acquièrent un caractère neuf et des fonctions particulières.[9]

Between those two fixed points in time, the meeting and the wedding, all that happens is thus merely incidental and without consequences. The extratemporal hiatus formed by the adventures leaves no traces on the characters. Time has, in a manner of speaking, stopped. Voltaire actually parodied this very idea in his own adventure novel inspired by the Greek genre: when Candide eventually reunites with Cunégonde, following a rather long and incredible series of wanderings, he finds her "rembrunie, les yeux éraillés, la gorge sèche, les joues ridées, les bras rouges et écaillés," which forces the hero to start back "saisi d'horreur," then to move closer to her "par bon procédé."[10] In this case, time has not stopped its course during the adventures. The chronotopes of encounter and of the road are accordingly founding themes of our literature, but Chrétien adapts and transforms them within the frame of his chivalric novels.

In *Érec et Énide*, he reverses the pattern of the Greek novel by resuming the adventure at the precise moment it should have ended, namely after the wedding of the eponymous characters. Érec is forced back on the road for an apparently obscure reason: no obstacle seems to be troubling the tranquillity of the wedded couple, and that is precisely what turns into an issue. Social pressure is at that moment interiorized by Énide who starts to give credence to the accusations of

---

8 Bakhtin, *Esthétique et théorie du roman*, 240.
9 "all the elements belonging to the various genres are here reshaped, unified, to form a new and specific novelistic entity. In a brand-new chronotope, a foreign world in the time of adventures, the elements from the different genres acquire a new aspect and particular functions." Bakhtin, *Esthétique et théorie du roman*, 241.
10 "sunburned, with bleary eyes, a withered neck, wrinkled face and arms"; "with horror"; "out of good manners." Voltaire, *Candide ou l'optimisme*, 155–56.

"recréantise"[11] (2446–600) against her husband, which compels him to live as an adventurous knight again. Chrétien later repeated this process in *Yvain, le Chevalier au lion* by dramatizing the plot at the moment it was supposed to end. Yvain overcomes all the obstacles in his way and marries Laudine, but is then reclaimed by chivalry to the point that he is rejected by his wife. Chrétien thus relaunches his novel by creating a narrative context close to his *incipit*, but this time the young man is entirely deprived of his character traits and becomes the very archetype of knighthood. In other words, the poet transforms the knight's quest into a true quest for the meaning of life in which the passage of time obsesses the characters and paces their adventures: Yvain hurries, for instance, to reach the fountain before Arthur, only misses Esclados by a few seconds, forgets the time limit fixed by Laudine, and so on. Chrétien's use of chronotopes allows him to insist on the fact that adventure is, by definition, the irruption of the unexpected into the temporal frame and the rejection of the notion of fate.[12]

Besides, the poet not only disrupts the classic plot of the Greek novel; he also contributes to the evolution of the novelistic genre by composing works that are increasingly less linear. Whereas his predecessors merely attempted to describe the progress of the hero's adventures following their logical order, Chrétien progressively introduces ellipses. He breaks the narrative by jumping from one character to another and by ignoring temporal logic. In *Lancelot ou le Chevalier de la Charrette*, for example, he momentarily abandons Lancelot in order to focus on Gawain, who had previously sworn to cross the Underwater Bridge. Chrétien here starts to use "une technique qu'il exploitera dans *Le Conte du Graal*, la quête menée en parallèle par les deux héros, selon les principes d'un déroulement temporel et d'un étalement en synchronie."[13] And just like Énide's internalizaton of social pressure, the discourse of the vernacular writer, as we have seen before, cannot but be influenced by an intrinsic social consciousness that merges polyvocality with the ideological vibrancy of an evolving society. It is accordingly not surprising that Chrétien, at this stage of his career, starts to give more and more importance to speech, to its use and power. Speech had already played a role in *Érec et Énide*—as seen in the strength of the royal speech or Érec's interdiction to break the silence—but it is

---

11 *Recréantise* is a form of idleness, associated with the abandonment of fighting, and thus cowardice.
12 Chrétien de Troyes, *Le Chevalier au lion*, 37.
13 "a technique he will later exploit in *Le Conte du Graal*, namely the parallel quests of two heroes, according to the principles of a temporal progression and synchronous unfolding." Chrétien de Troyes, *Le Chevalier de la charrette*, 19.

in *Le Chevalier de la Charrette* that it becomes decisive for the plot. It is dialogue that starts the adventure and paces the entire novel:

> Parole d'emblée problématique puisqu'elle est promesse en blanc, hasardeuse et à hauts risques, à l'image d'une narration un peu aveugle qui se règle au gré des rencontres. Parole déceptive par ses manques tels le silence inquiétant du nain (v. 418), et par ses excès comme la rumeur trompeuse et mensongère (v. 4165 et ss.; v. 4258). Parole informative dans le fil du récit: les dialogues reflètent l'histoire des personnages, soit pour les condamner, soit pour les distinguer.[14]

In the same way, Chrétien ranks certain forms of speech and does not hesitate to condemn those he judges reprehensible: ostentatious speech is attributed to proud knights, whereas he emphasizes Gawain's well-worded speech to his uncle (240), he criticizes Meleagant's style when he addresses his father (6266–72). The king of Gorre is actually described as being gifted with wise and measured speech, yet his tendency to over-mannered discourse prevents him from convincing Guinevere to be warmer with Lancelot, and from persuading his son to calm down.

This "social" speech is accordingly unadapted and constantly out of touch with what is happening and therefore fails to convince. Chrétien here opposes to this social speech a much more intimate variation, consisting of introspective monologues, and which the poet reserves for Lancelot, Guinevere, and Meleagant. This internalization of feelings gives us a glimpse of the main characters' moods, as they are prisoners of a social order in which the secrecy of feelings prevails.

Thus, with chivalric novels, both the author and the audience had a verbal literary consciousness that was marked socially and ideologically by their living in a class-based society. Bakhtin explains that this verbal literary consciousness was linked with the assimilation of a heterogeneous society within an ordered system:

> La traduction, le remaniement, la réaccentuation, la réinterprétation, une orientation réciproque, à divers degrés, avec le discours d'autrui, l'intention d'autrui, tel fut le processus de formation de la conscience littéraire qui donna le jour au roman de chevalerie.[15]

---

14 "Speech that is problematic from the outset since it is a hazardous and high-risk promise, in the image of a somewhat blind narration which unfolds as encounters happen. Speech made deceptive by its deficiencies, such as the dwarf's troubling silence (418), and its excesses, like the misleading and false rumor (4165ff.; 4258). Speech that is informative in the story line: dialogues give the history of the characters, whether to condemn them or distinguish them." Ibid., 41.
15 "The translation, redesign, re-accentuation, reinterpretation, reciprocal orientation, to different degrees, towards the speech and intention of another, all participated in forming the

The literary object and language were not, therefore, unified in the novel, and therein lies its originality. They seem to be unified, as in the epic, but the integration of a foreign culture and language changes everything, for European novelistic prose was born and created in the process of free and transformative translations of the works and voices of others. As Bakhtin shows with the example of Wolfram von Eschenbach's *Parzifal*, the evolution of novelistic prose in Germany, based on the translation of French prose and verses, is emblematic: since the linguistic consciousness is not dominated by a single language, it is necessary to separate the language from its subject matter in order to integrate the latter.[16]

Proud and aware of the magnitude of his accomplishment, Chrétien did not miss the chance to remind us of his importance in the evolution of the novelistic genre: he presents himself in the first line of *Cligès* as "Cil qui fist d'Érec et d'Énide."[17] Instead of making a reference to a Latin text, or to a translation like *Philomena* (an adaptation of Ovid's *Metamorphoses*), he chooses to mention an original work. And his phrasing is not accidental since it consciously evokes the beginning of the *Aeneid*, "Ille ego qui quondam gracili modulatus avena" in which Virgil signals that he is also the author of the *Eclogues* and the *Georgics*. Chrétien thus tries to establish a link between his own work and a classic of Latin literature; a link that he further highlights by producing a Virgilian echo in the very name of his character, Énide. The novel ceases, as a result, to be merely an adaptation and rivals the prestige of Latin. Chrétien even declares in the opening of *Érec et Énide*,

> Des or comencerai l'estoire
> Qui toz jorz mes iert an mimoire
> Tant con durra crestiantez:
> De ce s'est Crestïens vantez.[18]
> (23–26)

The *trouvères* and nobles at Henry II's court could not but think that the progress of the Romance language was heralding a linguistic and ideological transfer from Rome to England, a transfer made possible by Aeneas's legendary exodus and the conquest of Britain by his descendant, Brutus.

---

literary consciousness that gave birth to the chivalric novel." Bakhtin, *Esthétique et théorie du roman*, 192.
16 Ibid., 193.
17 "Him that made Érec et Énide"
18 "And now I shall begin the tale / which will be remembered / so long as Christendom endures: / This is Chrétien's boast."

From Chrétien to the *Roman de la Rose*

Chrétien left his mark on the Golden Age of courtly love poetry and greatly influenced the evolution of the novelistic genre. Although we cannot assert that his Arthurian cycle transformed European literature on its own, Chrétien's work made possible the *Roman de la Rose*, written by Guillaume de Lorris between 1230 and 1245.

Guillaume's monumental poem and Chrétien's *Conte du Graal* may be separated by half a century, but the *Roman* represents the artistic outcome of the *fin'amor* tradition and, despite several differences with Chrétien, it inherits the conventions established by the *trouvère* from Troyes. Indeed, Guillaume took over the key elements developed by his predecessor but pushed the tradition forward in another direction, far from the chivalric romance, and closer to the poet's interests, namely the world of dream visions. Whereas Chrétien had described the doubts and states of mind of his characters by contrasting monologues with silence, Guillaume turns those concerns into the heart of his narrative through a sublimated use of allegory. As Lewis observed, "[i]t is of the very nature of thought and language to represent what is immaterial in picturable terms."[19] And even though it is inherited from the personifications of Latin poetry, medieval allegory represents a real evolution: because of its use in antiquity, it still feels like a natural mode of expression, but it now serves the "subjectivism of an objective age."[20] It allows the expression of the feelings and doubts of a *fin'amor* society dominated by secrecy. When, for instance, Chrétien puts a cart on Lancelot's path, which makes the character hesitate, he allegorizes the constant opposition in the courtly tradition between reason and love. Dante himself thought it necessary to clarify this use of allegory, noting that there is nothing mystical about it:

> Potrebbe qui dubitare persona degna da dichiararle onne dubitazione, e dubitare potrebbe di ciò, che io dico d'Amore come se fosse una cosa per sé, e non solamente sustanzia intelligente, ma sì come fosse sustanzia corporale: . . . Amore non è per sé sì come sustanzia, ma è une accidente in sustanzia.[21]

In that case, any physical representation of the god of Love is just a figure of speech since love only exists in relation to the people experiencing it; it is not a

---

[19] Lewis, *The Allegory of Love*, 47.
[20] Ibid., 30.
[21] "It might be that a person might object, one worthy of raising an objection, and their objection might be this, that I speak of Love as though it were a thing in itself, and not only an intelligent substance, but a bodily substance: . . . Love is not in itself a substance, but an accident of substance." Dante, *Vita Nuova*, 129.

substance existing in itself and for itself, but the accidental result of the meeting of two lovers.

The poets of the *Roman de la Rose* and of the Arthurian cycle accordingly use allegorical language in different ways. Chrétien has often been described as a talented psychologist, but Lewis notes that he could not slip in psychology without falling at the same time into allegory.[22] One may find in his work thousands of lines in which the poet refers to the accomplishments of his knights, punctuated with monologues whose refinement of feeling is often allegorical. The episodes of the cart or of the simulacrum of rape in *Lancelot* perfectly illustrate this point. Yet, feelings and adventures seldom mingle. What is experienced by Lancelot and Guinevere is never truly represented by their adventures, which in turn do not explain the nature of their feelings.

The strength and originality of Guillaume's poetry come from his treatment of allegory, which gives more scope to the verisimilitude of feelings compared to Chrétien's work. It has been said that an intensive use of allegorical language might have as a consequence the retreat of the author into a fantasy world, whereas the only real risk is that of losing sight of the object disguised by this rhetoric. Dante reminds us once more that "grande vergogna sarebbe a colui che rimasse cose sotto vesta di figura o di colore rettorico, e poscia, domandato, non sapesse denudare le sue parole da cotale vesta, in guisa che avessero verace intendimento."[23] Such is not the case with Guillaume, who uses allegory to talk about the sentimental world. Because of the nature of his work and its intertextuality, Chrétien could play with verisimilitude and fantastical effects in such a way as to turn places and characters into romantic idealizations. But despite the abstract character of his poetry, Guillaume deals with essentially human facts. What could we say about the land of Gorre in *Lancelot*? It is apparently a real country, yet it is so difficult to reach that none of those who go there are able to get back. On the other hand, in the *Roman de la Rose*, Danger is an allegorical representation and thus by definition an abstract notion, yet it is much more tangible than Gorre. How many lovers have been confronted at one point in their life with Danger, while none has truly trodden the lands of Meleagant?

Guillaume finds in Chrétien this imaginative passion but transforms it into the heart of a story dealing with the feelings and values of his time. After having defined the frame of his narrative and the nature of his narrator/poet, Guillaume

---

22 Lewis, *The Allegory of Love*, 113.
23 "it would be shameful if someone composing in rhyme put in a figure of speech or a rhetorical flourish, and then, being asked, could not rid his words of such ornamentation so as to show the true meaning." Dante, *Vita Nuova*, 134.

starts describing his journey into an orchard surrounded by a wall on which are represented the figures (Hate, Felony, Villainy, Greed, Covetousness . . .) that may not enter this haven of courtesy. He is let into the garden of Déduit (Pleasure) by Oiseuse (Idleness) and there meets, as Armand Strubel notes, figures that "incarnent des vertus aristocratiques, dont la première est Courtoisie, mais aussi des conditions sociales ou des circonstances,"[24] offering an almost perfect symmetry with the images immortalized on the wall. The dreamer does not linger in the company of these values and starts to explore the garden, without knowing that he is being hunted by Love, and eventually discovers the fountain of Narcissus. Although he is aware of the danger represented by the fountain—the danger of passive contemplation, but also of courtly lyricism without foundations—he stops there and notices the rosebud. And that is when the *inamoramento* occurs: Love shoots him with its arrows and transforms the dreamer's interest for the rose into a true passion, each projectile making him suffer a little more to the point that he thinks:

> Mieus voudroie estre morz que vis,
>   Et en la fin, ce m'est avis,
> Fera amors de moi martir.[25]
>   (1832–35)

The dreamer has accordingly no other choice but to surrender and become the servant of Love, who teaches him how to behave as a courtly lover in love with a lady, and describes the trials ahead. Following his new master's advice, the dreamer finds a companion able to share his grief and secretly help him, in the person of Bel Accueil (Fair Welcoming), son of Courtesy. Thanks to him, he crosses the thorns surrounding the rosebud and heads towards the object of his desire when Danger, guardian of the roses, stops him with Malebouche (Foul Mouth), Honte (Shame), Peur (Fear), and Jalousie (Jealousy). The lady's good intentions, represented by Bel Accueil, are therefore suddenly destroyed because of the dreamer's haste. She is taken over by the social and psychological values preventing a young girl from giving herself away to a man.

This use of allegory allows Guillaume to reduce the importance of the notion of "character" by notably redistributing the aspects of the lady's personality. Indeed, a "man need not go to the Middle Ages to discover that his mistress is many women as well as one, and that sometimes the woman he hoped to meet is

---

[24] "personify aristocratic virtues, the first of which is Courtesy, but also social conditions and circumstances." Guillaume de Lorris and Jean de Meun, *Le Roman de la Rose*, 85.
[25] "I would rather have been dead than alive, / for in the end I believe, / Love would make a martyr out of me."

replaced by a very different woman."[26] Nevertheless, although Guillaume strips his characters of their attributes, he does not entirely abolish the notion of the "hero." Lewis believed that this process tends to turn the narrator into the bland witness of adventure,[27] but that is not correct for Guillaume produces here an effect close to what would later be undertaken by Dante or Chaucer. The entire poem is, as we have seen, presented in the first person, but this "je" is actually much more complex since it goes through a process of multiplication in chronological layers.

On the one hand is the present of writing, namely Guillaume telling the story of his dream, and on the other, the past of adventure with a "je" shared between the dreamer and actor; in other words, between Guillaume at the age of twenty and his counterpart who is wandering in the dream world. The statements unifying these various representations of the first person are in fact many since the poet does not hesitate to highlight the prospective and retrospective aspects of his work by explaining clearly that his dream has since come true.[28] The allegorical aspect of the *Roman* gives to this "je" a universal reach, detached from Guillaume, and representing every twenty-year-old man experiencing love for the first time. Furthermore, this first-person narration encounters an equally complex "tu." According to the allegorical model, the rose should represent the lady—which is true at one point (33–44)—but it is progressively described with a botanic vocabulary unsuited to a young girl (1634–78). The rose is not only both flower and woman, it is also a purpose, the idealization of the quest's accomplishment. When the dreamer first moves towards the rose, the "tu" suddenly explodes putting Guillaume face to face with several interlocutors (Bel Accueil, Danger . . .) representing all the possible reactions of a young lady in a similar situation.

The dream world is, besides, rather peculiar. From a pictorial perspective, the dreamer experiences the events from inside and does not consider himself as a character among others, which is remarkable since the dream is a complete production of the subconscious. Yet Bakhtin remarks that if we were to narrate a dream to someone, we would go through some sort of pictorial transposition

---

26 Lewis, *The Allegory of Love*, 118.
27 Ibid.
28 See for example 1–20, 2055–74.

since all the characters, including the dreamer, would become for the listener exterior characters:

> C'est ce qui différencie le monde de la création artistique du monde de la rêverie et de la vie réelle: dans l'un des cas, tous les personnages sont figurés sur un même plan plastique-pictural de la vision, dans l'autre, le héros principal . . . n'est pas figuré extérieurement et n'a pas besoin de son image.[29]

This is when the artist must don the exterior flesh of the dreamer. But the reader often crosses the boundary separating the worlds of artistic creation and dream: this passive reverie is then determined by the narrative that makes us identify with the hero, whose completion and physical aspect will be ignored so that we ourselves may become the hero.[30]

In other words, the allegory in the *Roman* allows the transformation of the dreamer into a character having one foot in each world: he is both the main character of the story and an intangible dreamer. Guillaume thus turns the hero into a persona who is the witness of a formidable cacophony and of a continuous dialogue between foreign and contradictory voices. When he breaks the strict limits that until then framed the characters in the novelistic genre, Guillaume sets up a dialogic relation between the components of his work. Strubel remarks that the

> débat entre Jalousie, Honte, Peur et Danger,[31] pourrait être comparé à l' "analyse psychologique" des romans modernes, à l'exploration des sentiments et réactions contradictoires, chez l'être aimé, après une étape importante (le baiser); il s'agit là d'une psychologie éclatée, sans frontière entre "intérieur" et "extérieur."[32]

This orchestration of discourse and opposition between the intentions of his allegorical figures, is what Guillaume contributes to the development of the polyphonic novel. Whereas Chrétien's handling of the various uses of speech had suggested dialogism, Guillaume makes way for polyvocality. Yet he completely ignores multilingualism: although different voices are opposed in the *Roman*,

---

29 "This is what differentiates the world of artistic creation from the world of dream and reality: in one case, all the characters are featured on the same pictorial-plastic plane, in another, the main hero . . . is not featured externally and does not need his own image." Bakhtin, *Esthétique de la création verbale*, 49.
30 Ibid., 49–50.
31 3497–728
32 "debate between Jealousy, Shame, Fear and Danger could be compared to the 'psychological analysis' of modern novels, to the exploration of feelings and contradictory reactions in our loved one after an important step (the kiss); it is an exploded psychology without border between the 'interior' and the 'exterior.'" Guillaume de Lorris and Jean de Meun, *Le Roman de la Rose*, 247.

they remain the voices of the same social class since the values opposed to the aristocratic way of life are not welcome in the garden of Déduit.

Guillaume's poem is interrupted shortly after the imprisonment of Bel Accueil. The dreamer suddenly finds himself cut off from his only support, which leaves us—if we ignore the anonymous ending supposed to conclude the poem—with a few lines recounting the complaints of the young man. Jean de Meung decided, however, to conclude the *Roman* in a more satisfactory way between 1270 and 1280, and although he takes up the narrative right where Guillaume stopped, he does not follow the pattern established by his predecessor. The courtly tone inherited from aristocratic conventions starts to disappear to the benefit of a much more moralizing and folkloric vision. Indeed, Guillaume's poetry is essentially dominated by an aesthetic of contemplation respecting the courtly code and showing the beauty of seduction. His *Roman* accordingly follows the rules of *fin'amor*—the very same rules given by Love to the dreamer may even be found in the greatest poems of the following centuries, such as Dante's *Vita Nuova* or Chaucer's *Book of the Duchess*. Jean, on the other hand, reduces Guillaume's undertaking to a simple narrative allowing him to exhibit, more or less chaotically, a display of pedagogy and pedantry mixed with satire, ferocious irony, and laughter. Jean even substitutes for the codes, litotes, and euphemisms of *fin'amor* a glorification of physical desire and natural instincts.[33] The chivalric novel is fundamentally opposed to common parlance and popular discourse; it resists the polyvocality of the novel since it brings to light a noble, idealized world, cut off from the vulgarity of the ordinary.[34] It presumes to impose its norms on the common language, "d'enseigner le beau style et le bon ton, la façon de converser en société, de rédiger une lettre, et ainsi de suite,"[35] while the novel usually plays with the freedom made possible by contrasts.

Things started to change with the emergence in Artois and Picardie of the bourgeois tradition during the twelfth and thirteenth centuries, thus responding to the expectations of the new middle class. Combining genres coming from the Orient and antiquity, the bourgeois tradition includes fabliaux, satiric and comic poems, animal fables, and attempts to describe a more ordinary and realistic world. Its treatment of a subject is usually down to earth, vulgar or even obscene. What Bakhtin defines as grotesque realism, that is to say, a complete imagery system used by popular comic culture, systematically highlights the body and the flesh so as to reduce all that is spiritual and ideal

---

33 Guillaume de Lorris and Jean de Meun, *Le Roman de la Rose*, 7.
34 Bakhtin, *Esthétique et théorie du roman*, 198.
35 "to teach the beautiful style and the right tone, the way to speak in society, to write a letter, and so on." Ibid.
36 Bakhtin, *Rabelais and His World*, 19–20.

to the corporal level.[36] As Charles Muscatine remarked, this tradition "has an almost total incapacity for disgust or for pretension,"[37] which allows it to link the divine and the earthly, the top and the bottom:

> Degradation and debasement of the higher do not have a formal and relative character in grotesque realism. "Upward" and "downward" have here an absolute and strictly topographical meaning. "Downward" is earth, "upward" is heaven. Earth is an element that devours, swallows up (the grave, the womb) and at the same time an element of birth, of renascence (the maternal breasts). Such is the meaning of "upward" and "downward" in their cosmic aspect.[38]

Jean thus opposes the dreamer's courtly love ideology with a completely different vision of the world during his encounter with Raison. While Love had forbidden the young man the use of "orz moz" and "vilenies" (2107–8)—especially around a lady—Raison starts employing the word "coilles" (see notably 5533), which profoundly outrages the dreamer. But this violation of the lover's aristocratic values is further accentuated by the fact that Raison is a feminine figure symbolizing wisdom. Raison defends her use of the word (6941–74) by stating that there is nothing wrong in pronouncing this sort of word without glossing it: it is perfectly natural to use the word *coilles* to describe the male reproductive organ since it serves a divine purpose. After all, as Alison reminds us in *The Wife of Bath's Tale*:

> So that the clerkes be nat with me wrothe,
> I seye this: that they maked ben for bothe,
>   That is to seye, for office and for ese
> Of engendrure, there we nat God displease.
>   (125–28)

This insistence does not please the lover who is forced to contradict his own courtly values by calling Raison a ribald. For him, if God has indeed created these things, he is nevertheless not responsible for the creation of such a vulgar word (6975–82). Raison then comments on the linguistic hypocrisy of these conventions by explaining that had she called the *coilles* relics, he would have found the word so beautiful that he would have adored them in churches and kissed them, crimped with silver and gold (7102–20). Besides an obvious reference to the medieval use of false relics, this commentary is to be compared with the end of the poem, in which the dreamer penetrates the reliquary to pluck the rose—an act described with a certain number of innuendos on the

---

37 Muscatine, *Chaucer and the French Tradition*, 59.
38 Bakhtin, *Rabelais and His World*, 21.

consummation of love. Armed with an "[e]scharpe et bourdon roide et fort"[39] (21358), the lover moves towards the arrowslit through narrow paths with "grant esfort"[40] (21357). Jean shows here that systematic use of rhetoric and elaborate periphrases may be just as obscene as one apparently vulgar word.[41]

This lowering is thus inherently ambivalent since it allows the coexistence of the satisfaction of natural needs with a desire for renewal, something that modern parody no longer does because the aesthetic, cultural, and literary rules of our age have deprived parody of its regenerative value. Whereas folkloric parody celebrated renewal, modern parody praises negation. The grotesque realism of the bourgeois tradition has thus a particular conception of time, in which everything mingles—beginning, end, birth, and death. By relying entirely on the ambivalent relation between opposites, the tradition takes its distance not only from our conception of parody but also from the Renaissance and the aesthetic of the body inherited from classical antiquity where the body is glorified, purged of its impurities, and presented at an age far from the thresholds of birth and death.

The bourgeois tradition has, as a result, a specific conception of dialogue. *Fin'amor* had slowly integrated polyvocality and dialogism into the novelistic genre while ignoring the social diversity of language. The bourgeois tradition, especially the fabliau, has, on the other hand, a much more dramatic conception of dialogue, giving us the impression of hearing the sounds and voices of everyday life. Muscatine notes, however, that this sort of language reproduction "is no less an artifact than the patterned discourse of the courtly tradition, but it is based more closely on speech as heard, especially as heard on the street corner and in the kitchen."[42] Vulgarity, jargon, and regional dialects are therefore used to simulate the realism and comedy of everyday life. *La Paix aux Anglais* reproduces, for instance, the vocabulary and the way of speaking of an Englishman talking in French, while in *Privilège aux Bretons*, a peasant is described as addressing the king in a Breton dialect—which brings to mind the clerks in *The Reeve's Tale*. The characterization associated with this style of representation thus strongly resonates with the modern reader who may notice echoes of the vivacity of Charles Dickens's novels, for example. It allows the author to create bigger than life characters, like the prostitute in the *Dit de Richeut* who bequeathed many of her qualities to Alison in *WBT*.

---

39 "scarf and strong and stiff pilgrim's staff."
40 "great efforts."
41 Fyler, *Language and the Declining World*, 77.
42 Muscatine, *Chaucer and the French Tradition*, 64.

Jean does not merely use laughter as a therapeutic instrument, he transforms it in order to sustain his philosophical vision of the world while protecting the ever-meaningful relation he had as a poet with courtly love poetry. Thus, when the dreamer finds himself isolated from the object of his desire and accordingly cut off from Doux Penser (Sweet Thought), Doux Parler (Sweet Talk), and Doux Regard (Sweet Glance), he starts to lament and blame Oiseuse. But he cannot back down without breaking the oath made to Love and betraying the courtesy exercised by Bel Acceuil. As a consequence, he decides to suffer as a martyr until Raison starts a three-thousand-line speech questioning the dreamer's allegiance to Love. For Strubel, Raison's intervention becomes

> un prétexte à de longs développements didactiques. . . . Avec Jean, un certain nombre d'acteurs (Raison, Ami, la Vieille, Nature, Faux Semblant) se transforment en personnifications purement discursives, et leur interaction se réduit à un débat d'idées; les figures correspondent à des thèses, des doctrines, des visions du monde contradictoires ou parallèles, et l'initiation amoureuse devient apprentissage philosophique, moral.[43]

Jean thus takes a radically different direction. Guillaume had established a dialogic relation between the narrator/poet and the different psychological aspects of the romance, but Jean chooses an essentially rhetorical opposition between visions of the world and forms of philosophical discourse sustained by the bourgeois tradition. Nonetheless, despite this philosophical inflection and the development of the bourgeois tradition in the poem, Jean is forced to completely transform one of the foundations of Guillaume's narrative. Indeed, when Love summons his barons in order to organize the siege of Jalousie's castle (10443–678), he lists his subjects and names, among other people, Guillaume de Lorris and Jean de Meun, who continued writing the *Roman* more than forty years after the death of its original author. The situation is at this moment rather complex since Love's order to take the fortress to facilitate Jean's task refers to a past event (the past tense of adventure), told in the present tense of writing, but taking place in the near future (the assault to come). Thus, by referring to Guillaume, the lover/dreamer, whose story is now narrated by someone outside of the dream, Love engages in a prospective-retrospective[44] that destroys the chronological stratification (dream,

---

[43] "a pretext for long didactic disquisitions. . . . With Jean, a certain number of actors (Reason, Friend, the Old Woman, Nature, False Seeming) turn into purely discursive personifications, and their interaction is reduced to a debate of ideas; the figures correspond to theses, doctrines, contradictory or parallel visions of the world, and the initiation of love become philosophical, moral education." Guillaume de Lorris and Jean de Meun, *Le Roman de la Rose*, 277.
[44] Ibid., 623.

moment of adventure, time of writing) developed by Guillaume in his part of the poem.

Besides, this also annihilates the narrative structure set up by Guillaume, along with the relation between the dreamer, the man acting the adventure, and the author. The "je" used in the first part of the *Roman* cannot possibly exist here. Accordingly, when the lover starts speaking again (12537–44) after hundreds of lines of silence, Jean takes his distance from him and demotes him to the role of passive witness. The dramatic markers noting the speaking order of the characters illustrate this change with the opposition between "L'amant" and "L'aucteur." Jean continues to multiply the narrative voices throughout his continuation of the poem, which reaches its climax when Genius compares his ideal garden with Déduit's. In the next four hundred lines (20283–671), Jean thoroughly modifies the constitutive elements of the garden as imagined by Guillaume and even allows Genius to attack the main quality of the crystal lying in the fountain of Narcissus, namely the duplication of reflection. To the surface, "miroitante et funeste à Narcisse, qui renvoie à un passé inquiétant, se substitue un fond lui aussi réfléchissant, non pas du propre visage du jeune homme et de son désir, mais de l'objet futur du désir."[45] By attacking the reflective capacity of the crystal, Jean also attacks the symbol of the duplication of authorial voice.

Thus during the speech on Pygmalion and his progeny at the end of the poem, the narrator retrieves the first-person narration: it is not the dreamer who then speaks, but the narrator, Jean, and at this stage of the narrative we easily pass from one to the other without further distancing. Jean's conclusion creates a paradox for the reader, one that "calls into question the reader's understanding of the meaning and ending of literary texts": both Guillaume's poem and Jean's ending have been accepted as forming one *Roman*, yet "the later poet calls attention to the change in authorship in such a way as to emphasize his manipulation of the reader's conception of literary closure."[46] The chronological layers and the distribution of instances imagined by Guillaume have long disappeared in favor of a much more open and bivocal narration.

The novelistic genre evolved a lot after the appearance of *fin'amor* in Provence. Chrétien was the first to place love at the heart of chivalric novels and to play with language and discourse. Yet it is truly with Guillaume and the *Roman de la Rose* that the genre wholly embraced polyvocality and dialogism by reducing the force of the authorial voice to the point of transforming it into

---

[45] "shimmering and fatal to Narcissus, that recalls a worrying past, is substituted an equally reflective bottom, showing not the young man's face and his desire, but the future object of desire." Guillaume de Lorris and Jean de Meun, *Le Roman de la Rose*, 127.
[46] McGerr, *Chaucer's Open Books*, 38–39.

one of the components of the great novelistic dialogue. Nonetheless, despite these first dialogic signs, the aristocratic principles at the heart of *fin'amor* left little room for social variation. It would take Jean's continuation and the development of the bourgeois tradition to allow different voices, belonging to different classes, to be heard for the first time in the novelistic genre. Chaucer's reception of the literature of the Oïl region was essential, especially in his understanding of unresolved ambiguities and the subversion of closure that reflect "the self-consciousness about language and fiction that modern critical theory attributes to modern literature alone."[47] But in order to truly understand how he exploited the genre, it is necessary to have a look at another huge influence, Stilnovism.

Dolce Stil Novo

While the courtly love tradition was spreading through the north of France, another branch inspired by troubadour philosophy and poetry began to develop on the other side of the Alps. Under the reign of Frederick II, the canons of *fin'amor* spread from his Sicilian court to most of the peninsula, which greatly modified the literary and cultural Italian landscape. For instance, a certain Ser Durante composed *Il Fiore*, and if the author was indeed Dante himself then it would mean that he personally participated in the assimilation and translation process of the *Roman de la Rose*. Brunetto Latini remains, however, the first great imitator of that tradition. His *Tesoretto* (composed during his exile in France between 1260 and 1266) became a source of inspiration for the artists of the Trecento. Boccaccio's *Amorosa Visione*, his first Florentine work, is thus undoubtedly indebted to Brunetto since the poem continues the same artistic undertaking, namely the adaptation in an Italian vernacular of the French narrative models.[48] Boccaccio's poem is particularly important in the evolution of this tradition because it was in many ways a conduit: the *Amorosa Visione* directed Petrarch towards the *Roman de la Rose*, a work he had until then ignored, and led to the composition of his *Trionfi*.

This first phase of assimilation did not last more than a few years and contributed to the evolution of a new approach to courtly love poetry. The "dolce stil novo," mentioned by the spirit of Bonagiunta Orbicciani in the *Divina Commedia* (*Purg.* XIV. 57), owes to the troubadours and *trouvères* its conception

---

47 McGerr, *Chaucer's Open Books*, 41.
48 Wallace, "Chaucer and Boccaccio's Early Writings," 142.

of love but has a different spiritual orientation. Thus, when Guido Guinizelli composed *Al cor gentil rempaira sempre amore* during the second half of the thirteenth century, he laid the foundations of the first modern Italian literary movement by choosing to elevate himself above the literary concepts developed by the Sicilian and Provence schools. Erich Auerbach remarks that love, in Provençal poetry, is not fundamentally either pleasure or passionate madness—although both are represented—but the mystical purpose of a noble existence.[49] Even if Guinizelli's work does not disavow these schools' teachings, it highlights the sublimated representation of the lady and frees love from the constraints of the reigning model of his time.

Al cor gentil represents the transformation of the chivalric world into a metaphoric place, the "cor gentil" or courtly heart. It puts love and the *cor gentil* on equal terms as soon as the first verse by explaining that they were both created at the same time and that both entities are just as indivisible as the sun and the moon. By seducing the heart thanks to her beauty, the lady brings out its best qualities: virtues and nobility thus shine in love like a precious stone illuminated by the sun. The poet concludes his work by imagining how God will judge him. God can only reproach him with loving and glorifying a mortal with all his heart, to which Guinizelli answers that his lady had the features of an angel from Heaven and that he cannot be blamed for his love. In a few lines, Guinizelli sets up the entire *Dolce Stil Novo* philosophy by turning the lady into the path to the divine, rather than the divine itself as the troubadours and *trouvères* had done. Conscious of the importance of Guinizelli's contribution to Italian literature, Dante did not fail to salute him in the *Commedia*. Like a happy child restored to his father, Dante offers his service to Guinizelli, which surprises the poet then trapped in the purifying flames of Purgatory (XXVI. 94–102). But while Dante is attempting to justify his devotion by mentioning Guinizelli's sweet poetry, he is interrupted by the poet himself who shows him another soul. Dante here demonstrates his perfect knowledge of courtly love poetry: like Guillaume, who could not have written the *Roman* without Chrétien, Dante mentions the man who—at least for him—is the greatest vernacular artist in "[v]ersi d'amore e prose di romanzi" (118),[50] namely the troubadour Arnaut Daniel. Daniel pronounces words that are the very essence of the *Dolce Stil Novo*: speaking in the Provençal vernacular, he confides to

---

49 Auerbach, *Studi su Dante*, 24.
50 "in lines of love and novel prose."

Dante that he had granted terrestrial love too much importance, but rejoices nonetheless that he may now expiate his sins and one day reach Paradise (139–47).

Dante's embrace of it would eventually establish the credentials of Stilnovism, until then known only to its founding members. Indeed, the movement that inspired Dante's poetry was not vast, but merely represented the formal culture of a small circle of artists who welcomed, consciously or not, the *fin'amor* tradition.[51] Dante inherited the mysticism of Stilnovism and the rhetoric of *fin'amor*, but he managed to produce an original work intensifying feelings and confining its focus to unique experiences. For Auerbach, no other Stilnovist poet managed to present the richness of the heart with such simplicity and in such a fresh language.[52] In the *Vita Nuova* (written between 1283 and 1295), Dante showed his faithfulness to the canons of *fin'amor* and presents his relation with Beatrice in a very conventional way—he follows, for instance, the advice given by Love to the dreamer in the *Roman de la Rose*. Nonetheless, unlike Boccaccio who expressed his pain in *Il Filostrato*, Dante developed a work that would later become the foundation of Dantean mythology. Unable to seduce Beatrice, he is doubly deprived of her presence by his amorous failures and her sudden death. This event provoked a change that profoundly transformed Dante's work: the young man who, upon seeing Beatrice, came to think "[e]cce deus fortior me, qui veniens dominabitur michi"[53] (*Vita Nuova* II), gained the philosophical, literary, and theological maturity witnessed in the *Divina Commedia* (1307–1321), in which Beatrice becomes among other things the symbol of the Stilnovist lady. She is no longer an object of courtly love poetry veneration, but the path to Paradise.

The appearance of this literary movement, associated with the rule of the Hohenstaufen dynasty in Sicily, allowed the re-inclusion of Italy in a medieval European culture from which it had been cut off for centuries. Indeed, the country suffered not only from a lack of unity but also from infighting between different cities that had turned strife into a permanent way of life. During the Trecento, several families shared the peninsula: Genoa, for example, fell briefly under the influence of the Visconti between 1353 and 1356, before undergoing the rule of a series of dictators overthrown one after the other. The Visconti still controlled most of northern Italy and dominated Milan from the 1320s, while their influence on Piedmont and Lombardy kept growing. From 1355 onwards, the family was led by Galeazzo II, then after 1378 by his brother Bernabò,

---
51 Auerbach, *Studi su Dante*, 25.
52 Ibid., 51–52.
53 "Here is a God more powerful than I who comes to rule over me."

whom Chaucer describes as the "God of delit and scourge of Lumbardye" (*The Monk's Tale*, 2400).

Naples and Sicily basically ruled the rest of the country. The Neapolitan influence had strongly decreased in the 1370s but still retained an echo of the splendor and greatness that, under the reign of Robert I (1309–1343), had impressed the young Boccaccio. When Chaucer visited the country for the first time in 1373, he discovered a different landscape from his native England. While the English people was gradually being unified around a single language and a common cause, in opposition to France, the Italians inhabited what John Larner describes as "a land deeply divided, politically, economically, socially, and one about which any generalization at all might seem precarious."[54] The difference between the cities was not only political and social but also linguistic. As we have seen in the previous chapter, Chaucerian England was the heir of centuries of multilingualism and cultural transfers. The Italy Chaucer visited was not that different. Linguistically speaking, Trecento Italy might be compared to the Anglo-Saxon Heptarchy: the Italian cities were at war, yes, but they were also strongly divided by their respective dialects. The very notion of "dialect" tends to imply the existence of standard variety of Italian, whereas the idiom spoken in Genoa was as foreign to a Milanese as English is to a Spaniard. Fra Bernabò Reggio was, for example, described by his friend Fra Salimbene de Adam as a fine linguist because he could speak French, Tuscan, and Lombard.[55] Italy was, in other words, more a literary conception than a physical reality since only the values of courtly love poetry seemed to grant a sense of unity to its native poets. Dante even laments this aspect of Italian culture:

> Non ti maravigliar s'io piango, Tósco,
>
> . . .
>
> le donne e i cavalier, gli affanni e gli agi
> che ne invogliava amore e cortesia
> là dove i cuor son fatti sì malvagi![56]
> (*Purg.* XIV. 103–11)

Yet Dante's importance to this literary movement quickly became a source of anxiety for his successors, most notably Boccaccio and Petrarch. Whereas Dante had successfully found his place among Guinizelli, Virgil, or Arnaut Daniel, his literary heirs were instead faced with the anxiety of influence, as Harold Bloom

---

54 Larner, "Chaucer's Italy," 7.
55 Ibid., 9.
56 "Do not wonder, Tuscan, if I weep . . . the ladies and the knights, the toils and the ease, that love and courtesy made us wish for, there, where hearts are grown so sinful."

named it. Thus, when the young Boccaccio started writing in the vernacular, he found himself confronting Dante, but also Petrarch and upon discovering the work of the latter, was seized with a sense of inferiority that forced him to burn most of his work. Petrarch himself blamed Boccaccio for this: "[i]ndignum odium, immeritum incendium . . . uide ne superbiae uerae sit, ut ego etenim, te antistitem cui utinam par essem, ut te praecedat ille nostri eloqui dux uulgaris."[57] Petrarch, too, had suffered from this anxiety to the point that his contemporaries started to believe he despised Dante's work. Actually, as he explained to Boccaccio in a letter, he felt no hatred towards the Florentine, on the contrary, he consciously chose to avoid his work as a young man so as not to become a mere imitator.[58] He considered that Dante belonged to a different age, another generation, and preferred to develop his own style. Larner notes on that subject that

> The very greatness of Dante imposed its own barrier here. However useful it might be for a foreigner to introduce into his work Dantesque phrases, ideas and themes, for an Italian their unsolicited arrival in his mind and on his page could often have the effect—as the poetry of Boccaccio reveals—of a jarring reiteration in an inappropriate context of the all-too-familiar.[59]

Petrarch accordingly avoided Dante and turned towards Latin Humanism, while Boccaccio ended up by accepting his influence in the domain of vernacular literature. Italian high culture thus became particularly difficult to adapt for foreign writers and the rare authors who did so, like John Tiptoft or Humphrey of Lancaster, were rather isolated. Chaucer's discovery of Dante's work and of Stilnovist poetry may even be considered as a happy coincidence. It was not strictly necessary to cross the Channel during the fourteenth century to experience culture shock, for London was a remarkably cosmopolitan city even then: "by far the largest urban conglomeration in Britain, . . . it was at the heart of wide and spreading trade networks that stretched right across the known global business routes."[60] Chaucer probably had repeated contacts with the Italian merchants settled in Southampton or on Lombard Street in London because of his father's trade relations. These tradesmen mainly used French as the *lingua*

---

[57] "Such useless hatred and undeserved fire! . . . Beware that it is not pride that prevents you from accepting a second or third place for I might surpass you when I wish to be your equal, or that the master of our vernacular literature [Dante] be preferred to you." Rossiter, *Chaucer and Petrarch*, 71.
[58] See, *Letters on Familiar Matters*, vol. 3, XXI, 15.
[59] Larner, "Chaucer's Italy," 24.
[60] Butterfield, *The Familiar Enemy*, 203.

franca but Chaucer somehow picked up on a variety of Italian dialects—which was rather extraordinary at the time—and this partly explained his role in a diplomatic mission that ended up being crucial to the future of English literature.

He left England in late 1372 for Genoa but was forced to stay in Tuscany to meet the Bardi, the great Florentine bankers and main financial supporters of Edward III, and there discovered Dante's poetry. Indeed, following Boccaccio's lobbying, the authorities had agreed to celebrate the seventieth anniversary of Dante's exile. Although Chaucer was no longer there to witness the festivities (Boccaccio's petition was given to the authorities in June 1373, one month after Chaucer's return to England, and he lectured on Dante in the Santo Stefano di Badia church in October), it is probable that the atmosphere in Florence had changed.[61] That would explain Chaucer's discovery of Dante's poetry. But as Larner suggests, had Chaucer followed Prince Lionel in 1368, he might have met Petrarch and been lectured on the futility of pursuing vernacular literature. Similarly, a visit in the 1390s would have immersed him in a culture that considered Tuscan poetry as a remnant from the past. Instead, Chaucer arrived in Florence in 1373, at the moment when Dante was about to be rehabilitated.

It is, in other words, within the *fin'amor* and *Dolce Stil Novo* traditions that the division of Italy was truly expressed. The works produced during the Trecento perfectly represent the division of the authorial voice: the poets were deeply wounded by the lack of unity in their country, and the fact that they lived in a place lacking in centralized authority helped the development of a certain polyvocality, associated with the peninsula's multilingualism. Their poetry acquired a therapeutic value and polyvocality rapidly became the literary expression of a psychological fragmentation. Dante expressed his pain when describing Italy, with evident anger and bitterness, not as a mistress of provinces but of a brothel, and as a ship without helmsman in a mighty tempest (*Purg.* VI. 76–78). Petrarch also lamented the fragmentation of this "Italia mia" (*Canzoniere*, 128). As a result, when Chaucer discovered their work, he immediately recognized this feeling without necessarily understanding the political situation of Italy. As W.T. Rossiter notes, "[i]t is this voice, first translated by Chaucer, that would become the touchstone for generations of poets who sought a way of sounding out their own dislocation."[62] One must not be surprised to find this dislocation later translated, for instance, in the "I" of *Troilus and Criseyde*.

---

61 Wallace, "Chaucer's Continental Inheritance: The Early Poems and *Troilus and Criseyde*," 21.
62 Rossiter, *Chaucer and Petrarch*, 48.

Chaucer's First Influences

Chaucer's poetry started to evolve while Europe was in the midst of an intellectual efflorescence. As the heir of Anglo-Saxon multilingualism and having been exposed since his early days to metropolitan polyvocality, Chaucer could not but help integrate into his poetry his reception of *fin'amor* and the Italianisms of his Tuscan models.

As we have seen, the literary production of the Middle Ages was based on a process of translation, but not in the modern sense of the word. The purpose was not to be as faithful as possible to the original work but to adapt it and reinterpret it. Medieval translation was, in other words, a creative evolution of speech in a new context. As Daniel J. Pinti observed, it is both a form of indirect, reported discourse with an implicit "he/she said" accompanying it, and dialogic because it is a response to a previous text.[63] If we consider translation as reported speech, then we cannot but recognize its inherently dialogic and responsive characteristics, for reported speech is "speech within speech, utterance within utterance, and at the same time also speech about speech, utterance about utterance."[64] It is heteroglossic and polyvocal, and more to the point, an interdiscursive form of dialogism.

And Chaucer was a remarkable translator, celebrated by Eustache Deschamps as the "[g]rand translateur, noble Geffroy Chaucier" who "[e]n bone anglés . . . translatas" the *Roman de la Rose*.[65] At the beginning of his artistic career, Chaucer spent most of his time attempting to incorporate the nuances of French courtly love poetry and realized how the English language was ill-adapted to transcribe the fluidity of French lines. "It has a winning and unobtrusive way," remarks Lewis, "which the harder-hitting style and deeper-chested voice of English cannot reproduce."[66] That did not stop the poet, however, who persevered even though he would keep complaining about the poverty of his idiom.[67] He quickly mastered the conventions and characteristics of the *fin'amor* tradition and of Chrétien's and Guillaume's poetry. He was both the *grand translateur* and one of the main representatives in England of grotesque realism and of the bourgeois tradition. His own social class meant that he was always in contact with the merchant world and with the polyvocality of the marketplace. He was greatly influenced by Jean's

---

63 Pinti, "Dialogism, Heteroglossia, and Late Medieval Translation," 110.
64 Voloshinov, *Marxism and the Philosophy of Language*, 115.
65 Paris, Bibliothèque Nationale de France, MS fr. 840, fol. 62.
66 Lewis, *The Allegory of Love*, 135.
67 He notably remarks in *The Book of the Duchess*, "[m]e lakketh both Englyssh and wit" (898).

continuation of the *Roman* and embraced the dialogic possibilities of his style. Whether in smaller poems or major narrative works, Chaucer always attempted to confront monologism with a more carnivalesque counterpart, to balance the top and the bottom. Cervantes later gave a splendid example of this literary encounter between the language of the chivalric novel and of the vulgar in the relationship between Quixote and Sancho. Two hundred years before the Ingenious Hidalgo started slaying windmills, Chaucer had staged this very encounter in his most famous poems, particularly in the *Canterbury Tales*, as we will see. Lyric poetic discourse is often opposed to polyphony, yet Chaucer developed it by playing with a variety of genres, for it is in the inferior genres like fabliaux and parody, far from the great chivalric tradition, that the bivocal European discourse truly developed.[68]

As for his relationship with Italian poetry, Chaucer went well beyond merely adapting Dantean lines. He also focused on the work of other members of the *Dolce Stil Novo*, namely Boccaccio and Petrarch. The complexity of their relationship with Dante considerably delayed the influence they might have had on Chaucer: even if he eventually translated some of their sonnets and narrative poems, they did not have as great an impact on him as his reading of the *Commedia*. But that does not mean he felt no connection with those poets. On the contrary, Boccaccio helped, for instance, Chaucer distance

> English from French, as well as enable English to gain new heights of francophone internationalism by his own relationship to French writing. For his own Neapolitan context for composing *Il Filostrato* meant that Boccaccio was trying out French-inspired lyric gestures from the trouvères and a newly intense first-person exploration of love from the *Rose*.[69]

Boccaccio's *Amorosa Visione* and Chaucer's *House of Fame* also have in common the fact that these are two poets working with a courtly love framework inherited from their French models, and keen to transcend Dante's poetry while attempting to understand their own connection as vernacular poets with the great classical writers. It is no accident, for instance, that Chaucer's first poems share with Brunetto's *Tesoretto* a same poetical form, close to Guillaume's octosyllabic rhyming couplets. Both poets are placed at the beginning of their respective poetical traditions and each is in search of his own versification, his own voice.

It is consequently possible to establish a parallel between the situations of the *trouvères*, troubadours, and of the Stilnovists. The poets contributed to the

---

68 Bakhtin, *Esthétique et théorie du roman*, 213.
69 Butterfield, *The Familiar Enemy*, 296.

evolution of *fin'amor* but also of the novel genre by assimilating, consciously or not, the details of a particularly complex political and linguistic situation. Whether it is the dislocation of Italy, multilingualism, the hazards of the translation process, or the simple desire to tell a story based on the psychological plurality of a character, it all ended with the progressive emergence in medieval poetry of aspects and characteristics of the novel as we have come to define it. But it would take Chaucer's hand to truly seize the dialogic elements that had appeared here and there, and transform them. His unification of French and Italian elements in a poetic work where grotesque realism mingles with the values and expectations of *fi-n'amor* and Stilnovism was paramount in the development of literary polyphony. He was first and foremost a courtly love poet who, seduced by Stilnovist aesthetics, ended up questioning the role of the *auctor* within the narrative. The Chaucerian narrator is accordingly one of the best illustrations of his reception of the codes of *fin'amor* and of Dantean poetry.

Chapter 3
Narrative Evolution and New Discursive Strategies

When Chaucer started writing his first major vernacular narratives, he did not yet possess the poetic and philosophical maturity that would eventually turn him into one of the most influential authors in the history of English literature. But this self-described "lewd compilator" (*Treatise on the Astrolabe*, 61) nevertheless managed, through a clever orchestration of the various voices heard in his intertext, to take part in an interdiscursive dialogue essential to the evolution of literary polyphony.

As we have seen in the previous chapter, some of the authors Chaucer would have to engage with were already considered monuments of their respective literary traditions. *Fin'amor* poetry's generative force had fertilized most of Chaucer's literary background and few could escape its influence. Dante was likewise considered a poet "to venerate or to ignore, but impossible to imitate,"[1] yet Chaucer somehow managed to integrate his voice without being crushed by it. It is still difficult however to clearly identify the nature of Dante's influence on Chaucer: he certainly translated and adapted situations and themes, but that is no more revealing than other elements inherited from medieval hermeneutics. As T.S. Eliot remarks:

> [T]he important debt to Dante does not lie in a poet's borrowings, or adaptations from Dante; nor is it one of those debts which are incurred only at a particular stage in another poet's development. Nor is it found in those passages in which one has taken him as a model. The important debt does not occur in relation to the number of places in one's writings to which a critic can point a finger, and say, here and there he wrote something which he could not have written unless he had had Dante in mind.[2]

In this chapter, we finally get back to Chaucer and look at how his reception of *fin'amor* literature and of Stilnovism transformed his vision of poetry and allowed the affirmation of the dialogic practice. As nobody would want this book to be longer, it will be a bit of a fast jog through his early poetry, for which I apologize. More would need to be said, and I believe that a separate book could be written on this subject for each of Chaucer's poems, but since my purpose is to track the evolution of the polyphonic practice, I will need to be brief.

---

[1] Boitani, "What Dante Meant to Chaucer," 115.
[2] Eliot, *To Criticize the Critic*, 132.

The Book of the Duchess

His first major narrative poem closely follows the development of French poetry and draws from the *Roman de la Rose*, Froissart, and Machaut. It is thus the first clear instance of courtly literature in English[3] and it seems to have been written by Chaucer to address the passing of Blanche of Lancaster.[4]

Despite the solemn aspect of this poem, it nevertheless conceals a narrative embracing the conventions of courtly love poetry. Indeed, *fin'amor* did not just have as subjects adultery or religious parody, but could also be tragic and violent, and as Brewer remarks, "[m]uch of its charm lies in the different forms of story and song that it takes at different periods with different authors."[5] Chaucer, in fact, develops a narrative inspired by the tradition that formed him and does not hesitate to borrow a great variety of structural patterns and themes, conventions, allegorical or rhetorical clichés, which he uses with prudence.

The structure and themes of *BD* are thus conventional. The structure resembles that used in the *Roman*, yet the opening is technically speaking an adaptation of the first lines of Froissart's *Paradys d'amour*. But if Chaucer imitates the subject of the French poem, he completely ignores its style and favors technical experiments. While Froissart composed lines of great simplicity and concision, Chaucer develops a much more conversational style in which one can already hear the poet's voice. He also produces lines ruled by *energeia*, "the animation of linguistic material in tension with a concrete metrical system based in the material itself."[6] *BD* is in that regard a remarkable example of polyvocal discourse since it shows Chaucer's first attempt at writing in English, and thus reveals a poet conscious of the implications of his accomplishment.

In *BD*, we actually find Chaucer writing a manifesto for the native vernacular.[7] We know that his total vocabulary consists of about 8,000 words, with 4,000 French words—between 1,100 and 1,200 have been introduced in written English by Chaucer himself.[8] But Chaucer's naturalized loanwords appear both with French and English stress, while with new borrowings he tends to favor English

---

3 Fumo, *Making Chaucer's Book of the Duchess*, 70.
4 It is always difficult to link Chaucer's biography and his writing. Julia Boffey and A.S.G. Edwards argue for instance that *BD* might have been composed either immediately after Blanche's death or later in 1374 when Gaunt erected a tomb in her memory, which is also the year when he granted Chaucer a life annuity. See Fumo, *Chaucer's* Book of the Duchess, 13.
5 Brewer, *An Introduction to Chaucer*, 44.
6 Ibid.
7 Barabar, "The Art of Expropriation: Chaucer's Narrator in *The Book of the Duchess*," 218.
8 Mersand, *Chaucer's Romance Vocabulary*, 45.

pronunciation (*fátal, múrmour* . . .) within the verse line. However, he does use new borrowings in rhyme with greater phonetic freedom, to attract attention to them. Chaucer's use of loanwords is accordingly highly polyvocal.[9] The beginning of the poem, as we have said, adapts Froissart, who had been writing in French at the English court. He was extremely popular there. When Chaucer accordingly adapts the first lines of *Paradys d'amour*, he re-appropriates the material:

Je sui de moi grant *merveille*	I have gret wonder be this *lyghte*
Comment je vifs quant tant je *veille*	How that I lyve for day ne *nyghte*
Et on ne poroit en *veilant*	I may nat slepe wel nygh *noght*
Trouver de moi plus *traveillant*	I have so many an ydel *thoght*
Car bien sacies que par *veillier*	Purely for defaute of *slepe*
Me viennent souvent *travillier*	That by my trouthe I take no *kepe*
Pensees et *merancolies*	Of nothing how hyt cometh of *goothe*
Qui me sont ens au cœur *liies*	Ne me nys nothing leve nor *looth*
Et pas ne les puis *deslyer*	(1–8)
(1–9)	

Chaucer's lines are almost monosyllabic; they have Germanic consonance and are rougher than the near monorhyme of Froissart's vowels. He thus frames the original material within a new linguistic system. Yet Chaucer still uses the French octosyllabic rhyming couplets, which creates a juxtaposition of linguistic-poetic registers. As Guthrie remarks, "[b]y advertising itself as English, it calls attention to its Frenchness as well."[10] It makes the interdiscursive interaction and multilingualism visible. And as the narrative develops, Chaucer unfolds a stylistic movement that first embraces the French register (poetically and thematically), before going back to English. The meeting with the Black Knight is especially relevant as Chaucer makes extensive use of the French register, with borrowings from the *Roman*, and Machaut's *Jugement dou Roy de Behaigne* and *Remede de Fortune*. The number of French loanwords matches, of course, this poetic movement towards *fin'amor*, yet only 20 percent of French words used by Chaucer in that part of *BD* correspond with words in the original texts (*joie/joye*, for example). The rest are Chaucer's own insertions because he does not merely translate, he interacts with his source material, he taps into the whole tradition, while simultaneously resisting and twisting it. He creates a linguistic and cultural atmosphere, rather than just blindly following the French poets. As the dreamer experiences the mysteries of love and the poet explores the poetic and linguistic possibilities of *fin'amor* in English, the narrative moves from a French to an English atmosphere.

---

9 Guthrie, "Dialogics and Prosody in Chaucer," 99.
10 Ibid., 103.

As often with Chaucer, everything is about dialogue. *BD* shows the poet's sense of discourse as an open and often unfinished interaction. Indeed, discourse is made of complex transactions, which may be open, failed, or completed. Chaucer seems to be especially interested in open transactions since they "suggest that reciprocity demands a listening talent in speaker as well as listener and that discourse is an open process that precipitates and generates new initiative, controversy, and revision."[11] A completed transaction cannot possibly interest Chaucer, for once the resolution is achieved nothing new is generated. The conventional style of *BD* implies the engagement of the listener with the speaker, yet rather than addressing the polemical confrontation of sources, Chaucer prefers elusiveness. No simple answer is given, but the conversation is engaged. In order to achieve this, he rapidly distances his narrator from the world surrounding him. Guy Bourquin has usefully identified four distancing phases: the narrator starts by describing himself as suffering from an unknown sickness cutting him off from his acquaintances (first phase), which forces him to take refuge in books (second). He then tells us one of the stories he has read (third) before eventually falling asleep and starting his dream wanderings (fourth), which are also divided into several segments.[12] This entanglement of sequences notably allows Chaucer to distance himself from the Black Knight, which multiplies the possible associations between the various constitutive elements of the poem.

The openness of Chaucer's poetry, even at this early stage, is necessary to the development of dialogism for it "gains its aesthetic validity precisely in proportion to the number of different perspectives from which it can be viewed and understood."[13] The coexistence of these perspectives, their very possibility, creates a sense of polemic and ambiguity, and thus dialogism. In Chaucer's early work, this ambiguity mainly comes from equivocation and the use of the narrative devices of the dream framework. The story of Alcyone and Ceyx, which the narrator reads before falling asleep, is for instance about grief and consolation. And it is superimposed via contiguity to the actual content of the dream, namely the Black Knight's sorrow. To that, Chaucer adds another layer in addressing the Knight's suffering cryptically with a play on words that starts at the beginning of the hunt:

> And al men speken of huntyng,
> How they wolde slee the hert with strengthe,

---

[11] Grudin, *Chaucer and the Politics of Discourse*, 28.
[12] Chaucer, *Les Contes de Canterbury et autres œuvres*, 750.
[13] Eco, *The Open Work*, 3.

> And how the hert had upon lengthe
> So moche embossed—y not now what.
> 		(350–53)

Before we even meet the Knight, Chaucer plays with the idea of wounds thanks to the multiple meanings associated with the spelling of "hert," which we could understand as hart, heart, and hurt. And when the Black Knight finally reveals the fate of his Lady, the hunting suddenly ends, leaving us once more with an ambiguous "al was doon, / For that tyme, the hert-huntyng" (1312–13). While the hart was distancing its pursuers, the Knight's heart tried to seize the memory of his Lady, but the intervention of the narrator allows him to speak about his grief and thus face it. The fact that the hunt, the dream, and the poem all end at the moment he accepts to clearly express what happened to his Lady reinforces the link between these different perspectives. In other words, the external exploration (the hart hunting), the internal exploration (heart hunting), and the hurt associated with it are equally superimposed metaphorically (external-internal hunting) as well as metonymically. As Nakao suggests, "[i]f the heart-hunting and the hart-hunting finish together, the poet seems to have avoided expressing the real social event straightforwardly. He wrote it in such an ambiguous way that the reader could get the message through the exercise of his or her inference."[14]

Chaucer, therefore, deprives his audience of the comfort of linearity and passivity and sets the stage for an interaction of fragments and languages reflecting a vast debate among his various sources. The dream framework indeed allows a constant juxtaposition of elements and scenes in which can be heard the Chaucerian polyvocality. Thus, when he tells the story of Alcyone and Ceyx, he adapts Ovid's narrative to his own purposes and refuses the lovers the reunion expected by the audience, leaving Alcyone alone with her grief. In a similar way, the Knight's Lady is not described conventionally and hierarchically, as she is in *Behaigne* (336–400) for instance. On the contrary, Chaucer contrasts Machaut's ease with the passion of the Knight who cannot help but describe his Lady as he had interiorized her. We are not dealing here with a lover describing the qualities of his love to an external observer, but with a widower remembering his wife, which results in a much more disordered intervention. In eleven lines, he goes from the grace of her singing to the gentleness of her words, to her kindness, her hair, and eyes (848–59). Machaut does not mention her "[r]ight fair shuldres" (952); it is only Chaucer who mentions her "straight flat bakke" (957) and hips of

---

14 Nakao, *The Structure of Chaucer's Ambiguity*, 40.

"good brede" (956). In Chaucer, the Knight's rhetoric is ill-adapted to his sorrow, because, as Bourquin remarks, the

> suite désordonnée des hyperboles, livrées dans une syntaxe frustre, sur un ton familier, proche de la langue parlée, confine à la naïveté et frise la parodie, voire l'héroï-comique—comme si le lecteur était invité à sourire des excès de certaines conventions littéraires.[15]

This description of the Lady through a rhetoric of borrowings inevitably reminds us of the poet himself, juggling with his sources to transcribe a poetical tradition he had strongly interiorized. The fact that the portrait of the Lady is also the beginning of *BD*'s movement away from the French register is further evidence of Chaucer's complex interaction with the tradition. Indeed, the "description in the *Behaigne* is an emblem of French romance, like the lines from Froissart's *Paradys*. The description in *BD*, juxtaposed with Machaut's image, is an emblem of English realism."[16]

The role of the narrator in *BD* is equally interesting in this respect. The notion of poetic persona[17] is by definition a characteristic of the Gothic age. The narrator/poet finds himself both in and out of the diegesis: he is not exactly the author's avatar, yet he is not completely fictitious. Machaut's narrator in *Navarre* describes himself, for example, as locked up in his house in Reims, terrified by the plague and the English army's siege of the city. We know this part of the story truly happened to Machaut, but what about his journey to the forest and his encounter with Bonneurté? It is quite obviously a fictitious event, yet Bonneurté reproaches him for the conclusion of *Behaigne* in which the king does not judge in favor of the lady. In other words, the poet's persona keeps sliding between reality and fiction. Although this narrative device is clearly inherited from the *Roman de la Rose*, Guillaume's successors seldom made such intensive use of it.

As we have previously noted, the multiplication of points of view in chronological layers, derived from allegorical models, allowed Guillaume to establish a dialogic relation between the narrator and the various representations of the lady. Chrétien's poetry was so complex that Guillaume had no other choice but to isolate the interior experience of the characters and to amplify this psychological component through

---

15 "disordered series of hyperboles, delivered in a crude syntax, in a familiar tone, close to the oral language, verges on naivety and approaches parody, perhaps even the heroicomic—as if the reader were invited to smile at the excesses of certain literary conventions." Chaucer, *Les Contes de Canterbury et autres œuvres*, 751.
16 Guthrie, "Dialogics and Prosody in Chaucer," 106.
17 David Lawton justly places the emphasis on narratorial voice rather than the narratorial persona because it seems "that in medieval poetry most narrators are part of, rather than subsume, the rhetoric of a work. They are elements in a larger strategy. Sometimes a narrator is no more than a product of rhetorical imperative, the decorum either of the style or the set of structural conventions adopted." *Chaucer's Narrators*, 8.

an intensification of allegory. Yet, although Machaut and his contemporaries inherit Guillaume's style, they have somehow lost—or chosen to abandon—this ability to organize an allegory around a psychological experience. As a result, even if Machaut brilliantly orchestrates the elements of the allegory of love (dream framework, personifications, aristocratic values . . .), he is forced to use it in a more mundane way and as Muscatine writes "[t]his general diminution of theme leaves him with a style too rich to be functional."[18]

As for Chaucer, he is famous for his representation of a narrator who is somewhat awkward in love matters, often incompetent, and who is supposedly an autobiographical portrait. Even if the origin of this narrative choice comes from the Gothic persona, Chaucer nevertheless manages to raise it progressively to a new level. But in *BD* he does not yet seem to be conscious of the potential of this particular narrative device and uses it rather superficially:

> the highly formalized narrator-persona of French courtly poetry, often melancholy and lovesick, is such a common figure that we should be very wary of assuming that the *I* of *The Book of the Duchess* represents Chaucer himself.[19]

Colin Wilcockson remarks that the comic elements and exaggerations allowing the introduction of comedy are not specific to Chaucer since they are also present in Machaut's poems.[20] Chaucer does not merely follow his French model; he presents an alternative to the 4,212 lines of *Behaigne* with a condensed text of 1,334 lines. He thus makes a leap forward with *BD*, where the audience can already notice the features of the future author of the *Canterbury Tales*.[21] Chaucer reinforces the irony by establishing a constant lag between the seriousness of the subject and the casualness of the tone, thus upsetting the expectations of an audience used to courtly values. He rejects the monological aspect of the refinement and solemnity of the aristocratic language in favor of grotesque realism, a polyglossic perspective, and open discourse. For example, he develops the passage in which Juno sends a messenger to Morpheus progressively, slowly increasing the pressure, so to speak. The messenger receives his instructions and thus takes the road:

> Til he com to the derke valeye
> That stant betwixe roches tweye
> Ther never yet grew corn ne gras,

---

18 Muscatine, *Chaucer and the French Tradition*, 99.
19 Chaucer, *The Riverside Chaucer*, 330.
20 Ibid.
21 Chaucer, *Les Contes de Canterbury et autres œuvres*, 752.

> Ne tre, ne noght that ought was,
> Beste, ne man, ne noght elles,
> Save ther were a fewe welles
> Came rennynge fro the clyves adoun
> (155–61)

If the syntax remains sober, the description is however quite elegant, and one can easily see here the influence of Ovid and Froissart. Yet Chaucer does not stop here, and while the audience is expecting an equally noble presentation of the sleeping god, the tone suddenly becomes much more carnivalesque:

> They had good leyser for to route,
> To envye who myghte slepe best.
> Somme henge her chyn upon hir brest
> And slept upright, hir hed yhed,
> And somme lay naked in her bed
> And slepe whiles the days laste.
> (172–77)

With this specific representation of sleeping gods, Chaucer destroys any possible reverence. This vision is besides reinforced by the messenger, who wakes up gods like a bartender wishing to get rid of drunken customers in the morning. He starts to shout "O, how! Awake anoon!" (179), before losing his temper and blowing his horn "ryght in here eere" (182), then finally yells "Awaketh!" (183). The poet thus moves from a conventional description to the exasperation of the messenger, effecting a transition from convention to laughter. The interaction between the messenger and the gods is a failed transaction, just like the transaction between the narrator and the book. It remains open since Chaucer chooses to ignore the conclusion of the story and just move on to the dream.

The irony is further reinforced by the naivety and lack of understanding—or refusal of understanding—of the narrator. The Knight consents to talk about his grief under one condition, "[t]hat thou shalt hooly, with al thy wyt, / Doo thyn entent to herkene hit" (751–52). He makes the narrator promise to be a good listener, which obviously creates a mutual engagement and mutual dependence in discourse. The narrator accepts of course, but despite his promise keeps on interrupting the Knight. And just as the fate of his Lady becomes obvious, he asks once more "[w]hat los ys that?" (1139), and suggests that maybe the Knight betrayed his Lady, which would explain their separation. When the Knight tells him "thow nost what thow menest" (1137), he underlines the thoughtlessness and incongruity of the narrator, which eventually leads to the climax of the poem, namely the Knight's declaration: "She ys ded!" (1309). It is by throwing at us this fact, which he had so long repressed and refused, that he liberates himself.

With an echo of line 204 ("I nam but ded"), Chaucer thus returns the poem to the English register with which he had started *BD*. But the knowledge acquired by the movement between French and English is invaluable to Chaucer, the Black Knight, and the dreamer. The Knight's courtship of the Lady was "an initiation into French poetic culture, and there is no sense in the poem that it has been a waste, that the Knight would trade his present knowledge for his former ignorance."[22] The admission of the Lady's death completes the transaction only in part, but this seems enough for the dreamer. The transaction seems completed, yet it generates another one that takes into account the various open interactions of the poem. The narrator announces that he is now ready to express his experience poetically:

> Having left the conspicuous transactions of his poem open—the problem of unrequited love, the Ceys and Alcyone story, and the dreamer's experience of the Black Knight's bereavement, which does not end the poem—and having reminded us of the poet's relationship to both the dream and the book, the speaker now initiates a further transaction, this time with the audience itself.[23]

Chaucer here suggests a new interaction, one that would take the dialogue outside of the diegesis. After having been an active participant in the interdiscursive dialogue that generated his narrative, he switches to an interlocutive dialogue in which his utterance itself directly addresses the audience. It answers and anticipates possible interpretations.[24]

That interaction still continues centuries after the poet's death and revocation of the poem in his *Retraction*. But at this stage of Chaucer's career, that particular form of dialogism is merely suggested and the poet just examines the ability of poetic discourse to help us understand our limitations; it both illustrates the ambiguities of the language shaping our perceptions and asks if poetry can prevent us from misreading partial answers as final ones.[25] The openness of the end of *BD* is an invitation to dialogue, rather than an active interaction: "Since the narrative depicts a reading experience that leads to a dream, which leads to a writing experience, which in turn leads to the reader's reading of the poem, *BD* suggests that the process of reading continues beyond the poem."[26]

---

22 Guthrie, "Dialogics and Prosody in Chaucer," 107.
23 Grudin, *Chaucer and the Politics of Discourse*, 35.
24 Perrin, "Polyphonie et autres formes d'hétérogénéité énonciative," 8.
25 McGerr, *Chaucer's Open Books*, 46.
26 Ibid., 45.

The House of Fame

During his trip to Italy in 1373, Chaucer discovered a new world whose richness would deeply transform his conception of poetry. Yet it seems that it took him several years to truly assimilate these influences. Indeed, if *BD* was written sometime between 1368 and 1374, Chaucer only started writing *The House of Fame* in 1379–1380, a few months after his second trip (1378) across the Alps. It was on this occasion that he discovered Boccaccio's poetry.

Any attempt to provide a literary response to the poetical vision offered by the *Commedia* was certainly not an easy task, especially in an idiom like Middle English. Boccaccio had previously tried to integrate Dantean motifs and structures in his *Amorosa Visione* but the effect on his work was to overwhelm it. Chaucer's undertaking in *Fame* was thus not without precedent, and not without risks. That is why he decided to build his "house of fame" on solid ground, employing codes and themes he had mastered: once more, he proposed a first-person narrative enclosed by a dream framework, written in octosyllabic rhyming couplets. No matter what Chaucer's objective is in this new work, it is obvious that he remains faithful to his convictions and courtly training, and if he does refer to Dante here, he is still the *lewd compilator* and *grand translateur* that we know, and thus systematically offers an ironic counterpart to Dante's poetry.

He accordingly develops his own vision of the Florentine poet's interests, while continuing to explore the motifs developed in *BD*: his narrator, this time aptly named Geffrey, is once again a character whose knowledge of love comes more from books than from personal experience, and who undertakes to narrate his dream. The reading of a book (Virgil's *Aeneid*) once again triggers the story, although Chaucer slightly changes things by turning the book into mural paintings seen by the narrator when he wakes up. In the dream, an eagle then arrives to take him to the House of Fame, where Chaucer analyzes once more the relationship between the poet, his sources, his responsibility as an artist, and the limits of his authorial powers. All these elements, already tangentially present in *BD*, are in *Fame* thrown into the foreground by the introduction of the eagle—a direct reference to the *Commedia*—which allows Chaucer to change his conception of narration. While the narrator of his previous poem was merely the product of the conventions of *fin'amor* poetry, Geffrey here leads the way to literary polyphony.

Chaucer often develops his stories in a secondary world that his narrators invariably know better than their own, namely the world of books. This presentation allows the poet to create some distance between the narrator and the adventures he narrates, but also gives him the ability to question his intertext and to mix the various voices of his influences. This reassessment of the tradition that trained him is already visible in *BD*, but this time Chaucer places it at the heart of *Fame*. The poem actually takes place in the world of literature. Whereas the dream framework allowed the other courtly poets to immerse their narrator in an allegory of love, Chaucer leads Geffrey in another direction. In Book I, the Temple of Venus is for instance covered with illustrations recounting the main events of the *Aeneid*, while in Book III the roof of the House of Fame is supported by some of the greatest names of European literature:

> . . . the gret Omer;
> And with him Dares and Tytus
> Before, and eke he Lollius,
> And Guydo eke de Columpris,
> And Englyssh Gaufride eke, ywis;
> (III. 1466–70)

Even the eagle supposed to take Geffrey out of his contemplation in Book II has a literary origin since it comes from the *Purgatorio*. It remains the most significant element ever borrowed by Chaucer from the *Commedia*: Dante and Geffrey both witness the arrival of that eagle with gold feathers (*HF.* V. 529–33; *Purg.* IX. 19–21) descending upon them like lightning (*HF.* 534–40; *Purg.* 28–30), and refer to the myth of Ganymede (*HF.* 588–91; *Purg.* 22–24). Nonetheless, Chaucer does not merely use the eagle as a way to advance his plot. On the contrary, as Karla Taylor notes, he "borrows not words, but an image and the process by which it is formed,"[27] and the eagle rapidly becomes in *Fame* the symbol of Dantean "visible speech."

When Dante is transported from the fifth to the sixth sphere of Paradise, he notices saintly beings floating in the air like birds that rise from riverbanks and while the poet is seduced by the beauty of the place, he sees them "segnare agli occhi miei nostra favella"[28] (*Par.* XVIII. 72). As they sing, they start to form shapes that spell words that Dante recognizes as being the first sentence of the *Book of Wisdom*, "Diligite iustitiam . . . qui iudicatis terram"[29] (91–93). At that moment, more beings are attracted to the M of the final word, which starts to take the shape of an eagle. This idea of speech taking visible form is not new in the *Commedia* and invariably implies, in such a theologically monumental work, the presence of a divine creator. Dante remarks for instance after the birth of the eagle, "Quei che dipinge lì, non ha chi il guidi"[30] (109). Yet this artistic beauty

---

[27] Taylor, *Chaucer Reads "The Divine Comedy,"* 22.
[28] "design before my eyes the signs we speak."
[29] "Love justice, you rulers of the earth."
[30] "He who paints there has no one as His guide."

had already been announced at the beginning of the *Purgatorio*. Indeed, Dante discovers there a bordering bank of white marble adorned by the divine creator with carvings so beautiful that "la natura lì avrebbe scorno"[31] (*Purg.* X. 33). These carvings representing humility illustrate famous historical and Biblical scenes, but the expressivity of the images is so strong that they provoke synaesthesia: looking at the carvings, Dante thinks he can smell the perfume of incense and hear the Archangel Gabriel speak, and people sing. It seems that the images come alive in front of Dante, a feeling reinforced by the poet's description of the carved scenes. They are not only "intagliato" and "effigiata" (carved and shown, 55, 67), which evokes the action of the artist working on the material, but also "imaginata" and "impressa" (imagined and imprinted, 41, 43). As a result, the "common metaphor of impressing further suggests the inward effect of the carvings on the mind of the beholder."[32] The artist's identity cannot be doubted, for none other than God might have produced visible speech taking physical shape in front of Dante:

> Colui che mai non vide cosa nova
> produsse esto visibile parlare,
> novello a noi perché qui non si trova.[33]
> (*Purg.* X. 94–97)

The eagle's metamorphosis and the disruption of the senses establish a strong link between divine and human creation. Indeed, the elements witnessed by the narrator echo another device developed, this time, by the creator poet. After having seen the series of images representing humility, Dante continues his journey through Purgatory and is then faced with a representation of pride. And it is, this time, his own visible speech that will illustrate this encounter. The first letters of the following twelve *terzine* (*Purg.* XII. 25–58) form a huge acrostic showing the word VOM (*uomo*, man). It appears one last time in the thirteenth *terzina* and concludes this visual composition with these lines:

> Vedea Troia in cenere e in caverne:
> o Ilión, come te basso e vile
> mostrava il segno che lì si descerne![34]
> (61–63)

---

[31] "even Nature, there, would feel defeated."
[32] Taylor, *Chaucer Reads "The Divine Comedy*," 23.
[33] "This was the speech made visible by One / within whose sight no thing is new—but we, / who lack its likeness here, find novelty."
[34] "I saw Troy turned to caverns and to ashes; / o Ilium, your effigy in stone— / it showed you there so squalid, so cast down!"

Dante's use of visible speech destroys any notion of artistic conduit and directly imitates the Divine creative principle, namely the Word. The acrostic works both visually and verbally since it allows Dante to show us that pride is, by definition, a human characteristic.

When Chaucer borrows the eagle from Dante, he also borrows the motif of visible speech. He never uses the acrostic, but the idea, presented in the Temple of Venus and in the physical transformation of rumors in the House of Fame, gives him the opportunity to explore the question of the role of poetry and of the human imagination. A fine example of Chaucer's handling of the *Commedia* can be seen in Book I when Geffrey is looking at the illustrations from the *Aeneid*. As usual, Chaucer does not translate Virgil's work literally since he also integrates Ovid's treatment of the myth of Aeneas. Yet, despite this interest in the classics, his reaction is determined by the tenth Canto of the *Purgatorio*. He discovers, for a start, the first words of the *Aeneid* engraved on a table of brass (I. 143–48), then rapidly begins to describe what seem to be mural paintings or engravings since he repeats several times "First sawgh I" or "And next that sawgh I" (151, 162, 174, 193, 198 . . .). Everything points towards plastic art. Yet Geffrey's description of the myth is punctuated with rhetorical devices such as amplification and repetition. If Geffrey is only looking at images, then why would Chaucer make such a use of literary rhetoric? Besides, Geffrey also seems to be looking at dialogues: he notices Venus consoling Aeneas, advising him to leave for Carthage (224–38), and decides not to bore his audience by repeating "[h]ow they [Dido and Aeneas] aqueynteden in fere" (250). Some accordingly see here words rather than images. But this diversity of opinion is not accidental since Chaucer consciously disrupts our perception of these two forms of representation. In other words, if images can be painted or engraved, then why not words? He refers to it briefly before going back to his usual humility topos:

> What shulde I speke more queynte,
>   Or peyne me my wordes peynte[35]
> To speke of love? Hyt wol not be;
>   I kan not of that faculte.
>   (245–48)

The Dido and Aeneas episode is thus presented by Chaucer as an interiorized experience. He mentions both what happens between the two characters and the

---

[35] The expression "my wordes peynte" has a double meaning. It refers to the principle of circumlocution but can also mean, in the context of visible speech, the visual representation of words.

effect produced in the mind of its receptor. Chaucer draws from Augustinian philosophy the aspects of the "visibile parlare" used by Dante. Saint Augustine indeed explains in *In Johannis evangelium tractatus* that the human mind does not react in the same way when dealing with a text or an image: to look at an image is sufficient to understand its meaning, while a text requires reading, an ability not mastered by everyone.[36] He further mentions in his *Confessions* that when events from the past are told, we do not remember them as they truly happened. On the contrary, the words we hear produce images representing these past events.[37] A distinction must accordingly be made between events and their extension in the human mind, and it is precisely this aspect that Chaucer exploits in *Fame*.

The scenes represented in the Temple of Venus thus become problematic. When Geffrey starts reading the words carved on the table, he does not give us a faithful reproduction of the *Aeneid*'s lines. Chaucer reinterprets Virgil's words: they penetrate Geffrey's mind and come out transformed by his voice. Thus, whereas Virgil writes "[a]rma virumque cano, Trojæ qui primus ab oris / Italiam, fato profugus, Laviniaque venit"[38] (1–2), Geffrey tells us:

> I wol now synge, yif I kan,
> The armes and also the man
> That first cam, thurgh his destinee,
> Fugityf of Troy contree,
> In Itayle, with ful moche pyne
> Unto the strondes of Lavyne.
> (I. 143–48)

The translation is almost perfect, yet one element is clearly foreign to Virgil: "yif I kan." What we have here is once more Chaucer's humility topos, but it is only the first element of a progression that will increasingly take us away from Virgil's voice. When Geffrey tells the story of Dido and Aeneas for instance, his version of the story has almost nothing in common with the *Aeneid* since the main character has become a rude man obsessed with his own glory. Upon discovering his betrayal, Dido is so upset she starts describing a vile polygamist who "wolde have fame / In magnyfyinge of hys name" (I. 305–6). Dido is no longer here the faithless widow immortalized by tradition but the poor victim of male dishonesty. Her relationship with Aeneas and the idea that she might have betrayed her late

---

[36] Saint Augustine, *Œuvres de Saint Augustin 72*, XXV, 2.
[37] Saint Augustine, *Les Confessions*, vol. 2, XI, 18.
[38] "Arms and the man I sing of Troy, who, first from its seashores, / Italy-bound, fate's refugee, arrived at Lavinia's / Coastlands."

husband are just elements in the constant rewriting of the myth. Whoever may be the author of the rewriting—Ovid (*Heroides*), Boccaccio (*De mulieribus claris*), or Chaucer (*House of Fame*, *The Legend of Good Women*)— it remains the case that he somehow used Virgil's poetic reinvention of that story. Virgil managed to convince his contemporaries and successors that the myth was real.[39]

Chaucer's presentation of the myth, though in appearance similar, is however slightly different since he clearly sets forward the fictionality of the narrative. He adds elements to the story, such as Dido's lament (I. 293–310), a detail for which "[n]on other auctour alegge I" (314). Chaucer's juxtaposition of materials allows him to show how they are often contradictory. In other words, he demonstrates that this addition to the myth is just as fictitious as what his predecessors wrote. They had reimagined the original story just as Geffrey reimagines the first lines of Virgil's poem. For human speech is fundamentally marked by transmission; our words, knowledge, and opinions belong to others. As Oscar Wilde wrote in *De Profundis*, there is almost nothing in the human language that allows us to avoid this dialogism: "Most people are other people. Their thoughts are someone else's opinion, their lives a mimicry, their passions a quotation."[40] In reproducing these texts with his own words, Chaucer questions the fictitious dimension of the story and introduces bivocal narration into his work. Bakhtin explains that our words must never entirely dissolve the originality of the words of another; a narration made with "our words" must retain a mixed character and reproduce, where needed, the style and expressions of the transmitted text.[41]

The modified quote from the *Aeneid* and the treatment of the Dido episode are perfect examples of this bivocal narration since Chaucer reproduces the original style while introducing his own voice in the final text. Such processing of his sources is new for Chaucer, for even if he was used to interacting with them, as we have seen in *BD*, he was seldom questioning the author's plan or the very purpose of literature. Dantean visible speech gave him enough material to rethink his own approach to art, to enrich his poetry, and made possible a creative evolution of speech in a new context.[42] If that dimension had been absent from the *Commedia*, if Dante had produced an essentially monological work, then Chaucer would probably never have acquired the capacity to develop this form of dialogism. Indeed, authoritarian speech does not authorize fluctuation,

---

39 Taylor, *Chaucer Reads "The Divine Comedy,"* 29.
40 Wilde, *Oscar Wilde: Plays, Prose Writings and Poems*, 612.
41 Bakhtin, *Esthétique et théorie du roman*, 160–61.
42 For Bakhtin, this creative evolution of speech is specific to a situation in which an author influences another without it turning into imitation. See Bakhtin, *Esthétique et théorie du roman*, 166.

nuances, or creative variations. It does not tolerate the least evolution and penetrates our verbal consciousness as a compact and indivisible mass to be accepted as a whole, or entirely rejected.[43]

This bivocal narration thus allows Chaucer to nuance the passage in the Temple of Venus, but more generally to transform Dantean speech, for it is this independence from Virgil that allows him to develop his version of visible speech. The carvings in Purgatory gave Dante the opportunity to connect visible speech with the divine and to associate pride with humanity. With his acrostic, Dante imitates celestial art and places himself under the protection of God: he puts his own artistic abilities at the service of the supreme artisan, this "fabbro" who turns the poet into the medium through which divine creativity is expressed. The eagle's metamorphosis in Paradise suggests, in other words, that the visible speech witnessed by Dante is not specific to the human mind, but a characteristic of the universe he is discovering.[44] Chaucer, however, does nothing to justify the authenticity of his story; on the contrary, he combines narrative devices supposed to assure us of its truthfulness, then suddenly abandons them, and deforms visible speech in order to showcase the illusory dimension of imagination. The fact that the story takes place in a dream is especially meaningful. According to the medieval tradition, only morning dreams had a prophetic value. Yet, the narrator clearly states that he went to bed at dusk and "fil on slepe wonder sone" (I. 114). Should we understand that it is all just a simple dream? The narrator himself seems puzzled. He wonders in the proem to Book I what is the cause and purpose of our dreams, "[w]hy this a fantome, why that a sweven" (11), and exclaims: "God turne us every drem to goode!" (1). Furthermore, he adds that no man has ever experienced "[s]o wonderful a drem as I" (62), without confirming whether that dream is prophetic, then asks his audience to trust him:

> That take hit wel and skorne hyt noght,
> Ne hyt mysdemen in her thought
>   Thorgh malicious entencion.
>   (I. 91–93)

Chaucer, therefore, presents arguments authenticating his vision, then reduces the strength of his own arguments by introducing contradictory elements that frustrate his audience's desire to know if the story is real.

His strategy equally forces us to question the origin of the images described in the Temple of Venus. When Geffrey eventually gets out of the Temple, he is

---

[43] Bakhtin, Esthétique et théorie du roman, 162.
[44] Taylor, *Chaucer Reads "The Divine Comedy,"* 30.

stunned by the beauty of what he has just seen but realizes that he is completely lost (I. 468–88). He does not know what to do and thus starts praying:

> "O Crist," thoughte I, "that art in blysse,
>   Fro fantome and illusion
>   Me save!"
>   (I. 492–94)

He does not ask Christ to wake him up or to help him find his way. Geffrey was quite comfortable in the Temple, where he recognized each word and image; but here he realizes that all these things could just be the product of his imagination, a mere impression of his mind with no foundation in the real world.[45] The true source of his fear therefore lies in the fact that he could be the victim of these "fantome and illusion."

It is precisely at the moment when Geffrey starts to doubt that the eagle[46] comes in to lead the dreamer towards a new adventure. This idea, represented throughout the poem by the word "tydynges" (repeated more than twenty times), illustrates Chaucer's quest for Dantean visible speech. But the nature of these tidings and their relationship with the narrator remain obscure. Are they news about love, fame, poetry? What does Geffrey really seek? When a spirit asks him what he hopes to find the House of Fame, he answers:

> The cause why y stonde here:
> Somme newe tydynges for to lere,
> Somme newe thynges, y not what,
>   Tydynges, other this or that,
>   Of love or suche thynges glade.
>   (III. 1885–89)

These tidings are essentially verbal creations, or as the eagle remarks: "[s]oun ys noght but eyr ybroken" (II. 765). The words uttered rise like compressed air towards the House of Rumor, which is described as some sort of whirling wicker basket. Rumors move freely within the House; however, they sometimes get stuck near a window and cannot get out without compromise:

> We wil medle us ech with other,
> That no man, be they never so wrothe,
>   Shal han on [of us] two, but bothe

---

45 Taylor, *Chaucer Reads "The Divine Comedy,"* 30–31.
46 The eagle symbolizes here Dante's representative; he is the avatar of literarity in the poem, but also evokes the Biblical eagle thanks to which those hope in the Lord will soar on wings like eagles (Isaiah 40:31).

> At ones, al besyde his leve,
> Come we a-morwe or on eve,
> Be we cried or stille yrouned.
>   (III. 2102–7)

Truth and lies thus mingle in the House of Rumors before they can reach the House of Fame, and that is the main source of ambiguity in the poem. Here, Chaucer questions once again the creative and deformative functions of imagination with a use of visible speech opposed to what he found in Dante's poetry since he directly echoes the various versions of Dido's story in the House of Rumors. He even suggests that these tidings largely depend on "Aventure," that is to say, chance or luck, "[t]hat is the moder of tydynges" (III. 1982–83).

The notions of fiction and imagination were highly problematic in the Middle Ages because they implied a confusion between creation and lies. Poets often had to authenticate their work by relying on religious teaching and cultural transmission. Dante uses visible speech partly to defend his poem, but Chaucer turns this very doubt into the heart of *Fame*. As Taylor notes, "[t]he journey of tidings through imagination and memory, far from resolving the impasse at the end of Book I, seems rather to magnify its troubling suggestion that reading and writing result in nothing but 'fantome and illusion.'"[47] If the tidings leaving the House of Rumors are really a blend of truths and lies, then there is nothing to prove that Fame has not granted her sanction to partly deceptive *tydynges*. Chaucer's use of Dantean devices allows him to question the fallibility of stories told by human beings.

This fallibility is further increased by the fact that most poets were then read in public, and in this situation, the author loses control of his creation. As soon as his words are uttered, they are assimilated by the audience and take physical shape in their mind, before being transformed again. And no poet was as conscious as Chaucer of the importance of orality: he never ceases to be part of the game and develops a close relationship with his public thanks to a conversational style and direct address. His use of visible speech around the House of Fame is, as a result, marked by this vision of orality. Indeed, the eagle explains to Geffrey that the news uttered on earth rises and takes the physical shape of its speaker before being received by its judge (II. 1070–82). But that is a vision diametrically opposed to what we have seen in the Temple of Venus or in the *Purgatorio*. We are no longer dealing with the graphic representation of historical or literary events, but with speech linked with its speaker: "They make visible the idea behind Chaucer's limited, well-defined narrators, that

---

[47] Taylor, *Chaucer Reads "The Divine Comedy,"* 33.

human beings speak in particular voices even when they claim to utter universal truths."[48] Thus, between Books I and III, Chaucer operates a complete return to his roots through a sensorial shift from sight to hearing: Geffrey sees Orpheus, Orion, and other legendary harpists playing music, along with musicians of lesser rank, but he also meets magicians, illusionists, and soothsayers (III. 1201–81). The list is so long that it could last "[f]ro hennes into domes day" (1284). The inside of the temple remains dedicated to written literature, though. And Chaucer reminds us that writing and orality are complementary since reading was done in public (the eagle even blames Geffrey for reading alone; II. 652–58). Although *tydynges* have an oral origin, they end up taking physical shape "[b]e hyt clothed red or blak" (II. 1078), which evokes medieval manuscripts where text was written in black and rubrics in red. Unlike the modern novel, which *is*, as Ardis Butterfield remarks, the book itself, "the medieval work is represented by the medieval manuscript only in a distorted and incomplete form."[49] There is indeed a lack of consistency between the production of the manuscript and the conditions of the original performance of the work. For although a scribe

> may be transcribing an oral event directly "from life" . . . in practice, most kinds of composition in the Middle Ages are produced, performed, received and reproduced in conditions which pass through various intermediary stages not just between the oral and the written, but between the public and private, individual and communal, and active and passive involvement on the part of authors, performers, audiences and scribes.[50]

Chaucer further blurs the boundary between orality and writing by giving a voice to the poets supporting the ceiling of the House of Fame. For example, Geffrey hears the poets who immortalized the Trojan War argue about the *Iliad*, with some spirits defending Homer, while Trojan supporters accuse him of having favored the Greeks (III. 1477–80). One supporter's conclusion, that Homer's version is a fable, indicates that the story of Troy is lost and the fragments we possess are only rumors and tidings, or as Paul Zumthor puts it, "une forme vide" rather than "une parole pleine."[51] Butterfield has rightly remarked that medieval works

> present acute problems of interpretation by their intimate associations with the circumstances of public performance. These circumstances, full of the contingency, riskand so-

---

48 Taylor, *Chaucer Reads "The Divine Comedy,"* 34.
49 Butterfield, *Poetry and Music in Medieval France*, 13.
50 Ibid.
51 "an empty shape" rather than "a full speech." Zumthor, *La poésie et la voix dans la civilisation médiévale*, 68.

cial tension of human exchange, and brought about by the physical presence of the people engaged in the act of communication, seem to be inherently irreproducible.[52]

Just as in Dido's case in Book I, it is the juxtaposition of points of view that allows Chaucer to emphasize the fictitious aspect of the story.

The poet once more uses the *Commedia* to defend his own vision of poetry. When Virgil appears for the first time, he looks at Dante and "per lungo silenzio parea fioco"[53] (*Inf.* I. 63). He only comes alive when the poet gives him a voice, yet that voice can only come from his readings of Virgil's work. This notion of voice is central in the analysis of Chaucer's reception of the *Commedia*. By stressing the importance of hearing in Book II, Chaucer wholly recasts the issue of authorial responsibility raised by visible speech. The eagle is the perfect illustration of this transition: he resembles his Italian counterpart until Chaucer makes him speak. It then becomes obvious that this eagle supposed to lead Geffrey is, in fact, one of the things the poet wants to show us. His discourse on the advantages of a simple speech "[w]ithoute any subtilite / Of speche, or gret prolixite" (II. 855–56) is more akin to Chaucer's own philosophy than to Dantean poetry. The eagle thus becomes the product of a new imagination as soon as it wakes Geffrey with an "Awak!" (556) that sounds strangely like the cry of an actual bird of prey. One can thus consider the eagle as the barometer on which the audience measures Chaucer's independence *vis-à-vis* Dante. An author borrowing from another writer tends to draw from what is immediately visible, yet *Fame* introduces an acoustic component. Indeed, Chaucer manages to implicate his audience imaginatively by a perfect reproduction of the voices of his characters, here the eagle and Geffrey. He creates a discursive interaction between the characters themselves, and with the audience.

The issue of the narrator's role is accordingly central. We have seen that in *BD* the persona was less a distinctive personality than "a means of incorporating speaker and listener, discourse and audience, into the very texture of the poem."[54] That is also true in *Fame*. Chaucer again uses a first-person narrative and defines his narrator conventionally, but Geffrey is mainly used to facilitate (inter-/intra-) discursive interactions and to define Chaucer's vision of Dante's literary philosophy. As we have seen, the Florentine poet gives a divine dimension to his creation notably through his use of visible speech. Chaucer, on the other

---

[52] Butterfield, *Poetry and Music in Medieval France*, 13.
[53] "seemed faint because of the long silence."
[54] Grudin, *Chaucer and the Politics of Discourse*, 31.

hand, defends the idea that speech depends on human imagination and voices, and that it is accordingly susceptible to fail.

One can already perceive the radical opposition between Dante's theological poetry and Chaucer's deeply human and terrestrial work. Geffrey notably allows the inclusion of laughter in the narrative, which systematically brings back to earth the Florentine's philosophy. The flight of the eagle is, for instance, a trope of great philosophical and religious value; it is meant to guide a character towards a superior state of consciousness, or closer to Heaven. Chaucer therefore makes use of grotesque realism,[55] to prevent the eagle from elevating too much. When he seizes Geffrey, he wakes him up then tells him twice "with wordes to comforte . . . 'Seynte Marye, / Thou art noyous for to carye!'" (II. 572–74), before continuing his flight "into glassy-eyed indifference with a tedious sight-seeing commentary."[56] Presenting his persona as a rather stout fellow—an aspect that henceforth becomes characteristic of the Chaucerian narrator—reinforces the carnivalesque dimension of his poem, given this image of the benefits of abundant food and drink that actually prevents the eagle from elevating too much. According to Bakhtin, this grotesque swing connects Heaven and Earth in a vertiginous movement, but the accent is placed not on the upward movement but on the descent.[57] As a result, as soon as Geffrey attempts to get closer to Dante, the eagle starts to talk and takes us brutally far from the walls of Florence. Before following Virgil, Dante wondered if he were worthy of accomplishing such a journey, reminding his guide, "[i]o non Enea, io non Paolo sono"[58] (*Inf.* II. 32). Geffrey equally wonders:

> Wher Joves wol me stellyfye,
> Or what thing may this sygnifye?
>   I neyther am Ennok, ne Elye
>   (II. 586–88)

To which the eagle cannot help but answer, "[t]how demest of thyself amys" (II. 596). Jupiter has no intention whatsoever to turn poor Geffrey into a star. The purpose of his journey is simply to reward him for his service to Cupid and Venus, "[a]lthough that in thy hed ful lyte is" (621).

Besides, the narrator also ends up asking if he is physically present in the dream, or if it is rather a projection of his soul—a recurring question in the

---

55 The essential principle of grotesque realism is degradation, the lowering of all that is abstract, spiritual, noble, and ideal to the material level.
56 Wallace, "Chaucer's Continental Inheritance," 24.
57 Bakhtin, *Rabelais and His World*, 371.
58 "I am not Aeneas, I am not Paul."

Commedia, notably throughout the *Inferno*, and more specifically in *Paradiso*, I. 73–74. But the eagle stops him and cries "Lat be . . . thy fantasye!" (992), before asking him if he wishes to take advantage of this unique opportunity to know more about the stars, an offer Dante would have eagerly accepted. Geffrey, however, politely refuses, noting "y am now to old" (995). This refusal is revealing of Chaucer's poetical and philosophical vision. Borrowing Mircea Eliade's anthropological terminology, Brewer remarks that "Chaucer refuses the role of *shaman*, priest, magician, prophet, with access to other-worldly experience: he chooses this life, this earth, these people."[59] He has no desire to learn more about the heavens and the universe this way; if he must learn about the stars it will be by studying them from Earth, as an astronomer.

Geffrey then continues to systematically lower the tone in describing everything he sees. For example, faced with the magnificence of the House of Fame, he regrets having such a small quantity of money in his pockets (III. 1347–49) and assures a spirit that he has no interest in fame, preferring "[t]hat no wight have my name in honde" (1877) after his death. Chaucer even shows his usual modesty at the beginning of Book III by paying homage—in his own way—to Dante. In the first Canto of the *Paradiso*, Dante begs Apollo to give him enough strength to complete the composition of the most complex part of his poem, and thus be worthy of his laurels:

> O buono Apollo, all'ultimo lavoro
> Fammi del tuo valor sì fatto vaso,
> come dimandi a dar l'amato alloro.
> Infino a qui l'un giogo di Parnaso
> Assai mi fu; ma or con amendue
> M'è uopo entrar nell'aringo rimaso.[60]
> (*Par*. I. 13–18)

Chaucer does the same thing in the invocation of *Fame*'s last Book, but mentions with self-derision that he will just kiss Apollo's tree:

> O God of science and of light,
> Appollo, thurgh thy grete myght,
> This lytel laste bok thou gye!

---

59 Brewer, *An Introduction to Chaucer*, 77.
60 "O Good Apollo, for this final task / make me the vessel of your excellence, / what you, to merit your loved laurel, ask. / Until this point, one of Parnassus' peaks / sufficed for me; but now I face the test, / that agon that is left; I need both crests."

> . . .
> Thou shalt se me go as blyve
> Unto the nexte laure y see,
> And kisse yt, for hyt is thy tree.
> (III. 1091–108)

Geffrey's journey is in other words built in parallel with Dante's, but it does not lead to the same revelations. Everything leads us to understand that the notion of truth in literature is essentially subjective. For Dante, visible speech is a divine creative process imitated by human beings, and thus finds its way into the authentication process of the *Commedia*. Chaucer, however, openly recognizes in *Fame* the conventional and discursive dimension of this poetic device: "it is fiction, it depends on the imagination, and its relation to truth is not easy to discern."[61] The poem consequently questions the authentication of narratives as a tacit contract between author and audience. The audience accepts to be taken to another world over which they have no control, but only on condition that they will not be deceived. Chaucer thus establishes an interdiscursive dialogue with Dante to emphasize the artificiality of this device. And once again, the poet gives us no clear conclusion or answers since *Fame* remains unfinished. Its ending departs from the traditional structure of the dream vision, and offers a revision of its codes: by omitting the genre's conventional closure, Chaucer manifests explicitly the resistance that at the end of *BD* had remained implicit.[62]

One may start to notice a pattern of rhetorical games in Chaucer's unwillingness to provide closure: he encourages us to question how a work's ending relates to its meaning and underscores how the conclusions we expect (human judgment and literary conventions—both of which abound in the *Commedia*) are "part of an ongoing process of interrogation and (re)interpretation."[63] The poem ends on an interrogative note that invites us to re-read.[64] Its failed discursive transaction does not lead us to an authoritative voice, but to a resonating silence that doubles the poem's undercutting of the authority of human voices. The poet reverses the situation and uses a "hyper-circular structure to 'turn dreams to good' or 'convert' the traditional dream vision into a vehicle for questioning the authority of vision literature and, by extension, literature in general."[65] The conception of (hi)story as successions of tidings and rumors and its opposition with

---

61 Taylor, *Chaucer Reads "The Divine Comedy,"* 38.
62 McGerr, *Chaucer's Open Books*, 61.
63 Ibid., 2–3.
64 Boitani, *Chaucer and the Imaginary World of Fame*, 7.
65 McGerr, *Chaucer's Open Books*, 62.

the superficial aspect of literature are among the elements developed in *Fame* and which will be revealed in all their complexity in *Troilus and Criseyde*.

From *Anelida* and *Arcite* to *The Parliament of Fowls*

Following the composition of *Fame*, Chaucer spent several years experimenting with various verse forms and *Anelida and Arcite* can be considered as the first text in which Chaucer attempts to use Boccaccio's *Teseida*. However, although he draws from the epic dimension of the Italian poem, its form remains quite conventional since it borders on the French complaint. Chaucer shows here the importance of his *fin'amor* inheritance, and this association between French form and Italian style partly explains the weaknesses of this particular poem. It is nonetheless remarkable for its division into Proem, Strophe (220–80), Antistrophe (281–341), Conclusion,[66] and for the use of the rhyme royal. By developing this verse form, Chaucer lays the foundations of several centuries of poetry in English since he is the first to adapt the Italian meter to Middle English. As Rossiter explains, "[t]his line would in turn become the normative meter for subsequent English sonnets; despite the various formal alterations instigated by Wyatt, Surrey and Spencer, few stray away from the rhythm which Chaucer decided on."[67] The rhyme royal owes much to Boccaccio's *ottava rima*,[68] whose narrative potential was much superior to the *fin'amor* octosyllabic rhyming couplets. Yet, at this stage of his career, Chaucer still lacks the experience to reveal the true potential of this verse form, and his story of *Anelida and Arcite* is unable to contend with the epic dimension of his source material.

He continued to experiment, however, and even borrowed Dante's *terza rima* in *A Complaint to His Lady* (probably composed after *Anelida*), but it is really with *The Parliament of Fowls* (1380–1383) that he managed to deploy the narrative mechanism that would later structure *Troilus and Criseyde*. Even if the fusion between his various sources is still not perfect, Chaucer balances his French and Italian influences in a narrative supported by a well-oiled rhyme royal that allows him to reproduce the epic aspect of Italian poetry while remaining flexible enough to preserve the conversational quality of his own style.

His *Parliament* is thus a new composition set within the now familiar dream framework. The narrator is equally familiar to Chaucer's audience by now since

---

[66] The virtuosity of this construction is probably inherited from Froissart and Machaut, but its difficulty might explain why Chaucer would never use it again.
[67] Rossiter, *Chaucer and Petrarch*, 113.
[68] Verse composed of eight iambic lines in abababcc.

he is presented as a bookish fellow who confesses in the first lines of the poem: "I knowe nat Love in dede, / Ne wot how that he quiteth folk here hyre" (8–9). He starts by telling us about his reading of Cicero's *Somnium Scipionis* (29–84) but is interrupted by dusk. Scipio himself then appears in a dream (106–19) and leads him through the Temple of Venus (120–94) to a garden in which Nature holds a bird assembly for Valentine's Day (295–699).

The first part of the poem is rather similar to *Fame* and addresses the same themes. Yet the carnivalesque spirit is much more present here, due to a passive narrator who does his best not to get involved in the adventure. One instance of this occurs when Chaucer presents his own version of the third Canto of the *Inferno*. When Dante is led by Virgil to the gate of Hell, he discovers that it bears an inscription "di colore oscuro"[69] (10) warning travelers of the dangers ahead:

> Per me si va nella città dolente,
> per me si va nell'eterno dolore,
> per me si va tra la perduta gente.
>   . . .
> Dinanzi a me, non fur cose create
> se non eterne, ed io eterna duro:
> lasciate ogni speranza, voi ch'entrate.[70]
>   (*Inf.* III. 1–9)

The crossing of the threshold is of great significance since it symbolizes, to follow Bakhtinian terminology, the narrator's penetration into the nourishing earth. This topographic journey, associated with Hell, binds together the earth (the grave), the body (the belly), and the mind (sin) and allows Dante's resurrection and extraction from his human condition. However, Chaucer once again uses carnivalesque lowering and reverses the top and bottom. His narrator therefore finds himself facing the entrance to a garden straight out of the *Roman de la Rose*, but before entering he notices its gate is topped by a double inscription "of gold and blak" (141). On one side, one may read a few lines praising the eternal beauty of the garden (127–33), while on the other side the narrator reads:

> "Thorgh me men gon, . . .
> Unto the mortal strokes of the spere
> Of which Disdayn and Daunger is the gyde,

---

[69] "of obscure color."
[70] "Through me the way into the suffering city, / through me the way to the eternal pain, / through me the way that runs among the lost. . . . / Before me nothing but eternal things / were made, and I endure eternally. / Abandon every hope, who enter here."

> Ther nevere tre shal fruyt ne leves bere.
> This strem yow ledeth to the sorweful were
> There as the fish in prysoun is al drye;
> Th'eschewing is only the remedye!"
> (134–40)

The association of a courtly garden with Hell might seem slightly excessive, but it allows Chaucer to insist on the discrepancy between the narrator and the world of love. He is terrified by that inscription and cannot move, but while Virgil comforts Dante by holding his hand, Scipio brutally pushes the narrator across the threshold and reminds him that his role in that story is minor: "Yit that thow canst not do, yit mayst thow se" (163). The narrator is not here to serve love and has consequently nothing to fear, Scipio had led him to the garden merely to show him "mater of to wryte" (168).

And Chaucer seems to enjoy writing about this garden. He elegantly adapts several stanzas of Boccaccio's *Teseida* (VII. 50–66) but never loses sight of his carnivalesque guiding principle. The garden is as beautiful as in the *Roman*, but when the narrator steps into the Temple of Venus he is faced with a sudden lowering of the sublime: he sees the god Priapus standing "in sovereyn place" (254), at the moment when the ass brayed, thus preventing him from raping Hestia. He is immortalized in this pose, "with hys sceptre in honde" (256) while men desperately try to crown him with garlands of fresh flowers. Chaucer's narrator goes through the garden without being worried and never faces *inamoramento*. As Brewer remarked, Chaucer's narrator is, in *PF*, nothing more than a pair of eyes.[71] Scipio has told him that he is there to watch and he does not miss the chance to look when he discovers Venus lying on a bed of gold in her Temple. The particularity of that scene does not come from Venus's presentation, but rather from the narrator's scrutiny. The passivity of the narrator turns into a form of voyeurism that distances us from Italian elegance and subtlety, as he sees the goddess

> naked from the brest unto the hed
> Men myghte hire sen; and, sothly for to say,
> The remenaunt was wel kevered to my pay,
> Ryght with a subtyl coverchef of Valence—
> Ther was no thikkere cloth of no defense.
> (269–73)

We have seen the effects produced by the distancing of the narrator in the *Roman*, and Chaucer manages here to give this narrative process a wholly new dimension. Indeed, he turns his persona into the herald of a wonderful cacophony, and of a

---

[71] Brewer, *An Introduction to Chaucer*, 79.

dialogue between foreign and contradictory voices, especially when he finally enters the parliament of birds. The voice of the author is then dissolved to the point of becoming merely one of the components of a discursive web allowing polyphony to occur. The narrator finds himself facing a multitude of birds making "so huge a noyse" (312) they seem to fill the entire area. All of the species present are placed according to their nobility and function, with the birds of prey perching obviously higher than those eating worms, and waterfowls. Nature, therefore, grants the male eagle, "[t]he foul royal, above yow in degre, / The wyse and worthi, secre, trewe as stel" (394–95), the chance to be the first to choose his mate. He promptly starts his plea, declaring his love for a particular bird, but when everything seems settled another eagle, of lesser rank, declares that he loves that female more. And then a third bird joins the dance, provoking discussions lasting "from the morwe . . . Tyl dounward went the sonne wonder faste" (489–90). Yet the narrator swears he has never head "[s]o gentil ple in love or other thyng" (485), and just as Chaucer's audience expects the crisis to resolve itself courteously, the rest of the fowls make such an outcry that the narrator thinks the wood has shivered to pieces.

This noble Valentine's Day gathering thus begins to look increasingly like an authentic parliamentary discussion. Respect and the values of courtly love cannot last longer than the patience of the members of the parliament, who start screaming "Have don, and lat us wende!" (492) and "Whan shal youre cursede pletynge have an ende?" (495) while fowls of lesser nobility merely join the current cacophony as best as they can:

> The goos, the cokkow, and the doke also
> So cryede, "Kek kek! kokkow! quek quek!" hye,
> That thourgh myne eres the noyse wente tho.
> (498–500)

Nature has consequently no other choice but to ask each group to elect a representative that will speak for them. Chaucer continues his parody of the political world and presents us with elected representatives who also cannot communicate calmly. The waterfowls, who up to this point had been shouting, pronounce "large golee" (556) and by mutual assent elect the goose for her eloquence.

Yet when the goose starts talking, the sparrow-hawk interrupts her twice and tells the parliament "Never mot she thee!" (569), which obviously provokes "[t]he laughter . . . of gentil foules alle" (575). In effect, each representative is then insulted or ridiculed one after the other in an increasingly growing confusion. The noblest eagle thus judges that the words of the duck come "[o]ut of the donghil" (597), while the merlin suggests to the cuckoo that the extinction of his species would not be a bad thing (615). Nature then closes the debate by giving the female the right to choose her mate. Chaucer thus opposes throughout this debate the legal aspect of a parliamentary discussion with courtly language in order to create a sense of irony that becomes the real object of the meeting. As Muscatine explains,

> The very inconclusiveness of the outcome shows that the pointed contrast of courtly and bourgeois attitudes is designedly balanced. It produces a comic reflection of one attitude on the other; each is partly admirable, partly foolish. The ending leaves us with no hard feeling.[72]

The narrator eventually wakes up in his bed and goes back to his books. The audience, therefore, is faced with a poem that gives us no answer.

Although *PF* has a formal conclusion, unlike *Fame*, it does not seem that the issues it raised can be perceived as resolved. Chaucer goes back to the closing conventions of the dream vision and delivers an "essay in poetics as well as a poem about its subject"[73] but without offering a single answer. Nature has been remarkably useless as a judge, the debate on the issue among the members of the parliament is a failed transaction, and the narrator has learned nothing at all from his experience and continues to read, hoping one day to find "som thyng for to fare" (698). Chaucer has gradually operated a transition from a sublime Italian vision to the parody of a parliamentary meeting in which everybody speaks without taking the debate forward. This popular counterweight to the seriousness and official constraints of feudal life, associated with the narrator's withdrawal, gives the poet the opportunity to lead his audience into a secondary world where laughter mingles the voices of men and women of all social classes. Indeed, *PF* presents "a wide range of voices, representing learned, courtly, and anticourtly perspectives, in explicit and unresolved competition with each other." Chaucer's polyvocal poetics is here strongly dialogic.[74] And although the polyphony orchestrated by the poet highlights the independence of each voice while suggesting a possible harmonious interaction, it also allows him to question the very literariness of his art.

The open-ended conclusion returns us to the beginning and once again turns the poet into a reader grappling with his sources. His narrator is not attracted by love; the only pleasure of this character lost in a dream vision is to watch, and as Juliette Dor notes: "[i]l n'entre même pas en dialogue intérieur avec ce qu'il découvre. Son but serait-il d'encore éviter d'affirmer son autorité

---

[72] Muscatine, *Chaucer and the French Tradition*, 119.
[73] Payne, *The Key of Remembrance*, 144.
[74] Strohm, *Social Chaucer*, 152.

d'auteur?"[75] Through this passion for books Chaucer shows that reading is an ongoing process continuing even after the end of a text, and that the juxtaposition of influences, his interdiscursive dialogue between his sources, is revealing of the human and fallible character of imagination and story-telling. Nothing is ever truly created,

> For out of olde feldes as men seyth,
> Cometh al this newe corn from yer to yere,
> And out of olde bokes, in good feyth,
> Cometh al this newe science that men lere.
>   (22–25)

On the whole, the juxtaposition of elements coming from stilnovism, *fin'amor*, and the bourgeois tradition draws the portrait of a poet with the ability to manipulate his audience. The circular structure of *PF* establishes a parallel between the parliament in the diegesis and the text itself. Indeed, both have as their subject "the attempt to determine the truth about love, and both present the issue of words and conclusions—or, in other words, in terms of meaning and ending."[76] More importantly, it clearly establishes Chaucer's discursive strategies and polyphonic abilities.

---

[75] "he does not even start an inner dialogue with what he has discovered. Would his purpose once again be to avoid affirming his authority as an author?" Chaucer, *Les Contes de Canterbury et autres œuvres*, 886.
[76] McGerr, *Chaucer's Open Books*, 93.

Chapter 4
Troilus and Criseyde and the Ambiguity of Double Enunciation

The years following the composition of *PF* are undeniably crucial in Chaucer's career. He continued to compile narratives and to popularize European culture in his vernacular, and in the 1380s alone, he produced three major works showing a radical evolution of his mode of poetical representation, namely a translation of Boethius's *Consolatio Philosophiae*,[1] *Troilus and Criseyde*, and *The Legend of Good Women*.

Troilus and Criseyde follows the *Roman de la Rose* insofar as it apparently presents a narrative inspired by vernacular poetry. But as Stephen A. Barney remarked, the resemblance ends there.[2] Indeed, Chaucer ignores in *TC* the allegory of love he had been using since *BD* and turns instead to a pseudo-historical mode of representation that condenses his sources within a diegesis dominated by Boethian philosophical gravity. In doing so, the controller of customs occasionally composing poetry suddenly became a "serious contender for the laurel, a learned European poet, the deliberate rival of the great Italians, a seeker of fame."[3]

The debate between the Trojan and Greek supporters at the end of *HF* perfectly prefigures *TC* since it once again suggests that (hi)story, as we know it, is made of a juxtaposition of often contradictory points of view. This time Chaucer draws from Boccaccio's *Filostrato*, a source that will undergo a new creative evolution of speech. For Chaucer does not merely translate Boccaccio, he adjusts it to a newly created context and works on a transvaluation, namely "a shifting of perspectives, an intensification, a 'thickening' of the texture of language and idea."[4] When we notice the intertextuality of the poem, we may become aware of the coexistence of the surface text and those underneath that have affected it. The result is a poem in which an attentive audience may perceive the echoes of Dante's and Boccaccio's voices, but with a distinctive English accent.

---

[1] We will not dwell on his translation of Boethius, as we are mainly trying to focus on Chaucer's fiction, but this particular work does mark a philosophical change in his poetry, which gained considerable depth. See for instance John M. Hill's book *Chaucer's Neoplatonism*.
[2] Chaucer, *The Riverside Chaucer*, 471.
[3] Ibid.
[4] Windeatt, "The 'Troilus' as Translation," 4.

https://doi.org/10.1515/9781501514364-005

Reprocessing Boccaccio's *Filostrato*

Troilus and Criseyde is clearly a poem about story-telling and one's relation to a text. It is about how language can be used to deceive, how it can be misunderstood or manipulated. This is not, of course, the first time Chaucer deals with his source material by introducing a notion of fallibility and failed discursive transactions. But with *TC*, he starts by operating a major reprocessing of Boccaccio's mode of representation and stylistic approach that gets the dialogue started at a formal level.

When Boccaccio settled in Naples, the court of Robert I was still at the height of its power and glory. Courtly love values and poetry had been spreading through the south of Italy since Charles of Anjou had turned what is now the region of Campania into the heart of a remarkable cultural and intellectual network in 1266. Charles himself admired poetry and music: he became, for instance, Jean de Meun's patron, used his influence to attract to Naples troubadours such as Adam de la Halle or Sordello of Mantova and was in effect influential in the implantation of French culture in Italy. As Wallace notes, "[a] good many French texts were copied at Naples during this period, including a number of translations from Latin into French executed for Italian patrons, who were evidently anxious to be included within the ambit of French culture."[5] *Fin'amor* was accordingly so well established in Naples that it profoundly marked Boccaccio a few decades later.[6]

It is in this context, during the 1330s, that Boccaccio, then in his twenties, started the composition of *Il Filostrato*. The poem, which evokes Boccaccio's recent heartbreak, channels most of his poetical influences, but without the necessary experience to integrate them homogeneously into the narrative. Quotations from Cino da Pistoia, Andreas Capellanus, and Dante can thus be found within the poem but without proper contextualization. Nonetheless, by choosing to set his love story during the siege of Troy, rather than in the more conventional dream vision, Boccaccio positions himself as what literary history would later call a "Renaissance" poet. Indeed, by isolating and developing an episode of the Trojan chronicles, which were legion at the time, he directly echoes the ancient Greek poets who had isolated and re-elaborated segments of the Homeric cycle.

Chaucer, for his part, became interested in this very subject less than fifty years later, when he was in his forties and living in London. It is, in other

---

[5] Wallace, "Chaucer and Boccaccio's Early Writings," 146.
[6] The coming to Naples in 1330 of Cino da Pistoia, whom Dante praised as the greatest Italian poet, must have marked Boccaccio.

words, not merely a difference in maturity that distinguishes the two men but also their belonging to two different worlds. Despite a somewhat similar origin, Boccaccio and Chaucer clearly did not have the same connection with their respective surroundings: even if the Italian had come closer to the court of Naples, he was never a member of its aristocratic circle and had to rely on his imagination to understand and visualize the values of *fin'amor*. Chaucer, on the other hand, had a much better understanding of the courtly world, even if he had little influence there. He joined the household of Elizabeth, Countess of Ulster, in 1357 at the age of seventeen and there learned to observe and listen:

> Chaucer, although of bourgeois origins, received a courtly education. Boccaccio, however, remained an outsider to the courtly world; his conception of *cortesia* is inevitably impoverished and debased. In Boccaccio's early writings, the popular appropriation of courtly vocabulary—a generative process bitterly observed by the aristocratic author of *Il Fiore*—is made absolute. It was perhaps for this reason that Chaucer nowhere acknowledges Boccaccio by name.[7]

Although he was influenced by courtly love poetry, Boccaccio was equally marked by the lyricism of the Stilnovists, which made his treatment of romance much more elaborate than it had been in Chrétien's time. His approach to the courtly world was imbued with sensuality and a cynicism completely foreign to French medieval poetry.[8] Chaucer thus rapidly decided to transform the vision of courtly love offered by *Il Filostrato* by rejecting a mere exposition of feelings. Just as Andreas Capellanus or Guillaume de Lorris had earlier attempted to instruct lovers, Chaucer illustrates this idea of teaching within a non-allegorical narrative. It is no surprise then that his treatment of this episode of the Trojan War is so different from Boccaccio's.

In *TC*, Chaucer faithfully follows the narrative of the *Filostrato*: the actions and reactions of the characters are fundamentally dictated by Boccaccio, as are his distribution of the narration and dialogues in verse. Yet he systematically steps away from the form imposed by the *Filostrato*. He no longer translates but rather reimagines his story and continues the bivocal narration he had started to develop in his previous poems. In doing so, he weakens the authority of the Italian poet in order to offer a radically different mode of questioning.

Chaucer was therefore not particularly receptive to the Italian sensibility—a poetical aspect specific to the so-called Renaissance. As we have hinted in the Introduction, the notion of "the Renaissance" was completely foreign to Chaucer and his contemporaries, and it would have been very difficult to translate into

---

7 Wallace, "Chaucer and Boccaccio's Early Writings," 159.
8 Muscatine, *Chaucer and the French Tradition*, 125.

Latin or English the difference that critics from the following centuries perceived between medieval and Renaissance art.[9] Thus whereas Boccaccio chose to focus on sentimentality, Chaucer preferred to exemplify emotions and create a dialogue between them. Troy is, in Chaucer's poem, a city besieged but strangely comfortable and warm: by merely summarizing the progress of the conflict, the poet moved away from a conventional approach and towards a depiction of feelings.[10] He favored a philosophical and rhetorical amplification and a reinforcement of the codes of *fin'amor* that allowed a return to the novelistic genre as conceived by Chrétien and Guillaume.

Right at the start of his proem, Boccaccio clearly establishes the link between the present work and his heartbreak. He invokes his lady, Filomena, asking her to guide him, whereas others "di Giove sogliono il favore / ne' lor principii pietosi invocare"[11] (I. st. 1). In his prologue, by contrast, Chaucer chooses to call on Tisiphone (I. 6) and thoroughly alters this prayer to Love. Indeed, whereas Boccaccio barely spends a verse on this subject, the good old rhetorician that is Chaucer devotes almost thirty lines to it (I. 22–49), returning to the love experience the sacred aura that Ovid and Andreas Capellanus had given it.[12] He thus starts his prayer by saying:

> But ye loveres, that bathen in gladnesse,
>   If any drope of pyte in yow be,
> Remembreth yow on passed hevynesse
>   (I. 22–24)

He then invites lovers to pray for those suffering like Troilus "[t]hat Love hem brynge in hevene to solas" (31), and that God may grant to those "[t]hat ben despeired out of Loves grace" (42) the possibility of leaving this world without delay and thus avoid the damnation promised to those who commit suicide. He also asks that we pray so that lovers may keep the favor of their lady, in accordance with the rules of Love (45–46). Chaucer goes back, in other words, to the very origins of *fin'amor* and clearly establishes that his vision of *Il Filostrato* is closer to Chrétien's sensibility or Dante's in the *Vita Nuova*.

He also operates another major change, this time concerning the behavior of the main character. Just before his meeting with Criseida, Boccaccio's Troiolo

---

9 Lewis, "What Chaucer Really Did to 'Il Filostrato,'" 28.
10 Lambert, "Telling the Story in Troilus and Criseyde," 62.
11 "ask Jove's favor / in their pious invocation."
12 Andreas's vision is of course less irreverent than the one presented by Ovid in *Ars amatoria*.

looks at the ladies in the temple in a very unconventional but perhaps more "realistic" way:

> ed ora questa ed or quella a lodare
> incominciava e di ta' riprendendo,
> sí come quelli a cui non ne piaceva
> una piú ch'altra, e sciolto si godeva.[13]
>   (I. st. 20)

If this image of young men gazing at girls and passing their time comparing them would not shock a modern reader, it is not, however, acceptable according to the codes of *fin'amor*. That is why Chaucer deliberately alters this passage to bring it closer to the courtly love tradition. Whereas Boccaccio condenses the *inamoramento* to two lines ("il quale Amor trafisse / piú ch'alcun altro";[14] I. st. 25), Chaucer goes back to the metaphor used by both Ovid and Guillaume and presents us with a god of love offended by Troilus's actions, and fully intentioned to show him "anon his bowe nas naught broken" (I. 208).

This intensification of Boccaccio's "Amor trafisse" equally gives Chaucer the chance to accentuate another characteristic of *fin'amor*, namely the resistance of the young man to Love's charms. In *Il Filostrato*, Boccaccio sums up this image briefly with a reference to the "ciechità delle mondane menti"[15] (I. st. 25) before focusing on the contrast between our expectations and what the course of events usually grants us. *Troilus and Criseyde*, instead, questions the relation between human hybris and the state in which the rebellious lover is plunged by the divinity.[16] If Chaucer reproduces stylistically the effect desired by Boccaccio—he starts for instance with an apostrophe "O blynde world, O blynde entencioun!" (I. 211)—he adds in contrast eighteen lines during which he illustrates Troilus's pride (214–31), before inviting his audience for four verses not to reproduce his mistake "[t]o scornen Love, which that so soone kan / The fredom of youre hertes to hym thralle" (233–34).

The English version of *Il Filostrato* abounds in examples of this reprocessing of the courtly code.[17] One example, in particular, shows the strength of Chaucer's

---

13 "[he] began to praise now this lady and now that, / and in like fashion to disparage them, / as one to whom none was more pleasing than another, / and took delight in his freedom."
14 "whom Love transfixed / more than any other."
15 "blindness of mundane minds."
16 Lewis, "What Chaucer Really Did to 'Il Filostrato,'" 39.
17 In "What Chaucer Really Did to 'Il Filostrato,'" Lewis discusses Chaucer's medievalization of the Italian text. If the idea behind this remains interesting, the concept itself deserves to be nuanced. Talking about medievalization here would establish a clear association of both poets

transformation of his source material. In Boccaccio's text, Troiolo long hesitates to give Pandaro the name of the lady he loves because of the family ties between her and his friend and advisor (II. st. 15). Yet when he eventually confesses the truth, Pandaro answers that he would have done his best to facilitate their meeting even if she had been his sister (st. 16). For Chaucer, the situation is different. Indeed, even if the main trigger of the crisis is identical, the poet alters the cause of Troilus's hesitation by favoring a courtly language that Boccaccio did not master. By reducing the importance granted to social disparities in *Il Filostrato*, Chaucer tightens the links between his different characters (Pandarus is close to Priam and Criseyde becomes involved with the royal family) and produces a social circle in which it is even more complicated to achieve and protect intimacy. The cult of secrecy, central in the courtly love relation, is as a result placed in the foreground. It is the fear of a possible scandal that momentarily paralyzes Troilus and prevents him from revealing the name of the lady he loves. That is why the role of Pandarus is so important in Chaucer's adaptation, for he works towards the concretization of the love of the eponymous characters, which he even considers as a game ("Here bygynneth game"; I. 868). He forces Troilus to bounce back and serve his lady, but also to confess his faults to Love: for him, the virtue of a Lady becomes the basis of his hopes (I. 897–900), while for Boccaccio's Pandaro, this same virtue is an obstacle.

All these transformations systematically reconnect Chaucer's text with medieval sources. As Lewis notes,

> I am prepared to show how many of the beauties introduced by Chaucer, such as the song of Antigone or the riding past of Troilus, are introduced to explain and mitigate and delay the surrender of the heroine, who showed in Boccaccio a facility condemned by the courtly code.[18]

But Chaucer's modification of his source also sets up an additional layer of meaning in the text. It emphasizes "the surface moral meaning of the expression based on the authoritative text and conceals the morally problematic emotional meaning behind it."[19] A consequence of this reprocessing is a curious return to the roots of the novelistic genre and a greater narrative ambiguity. Chrétien had

---

with time periods they were not even aware existed. As we have mentioned in the Introduction, Chaucer was not especially trying to be medieval or modern, he was merely innovating in his own time, which is just as true for Boccaccio who happened to have a different artistic sensibility. I prefer to talk about Chaucer's reprocessing of the Italian's treatment of *fin'amor*.
18 Lewis, "What Chaucer Really Did to 'Il Filostrato,'" 43.
19 Nakao, *The Structure of Chaucer's Ambiguity*, 68.

connected his stories with psychology and *fin'amor* doctrine. Yet, as we have noted, these elements were then isolated by his successors: Guillaume focused on the psychological component because of his use of allegory, while others chose to develop the historical dimension of their narrative. But by changing his mode of representation, Chaucer manages here to reassemble within a unique poem these various elements that had matured individually for centuries. These pseudo-historic narratives

> could explore nuances of human relations, develop moral and philosophical themes, rearrange and give point and conclusiveness to the structure of events, and represent details of settings, conversations, private complaints, public speeches, and the subtlest gesture.[20]

Chaucer breaks with the allegorical model and focuses not on the result of Criseyde's betrayal but on its psychological process. What we have come to name the historical novel, and which brought glory to Shakespeare, Stendhal, and Dickens, to name just a few, is simply the result of the development of a literary mode of representation endowed with a novelistic twist. It is another way for Chaucer to underline the artificiality of individual utterances. This deliberate manipulation of Boccaccio's mode of representation, this reprocessing of his narrative, shows how language can be "willfully ignored or manipulated, at the least deliberately delimited."[21] It is not the first time Chaucer tells us a story about a story others have told, but this time polyphony is made even more audible by an interdiscursive dialogue between his persona and his intertext.

Double Enunciation: Introducing Dante in *Il Filostrato*

Chaucer continued to develop his persona throughout his career. What started as a mere literary device inherited from the conventions of courtly love in *BD* quickly became a distancing mask allowing the poet to share his vision of the world and of literature. Nonetheless, despite the distinctive features of each poem, the Chaucerian narrator progressively takes on characteristics that he will keep, turning him into the main element of a double enunciation in which the narrator's voice is divided and he does not necessarily acknowledge responsibility for his discourse.

---

20 Chaucer, *The Riverside Chaucer*, 471.
21 Wasserman, "Both Fixed and Free," 210.

Bally established a distinction between modal and speaking subjects based on the dissociation between actual and pretended enunciations.[22] The speaking subject is an empirical being, responsible for the "activité effective (articulatoire, cognitive, sociale) en quoi consiste la parole";[23] the modal subject, however, is an image, he is not responsible for the enunciation but is the one presented by language as speaking and thinking what is being said. Bally noticed that the modal subject is very often at the same time speaking subject[24] but a detachment between the actual producer of speech and the one presented as assuming the responsibility is not rare. Gérard Genette thus established a clear distinction between the author of a novel, the actual source of the narrative, and the narrator, who is merely a fictitious image of the one telling a story about experienced events.[25] Chaucer's narrator in *TC* is the perfect illustration of this dialogical opposition between speaking and modal subjects.

The detachment between author, narrator, and character in *TC* owes much to Old French vision-poems (see for instance the opposition between the naive lover of the dream and the author) and, by extension, to the narrative process of the *Commedia*. Chaucer notably adopts here the division of the narrator into historian/witness as a commentary on Dante's own use of the device. Indeed, in order to ensure the authenticity of his story, Dante develops several processes, such as the presentation of the poet as *scriba Dei*. Since Dante presents his tale as an autobiographical narrative, he is forced to prove to his audience the goodwill and honesty of this first person. Autobiographies rely on this pact between the narrator and the reader to ensure the exactitude of the facts about to be narrated. And in the case of a spiritual autobiography, the situation is even more complex given that the narrator must convince us quickly that the "I" introduced at the beginning of the narrative is not the same as the one

---

22 Following Bally's work, Ducrot later noted that the speaker sometimes has two different faces: he may be a speaker *en tant que tel* and *en tant qu'être du monde*. The speaker *en tant que tel* is the one presented as responsible for the choice of words, style, ethos, and discursive pathos. He assumes the vulgarity of his characters, their emotions and psychological states, and is, in other words, responsible for the enunciation, although he might disagree with what is being said. The speaker *en tant qu'être du monde*, however, is an object of discourse among others, he is the one that discourse represents at the level of its propositional content, when the speaking subject considers himself the object of his discourse. See Ducrot, "Esquisse d'une théorie polyphonique de l'énonciation," 171–233, and Perrin, "Polyphonie et autres formes d'hétérogénéité énonciative," 15.
23 "actual activity (articulatory, cognitive, social) that is speech." Perrin, "La notion de polyphonie en linguistique," 268.
24 Bally, *Linguistique générale et linguistique française*, 37.
25 See Genette, *Figures III*.

pronounced by the narrator-author. In order to prove that his life has changed, Dante merges the opposition existing between fact and fiction through the use of spatial, temporal, and personal deixis creating two time periods, inhabited by two different "I." As Bianca Garavelli remarks, Dante makes a distinction

> fra due se stesso, un Dante personaggio che non sa nulla, che deve imparare tutto, e che prova le più intense emozioni; e un Dante nuovo, il poeta che ricorda, conosce già tutto ciò che Dante personaggio sta per affrontare, e ha conservato in sé la conseguenza positiva di quell'emozione momentaneamente insostenibile.[26]

Dante establishes this distinction between two different time periods in the first lines of the *Inferno*. He starts by remembering his journey in the *passato remoto*, a grammatical time used to describe events belonging to a closed past ("Nel mezzo del cammin di nostra vita / mi ritrovai per una selva oscura";[27] *Inf.* I. 1–2), before going back a few lines later to the moment of writing (4–6). The past times serve, in other words, when Dante remembers his pilgrimage, while the stored experience invariably appears in the present (see for instance *Inf.* II. 1–6). He rapidly creates a distinction between two different Dantes: the speaking and modal subjects are in fact the same person separated at the beginning by the events to be narrated but connected by a same complementary connection to the audience. In addition to the word "nostra" that joins Dante with his audience, this relation is reinforced by a use of spatial and temporal deixis that makes us companions of the poet whenever he goes back into the past ("io vi trovai";[28] 8). He accordingly makes a distinction between the "qui" and "or" (here and now) relative to the present of writing, and the "là" (there), "allor" or "poi" (then) of his past journey. This unique ability to jump between two versions of himself, as if they were two different characters, is especially visible in certain cantos, where the times of discourse and story arrange themselves in accord with temporal adverbs. When Dante is so weary he can no longer move without Virgil's assistance, the poet tells us for example: "Allor mi dolsi, ed ora mi ridoglio / quando drizzo la mente a ciò ch'io vidi"[29] (*Inf.* XXVI. 19–20).

---

26 "between two versions of himself, a Dante character who knows nothing, who must learn everything and experiences the most intense of feelings; and a new Dante, the poet who remembers, who already knows all that the Dante character is about to face and who has kept within him the positive consequence of this momentarily unberable emotion." Dante, *La Divina Commedia*, 7.
27 "When I had journeyed half of our life's way, / I found myself within a shadowed forest."
28 "discovered there."
29 "It grieved me then and now grieves me again / When I direct my mind to what I saw."

Dante thus develops in the *Commedia* a specific narrative frame through which he gives his persona (narrator-pilgrim—modal subject) a completely different voice from the one of the narrator-author (speaking subject). This withdrawal of the poet allows him not only to reinforce the pilgrim's role as witness (authenticating the work) but also to create a dialogue through this double enunciation. Dante tells us what the souls he encounters experience without breaking his frame: he literally makes us hear all these voices through direct speech, giving each character, whether angel or demon, the chance to speak. Reported speech is, of course, a form of dialogism,[30] and Dante's use of it allows him to multiply the number of speakers and leave them the responsibility of their discourse. When he must himself describe what the souls feel, he keeps his position of witness and merely shares his own impressions. He says for instance of Virgil's unstated feelings: "Ei mi parea da se stesso rimorso"[31] (*Purg.* III. 7). In doing so, Dante turns the author into a character whose importance is equal to the others', and whose voice does not dominate the debate.

The idea of separating pilgrim and author by these deictic units is further supported by discourse. That is notably why Dante uses the *passato remoto* instead of the retrospective *passato prossimo*, which would make more sense since both characters are just two aspects of Dante. But Paul explains in the First Epistle to the Corinthians that all die in Adam and are reborn in Christ (15:22), which turns religious conversion into a form of death. It is accordingly not surprising that Dante echoes the separation of souls between the *passato remoto* of their earthly existence and the present of their death: "Io fui da Montefeltro, io son Bonconte"[32] (*Purg.* V. 88). This opposition between *fui* and *son* is almost systematic and the rare instances where it is absent happen to be of particular importance. Beatrice uses, for example, the present of general truth and never, despite her death, falls into the past: "Guardaci ben! Ben son, ben son Beatrice!"[33] (*Purg.* XXX. 73). As Taylor remarks, "Beatrice's eternality . . . does transcend mundane distinctions between past and present, and she, in fact, helps Dante to recover his own past and reform it into 'la sua vita

---

30 Jacques Bres and Bertrand Verine remark that if there is no clear boundary between reported speech and polyphony in Ducrot's work, it is probably because such a boundary exists only in linguistic facts. They suggest that under the apparent duality of phenomena resides their fundamental unity, which only the tradition of linguistic studies prevents us from seeing: reported speech is a form of dialogism. See Bres and Verine, "Le bruissement des voix dans le discours: dialogisme et discours rapporté," 161–62.
31 "He seemed like one who's stung by self-reproof."
32 "I was from Montefeltro, I'm Buonconte."
33 "Look here! For I am Beatrice, I am!"

nova.'"³⁴ The impact of this use of the *passato remoto* is recognized by the souls, as is apparent in Cavalcante de Cavalcanti's reaction after asking Dante why his son Guido does not accompany him in his journey. The Florentine answers:

> . . . Da me stesso non vegno:
> colui ch'attende là per qui mi mena
> forse cui Guido vostro ebbe a disdegno.³⁵
> (*Inf.* X. 61–63)

Dante's interlocutor interprets this past time by its completed aspect and infers that his son has died: "Come / dicesti? Egli ebbe? Non viv'egli ancora?"³⁶ (67–68).

This particular use reveals more about Dante himself than about Guido's fate since it implies a distancing between the poet Dante and the pilgrim, now separated by spiritual death and resurrection in Christ. That generates one of the paradoxes of the genre of autobiography, namely the presentation of the main character as a completely different person from the one telling the story. The events have transformed Dante to the point that he speaks about who he was then as if he were dead, which also implies that audience members do not have to worry about his honesty. The very principle of conversion allows Dante to authenticate his narrative and support his role as witness. It is therefore not surprising to see the pilgrim going through several phases of confessions and retractions, notably for example when Beatrice appears for the first time and accuses him of having forgotten her in death (*Purg.* XXX). He thus reflects on his past as courtly poet in *Inferno* V, but also on his *rime petrose* when the furies cry: "Vegna Medusa: sì 'l farem di smalto!"³⁷ (*Inf.* IX. 52). The credibility of his double enunciation relies entirely on his penitence: Dante rejects his past in order to prove that he is not that man anymore and that we can, therefore, trust him as witness and guide.

In *TC*, Chaucer develops his persona by ignoring Boccaccio and following Dante. Just as Dante sets up a double enunciation in his autobiographical poem, Chaucer superimposes two different stories and two types of narration. Ducrot's definition of dialogism as a form of enunciative lamination between

---

34 Taylor, *Chaucer Reads "The Divine Comedy,"* 92.
35 "My own powers have not brought me; / He who awaits me there, leads me through here / Perhaps to one your Guido did disdain."
36 "What's that: / He '*did* disdain'? He is not still alive?"
37 "Just let Medusa come; then we shall turn him into stone."

enunciative staging and actual enunciation perfectly fits Chaucer's strategy here.[38] His narrator thus tells us the story of Troilus in the third person, while juggling with an "I" supposed to give credence to his self-appointed role as historian.[39] Since he does not use the codes of autobiography, he must convince us of the good faith of a narrator unknown to his audience and who seems to have not lived the events he supposedly witnessed. Chaucer here modifies *Il Filostrato* in order to transform the nature of the personal experience at the heart of Boccaccio's poem into a reading experience, just as in *Fame*. The whole poem is accordingly seen through the prism of reading, and as Nakao notes, "[t]he reason I use 'prism' here is that whether phenomenon or expression, when it passes through the observer's eyes, it does not necessarily produce a straight line, but a refracted line or even a diffused reflection in accordance with their perceptions."[40] His narrator thus shares the experience and emotion consequent upon his reading of the story, and given the nature of Chaucer's intertext, this leaves us with uncertainties, and therefore ambiguity, about what he truly observed, how he cognized it, and how he expresses it. That creates a distance between the third-person frame (where true drama happens) and the first-person one in which the narrator comments—or refuses to comment—on what is happening. This combination of subjective and objective elements allows Chaucer to authenticate his narrative by positioning himself at Dante's level. In the *Commedia*, the link between discourse and story creates a balance justifying the presence of this double enunciation; all the elements reinforce our trust in the narrator-author. The roles of historian, witness, and mediator that Chaucer attributed to his narrator turn him into the only character that actually reacts to the course of events:

> The Narrator is an I, a mask, worn by the person who speaks the script. This public apparition of an I is not, of course, Chaucer the man, not even Chaucer the poet . . . . The I is not then the voice of the "second author," as this apparition is sometimes called in dealing with a modern novel: it is rather the voice of a "third speaker."[41]

The Chaucerian narrator is, in other words, the central piece of the dialogical process developed by the poet. His voice, supposed to convey the author's words, is foreign, which turns the narrator into one character amongst others, a

---

38 See Ducrot, "Enonciation et polyphonie chez Charles Bally," 165–91.
39 Boccaccio completely ignored historical authentication, and even wondered "se fede alcuna alle antiche lettere si può dare" (if one can trust in any way ancient letters). "Proemio," st. 28.
40 Nakao, *The Structure of Chaucer's Ambiguity*, 36.
41 Shepherd, "Troilus and Criseyde," 71.

modal subject, just like the narrator-pilgrim in the *Commedia*. The latter is often wrong and need his guides, whether Virgil or Beatrice, to correct him and lead him on the path to redemption. Dante accordingly creates a particular situation in which the narrator-pilgrim becomes the herald of polyphony, while the poet-creator retains at certain moments his will to impose a monological vision of his work.

Yet this can only come from his exotopic knowledge of his main character. Exotopy enables looking at a character as a whole, whereas seen only from the inside of the diegesis they are only perceived as incomplete. It gives us enough distance to see what remains invisible to the characters—whether it is their death, future, or a background they are not aware of—and perceive them as finished beings.[42] The narrator in *TC* already knows the story he is telling us, just like the narrator-author in the *Commedia*; he is, therefore, conscious of his characters' fate and reacts emotionally to the events. As Bakhtin remarks, the monological novel works around two situations: either ideas are taken for their content and are thus true or false, or they are seen as indications of the psychology of the characters.[43] Dialogism, however, gives access to a third situation that ignores the true/false polarity: given that each idea is somebody's idea, it exists in relation to the voice expressing it, and the horizon it seeks. It is this reaction to the work that allows Chaucer to dismiss monologism by turning his narrator/mediator/historian—speaking subject—into one of the characters of the narrative, with a voice different from the author's. The fact that Dante wishes us to interpret his work in a certain way is an example of this bypassing of truth and lies; it is merely an idea, presented by a character whose journey is complete. He wants to share what he learned from this state of death/resurrection with the rest of mankind, but we are free to ignore him. Chaucer is a perfect example of this. If the *Commedia* had been a fundamentally monological poem, it would have been impossible for Chaucer to manipulate its text in this way and to refuse the philosophy and vision of literature offered by Dante.

With *TC*, Chaucer turns his poem into a reflection on reading literature. By systematically destroying the objectivity of the narrator, who cannot help but get involved in the existence of the characters, and hence move from being a speaking to a modal subject, Chaucer questions the artificiality of human creations. For the more deeply the narrator understands the object of his observation, the more sympathetic he is towards it, and "the more indecisive he is as to

---

42 Bakhtin, *Esthétique de la création verbale*, 36.
43 Ibid., 13.

how to make a judgment upon it."[44] By this stage of his career, Chaucer has long educated his audience into accepting that the world is made of several points of view. In his *Oxford Guide to Troilus and Criseyde*, Barry Windeatt mentions this multiplicity, and states that by "reaching out toward certain polarities within its vision, *Troilus* promotes a kind of multiconsciousness in which any interpretation of the text must be offset by its opposite or contain its contrary within itself."[45] Chaucer thus leaves the final judgment to us. Dante uses a narrative duplication to justify his story, but for Chaucer, the Dantean narrator's tendency to mingle with the souls he meets is bound to create a conflict between the allegedly objective narration and the subjective comments based on the moment's sensation. Besides, most of the work relies on Dante's memory, a memory limited by his human condition. Dante himself recognizes this problem several times, and Chaucer has already demonstrated the fallible and deforming aspects of human memory.

As a result, whether in the *Commedia* or in *TC*, the story depends on reliable sources (Dante presents himself as *scriba Dei* and legitimizes his adventure, while Chaucer relies on "myn auctour") but also on the transparency of narrators promising to transcribe their narratives without altering them. Unlike Boccaccio, the Chaucerian narrator does not feel, for instance, the need to deform the narrative to make it fit his own conception of love since he considers himself as foreign to this world. He even confesses in Book I that he conveys the details and meaning of his source, although it is in a foreign language:

> And of his song naught only the sentence,
>   As writ myn auctour called Lollius,
> But pleinly, save oure tonges difference
>   (393–95)

This confession inevitably reinforces the credibility of the narrator as a translator. And yet we have seen that *Fame* invites the audience to beware of the difference between an event and its verbal echo, between facts and their extension in the human mind: a story may very well reach Fame's House by mixing truth and lies not with the intention to deceive but because in becoming bivocal, a narrative is bound to be marked by the voice of its new speaker. As a result, the alleged transparency of the narrator, who continues a chain of transmission going back to the original events themselves and that were never affected by the passing of time, becomes suspicious. As Dieter Mehl notes, "the main function of the narrator is

---

44 Nakao, *The Structure of Chaucer's Ambiguity*, 38.
45 Windeatt, *Oxford Guides to Chaucer: Troilus and Criseyde*, 299.

not to force a particular interpretation on us, but to make us critically conscious of the process of composition and transmission."[46]

It is accordingly Chaucer's sustained dialogism that allows him to underscore the limits of the transmission process. After having followed Dante for a while in his desire to connect objective facts and subjective interpretation, both aspects of the double enunciation, Chaucer starts to undermine the credibility of his own narration. He is, for example, able to present the events pertaining to the Trojan War as a true historian, inviting the audience to learn more about it in other works, before being transported by his own feelings. When Troilus and Criseyde finally find each other, he proclaims:

> Awey, thow foule daunger and thow feere,
>   And lat hem in this hevene blisse dwelle,
>   That is so heigh that al ne kan I telle!
>   (III. 1321–23)

He seems to forget that these are fictitious characters and lets his joy alone speak. Chaucer thus moves from a detachment authenticating the role of historian of his narrator, to an emotional involvement turning him into the witness of the action, and therefore destroying his objectivity. Several times, he takes the decision to get involved with the story and even threatens the audience members who might dare criticize Criseyde's sudden love for Troilus. Such a person would be "envious" (II. 666) of the beauty of that feeling and might as well go to hell: "Now whoso seith so, mote he nevere ythe!" (670). And although he reasserts his transparency and faithfulness to his source in Book III (491–504), he then confesses to having somewhat disguised the truth ("I kan nat tellen al, / As kan myn auctour, of his excellence"; 1324–25) without indicating why. He furthermore refuses in Book IV to transcribe Criseyde's complaint owing to the fear that his frail language might "childisshly deface" (804) her sadness. Besides, her faithlessness upsets him so much that he cannot keep his distance. He prefers to be laconic when Diomede woos her and merely summarizes the situation by telling us: "What sholde I telle his wordes that he seyde? / He spak inough for o day at the meeste" (V. 946–47). In other words, even when he tries to be transparent, he cannot systematically transcribe things as they happened.

Indeed, the modal subject does not necessarily follow the point of view expressed. Even when modal and speaking subjects are the same person, which is technically the case here, one must not mistake personal thought

---

[46] Mehl, "Chaucer's Narrator: *Troilus and Criseyde* and the *Canterbury Tales*," 219.

and communicated thought. This distinction is of the highest importance and is, for Perrin, linked with the very nature of the linguistic sign.[47] The subject can enunciate a thought given as his own but foreign to him/her.[48] In other words, the modal subject may very well be divided when he/she expresses a point of view that is not his/her own, and which he/she refuses to claim as such. These points of view will be those of other characters or enunciators, as Ducrot calls them.[49] The narrator resists, for example, the evolution of the narrative and refuses to clearly say that Criseyde fell in love with Diomede ("Men seyn—I not—that she yaf hym hire herte"; V. 1050) whereas the lady confirms it herself a few lines later (1071). All that we know of that second love story comes directly from what Criseyde reports in direct speech, while the narrator had previously given us an abundance of psychological and physical details about her relationship with Troilus. In doing so, Chaucer forces us to contemplate again "the other 'objective' parts of his narrative . . . and find that they too contain the narrator's personal perspective."[50] He differentiates the voice—that is, the locutionary act—from the point of view, which takes a position on what is being reported. In that case, the narrator's involvement as modal subject underlines that the speaker's voice is defined by the fact that language is made of "mots, expressions, phrases, dont l'emploi instaure une forme de subjectivité distincte de ce qui est exprimé au plan des contenus. Ainsi un même point de vue associé à un contenu peut être pris en charge, concédé ou rejeté."[51] His role as narrator might make him responsible for the enunciation, but his involvement in the narrative allows him to report what the characters are saying and thinking while rejecting their point of view. Criseyde might very well say she loves Diomede, but that is just her point of view, her words reported in direct speech. The speaking subject has an exotopic understanding of her fate, but the modal subject refuses to hear her words. Voice is not only linked with what words say but what they show.[52] Chaucer is here experimenting with autodialogism, an intralocutive dialogue between the speaking subject and his own enunciation.

---

47 Perrin, "Polyphonie et autres formes d'hétérogénéité énonciative," 20.
48 Bally, *Linguistique générale et linguistique française*, 37.
49 See Ducrot, "Enonciation et polyphonie chez Charles Bally," 165–91.
50 Taylor, *Chaucer Reads "The Divine Comedy,"* 117.
51 "words, expressions, sentences whose use establishes a form of distinct subjectivity from what is expressed at the level of contents. Thus, a single point of view associated to a content may be adopted, acknowledged or rejected." Perrin, "La voix et le point de vue comme formes polyphoniques externes," 63.
52 Perrin, "Le sens montré n'est pas dit," 157–87.

In short, the narrative process developed by Chaucer consists in forcing us to concede (and, as readers, to experience) the inextricability of these two modes—that they not only can but do inevitably intermingle, thus producing an endless multiplication of intralocutive effects. What was supposed to be a perfect transmission actually becomes a work marked by the passing of time and whose content has been altered by the human mind. The very source supposed to assure us of the authenticity of the narrative, Lollius, is fictional, while Boccaccio's name is never even mentioned. The narrator's tendency to modify or ignore certain elements of the original text proves he is particularly incompetent as a historian, which further questions the reliability of his first-person involvement. Nevertheless, if we choose to follow the objective narration, we find ourselves at an impasse: Chaucer forces us to make a choice and to rely on the historical basis provided by Lollius, a basis that is in fact fictitious. Still, the other possibility should not be disregarded because the historian's loss of credibility tends to increase the imaginative participation of the subjective narrator.

Indeed, he sometimes entirely disappears in favor of the action: it is, for example, the case in Book II during the conversation between Pandarus and Criseyde (85–595), a long part of the poem in which we end up forgetting about the complexity of the narration. The narrator's interventions are limited to what someone present in the room might see. His performance is essentially dramatic and dialogic since he punctuates interventions in direct speech with "quod she" and "quod Pandarus." Yet the narrator also invites us in this episode to be the witnesses of the characters' feelings. But by notably presenting Criseyde's thoughts (449–62), the narrator who had until then been absorbed by the dialogue becomes omniscient. Troilus's passage underneath Criseyde's window is thus significant. Following Pandarus's departure, the narrator details the feelings of the lady (596–610), until her attention is drawn by the prince's triumphant passage. Henceforth, the recurrence of verbs of perceptions in the infinitive ("to loke," 630; "to seen," 632; "to byholde," 647) takes us into Criseyde's mind, and we are then told what she thinks in direct speech. As Taylor notes, "[t]he infinitives do not presuppose a seeing subject; they only indicate the possibility of seeing if such a subject were to be present."[53] Such imaginative participation reinforces dialogism since the narrator allows us to share Criseyde's perspective: it is her voice, not the narrator's, that transcribes her thoughts. The distinction here between enunciator (Criseyde) and speaker (the narrator) is particularly relevant because of the already existing double enunciation. The speaker uttering the

---

53 Taylor, *Chaucer Reads "The Divine Comedy,"* 123.

embedding enunciation—the narrative itself—has a dialogic relation with the embedded discourse held by the enunciator.[54] He lets Criseyde speak no matter what happens, whether he shares her point of view or not.

This artifice is also revealing of the fictional dimension of the poem. By passing from one frame to the other, the imaginative participation considerably reduces the credibility of the narrator as a historian. That is, for example, the case when he speaks out against whoever might dare question Criseyde's *inamoramento*. His reaction shows the narrator's personal desires, just like Boccaccio's narrator. Although he describes the night spent together by the young lovers, he asks without justifying it in any way "[w]hy nad I swich oon with my soule ybought, / Ye, or the leeste joie that was theere?" (III. 1319–20). This personal involvement is particularly obvious in this scene where he wishes he might stop time and forever leave Troilus in Criseyde's arms. This desire is highly indicative: the exotopy inherent in his role as witness-historian and speaking subject gives him the opportunity to get involved emotionally and to identify with the characters while knowing the end of their story. This attempt to stop time at the precise moment their love story is at its peak shows how the imaginative participation of the narration depends on his melancholy. The story he pretends to tell with the greatest honesty is, in fact, subject to the selective memory of the narrator, who only lingers on the episodes he loves the most. After Book III, the narrator clearly continues the narrative reluctantly.

In the end, Chaucer's narrator can only lose control, turning *Troilus and Criseyde* into the story of a man reacting to the love story he had read previously. The historian he pretends to be at the beginning of the poem progressively disappears in favor of a narrator whose role as a mediator between two worlds connects him to Pandarus, another character who wished more than anything to see Troilus and Criseyde together.

Dialogism and Mediation

The reprocessing of Boccaccio's poem allows more than just a return to the roots of the novelistic genre. Indeed, Troilus is no longer the young prince passionately in love described by the Italian; on the contrary, he becomes the very image of the courtly lover. He is idealized so as to fit the codes of *fin'amor*. But this dependence on tradition is so important that it ends up impairing the prince's abilities.

---

54 Bres and Verine, "Le bruissement des voix dans le discours," 167–68.

As Muscatine notes, "[t]he fact is, that as medieval romance goes, as the 'code' goes, Troilus is *too* perfect a courtly lover. In him convention has taken on the superior purity that is only possible in nostalgic retrospection."[55] He thus finds himself completely cut off from Criseyde and cannot act without a go-between. In the *Roman de la Rose*, when the lover is pushed back by Danger, he finds solace in the support of Ami, and this is also the case in Jean's continuation where Ami's part is reinforced by Duenna. Whereas Boccaccio granted his hero more freedom of movement—a freedom often concealing a critical and ironic look at the failures of courtly behavior—Chaucer gives a greater depth to this criticism while increasing its humorous dimension. Pandarus is in this regard more than a go-between; he becomes a function: he is a tactician desperate to bring the lovers together. His actions are adapted to the situation, as seen in his suggestion to kidnap Criseyde before she is handed over to the Greeks.

But the highlight of Pandarus's strategy remains the consummation scene. In Book III, Pandarus organizes a dinner to which he invites his niece and her attendants, yet once the dinner has ended, he uses the violence of the rain as an argument to convince Criseyde to spend the night at his place. Once his niece has settled in, he fetches Troilus who had spent the evening hiding nearby and promises him "thow shalt into hevene blisse wende" (704). Chaucer here opposes to Troilus's courtly conventionalism, the naturalism of a Pandarus who cannot, at this precise moment, lose sight of reality: whereas Troilus keeps on invoking the grace of the gods (705–7; 712–35), Pandarus brings him brutally (and not without humor) back to earth and asks him: "Thow wrecched mouses herte, / Artow agast so that she who the bite?" (734–37). The constant presence of Pandarus makes this scene fundamentally comic since he becomes a cumbersome—but efficient!—variant of the traditional figure of the *fin'amor* advisor. However, unlike Ami in the *Roman*, Pandarus plays the go-between to the point that he actually throws Troilus into Criseyde's bed (1096–97), thus giving his name to the English synonym of "pimp," namely "pander." Putting his niece, who is then under his protection, in this situation raises all sorts of ethical and moral questions. Yet Chaucer is not Dickens, and the purpose of this strategy is quite distinct.[56] Indeed, once in bed, the roles reverse, and Pandarus loses control of the situation. Since he is only defined by his function as a go-between, he

---

55 Muscatine, *Chaucer and the French Tradition*, 137.
56 In *Nicholas Nickleby* Dickens presents a similar situation: Ralph Nickleby invites his niece Kate (under his protection since the death of her father) to a dinner at his place, yet it rapidly becomes obvious that the purpose of this invitation is to use the young girl's charms to facilitate his transactions with members of the nobility.

is forced to disappear. When the two lovers find themselves together in the room, he seems to withdraw:

> And with that word he drow hym to the feere,
> And took a light, and fond his contenaunce,
> As for to looke upon an old romaunce.
> (978–80)

This is rather confusing, and the meaning of this passage remains problematic. The candle that he lights may represent the pleasure he gets from this love story (Chaucer develops several images related to fire: 710–11, 855–59), nonetheless "looke upon" can, in this context, mean both "read" and "look." The question is: which love story is he referring to? It could either be an actual book or the love story he has himself written. The contrast between a courtly and naturalistic vision of the scene produces an ambiguity allowing a double reading of the same situation. This balance between Pandarus's voyeurism—evoking our own—and the narrator's distance vis-à-vis this scene is thus fundamental: "Retreating into the old books that both join and separate the narrator and characters, Chaucer intermittently views the love scene from afar."[57]

By introducing a reflection on the external view, Chaucer radically transforms the character created by Boccaccio and introduces a correspondence between the narrator and the go-between. At the beginning of the poem, the narrator announces his intention to be a mediator and implores Tisiphone to turn him into "the sorwful instrument, / That helpeth loveres, as I kan, to pleyne" (I. 10–11). His stated aim is, consequently, to translate "myn auctour called Lollius" (I. 393–94) and instruct his audience so that we might apply courtly love values in our daily life. He is in effect very different from Boccaccio's narrator, who is himself lost in the maze of love. Yet his role as the servant of Love ("For I, that God of Loves servantz serve"; I. 15) cannot but remind us of Pandarus's own actions in the narrative. The resemblance is in fact not superficial. In addition to their role as mediators, they are described as being completely incompetent in love: Pandarus explains for instance "I have myself ek seyn a blynd man goo / Ther as he fel that couthe loken wide" (I. 628–29), while a similar construction is used to describe the love woes experienced by the narrator ("[a] blynd man kan nat juggen wel in hewis"; II. 21). Besides, during the invocation in Book I, the narrator implores the goddess to help him compose "[t]hise woful vers, that wepen as I write" (7), whereas Pandarus advises Troilus to write a letter to Criseyde and "[b]iblotte it with thi teris ek a lite" (II. 1027).

---

57 Taylor, *Chaucer Reads "The Divine Comedy,"* 51.

Both characters also share a tendency to rely on their essentially bookish knowledge of the world and on their rhetoric. Pandarus's use of the story of Horaste just before the consummation scene is a good example: foreshadowing Criseyde's betrayal, this alleged romance between his niece and Horaste allows Pandarus to push her into Troilus's arms. Pandarus shares these rhetorical tendencies and bookishness with the narrator and prefigures another emblematic literary character, namely Voltaire's Pangloss, whose vision of the world is more encyclopedic than real and whose help is often essentially rhetorical and useless. When Candide attempts, for instance, to save James the Anabaptist from drowning, Pangloss stops him by demonstrating "que la rade de Lisbonne avait été formée exprès pour que cet anabaptiste s'y noyât."[58] Whereas Candide wants to take action, his mentor merely philosophizes. Pandarus is however sincere in his desire to help Troilus: he does not belong to the courtly world, but, unlike Pangloss, inhabits a world in which speaking means taking action. He thus progressively disappears when the situation starts to deteriorate. Being unable to intervene, he speaks one last time in the poem, telling Troilus "I kan namore seye" (V. 1743).

This reprocessing of the original narrative is in effect an extremely important commentary on the oral tradition and on books as custodians of human knowledge. The constant appeal to a form of past authority ("myn auctour") allows Chaucer to authenticate *Troilus and Criseyde* and to question the very authority of this tradition.

By going back to the basics of *fin'amor* and Dantean themes, Chaucer connects his ancient romance with a key episode of the *Commedia*, namely *Inferno* V. The meeting between Dante and Paolo and Francesca, the two lovers whose story started with the reading of a book, gives the Florentine poet the opportunity to reveal the potential nefariousness of romantic fictions. Chaucer was quite clearly attracted by this notion, and it is therefore not surprising to see a strong resemblance between *TC* and *Inferno* V: both works focus on the intermediary role literature may play between two lovers, by connecting their idyll with bookish knowledge. The possible consequences of reading are used as a catalyst in Dantean philosophy since the entire poem relies on the effect produced by the reading of Virgil. And just like Dante, Chaucer turns the narration in *TC* into the narrator's reaction to the reading of his *auctour*.

The relation that Dante has with his guide throughout the pilgrimage is, of course, presented as being similar to a pupil/master relationship, but the very existence of Virgil in the poem is literary and thus depends on the relationship

---

[58] "that the roadstead of Lisbon had been made on purpose for the Anabaptist to be drowned there." Voltaire, *Candide ou l'optimisme*, 37.

between reader and author. As we have remarked in the previous chapter, Virgil only comes alive when the poet gives him, after a "lungo silenzio," a voice that comes from reading his work. As a result, even though Virgil defines himself historically as having lived under the reign of Augustus "al tempo degli Dei falsi e bugiardi"[59] (*Inf*. I. 72), he remains present throughout the poem as an author and very soon mentions his most famous creation:

> Poeta fui, e cantai di quel giusto
> figliuol d'Anchise che venne da Troia
> poi che il superbo Ilión fu combusto.[60]
> (*Inf*. I. 73–75)

His presence in the other world is, in fact, fundamentally literary and both Dante and Statius are there to bear witness to the reverberations produced in their lives by the reading of his work. Dante quickly confesses to Virgil, "[t]u se' lo mio maestro e il mio autore"[61] (*Inf*. I. 85), while Statius presents himself in Purgatory as one of the many poets whose enthusiasm was inflamed by the divine fire of the *Aeneid* (*Purg*. XXI. 94–99). Yet Virgil's message supposed to prophesy a return of the imperial golden age has since his death been reinterpreted as a prefiguration of the Incarnation.[62] In effect, his writings have sparked many vocations and if, according to legend, Dante returned to religion because of Virgil, Statius clearly states "[p]er te poeta fui, per te cristiano!"[63] (*Purg*. XXII. 73). When Beatrice finally takes over, Virgil progressively disappears. His voice fades away: Dante first quotes the *Aeneid* (*Purg*. XXX. 21), then moves to a paraphrase (46–48), and finally repeats the name of his silent guide (49, 50, 51). Having lived at the time of the false gods, Virgil cannot reach Heaven and is more than ever defined by his poetry.

Reading can thus radically influence one's life: in the case of Dante and Statius, the effect was positive, but for Paolo and Francesca it led to eternal damnation. This contrast is at the heart *Inferno* V and shows the Florentine's sense of how to properly use literature. This particular Canto bears witness to the Stilnovist's concerns about the spiritual consequences of the *fin'amor* way of life. All the elements of this episode, its language and its characters, refer to this

---

59 "the season of the false and lying gods."
60 "I was a poet, and I sang the righteous / Son of Anchises who had come from Troy / When flames destroyed the pride of Ilium."
61 "You are my master and my author."
62 See the fourth *Eclogue*, 5–7.
63 "Through you I was a poet and, through you, a Christian."

tradition. Achilles is thus described by Virgil (65–66) as a romantic character, rather than as the heroic figure he is supposed to be, while Dante mentions "le donne antiche e i cavalieri"[64] (71). Francesca, whose name directly echoes French culture, evokes, in addition, the shadow of Guido Guinizelli when she states: "Amor, che al cor gentil ratto s'apprende"[65] (100). Paolo and Francesca's myth is, as a consequence, anchored in the *fin'amor* imaginary and makes specific use of the *Lancelot* in prose. Indeed, this version of the legend mentions the presence of a go-between named Gallehault, who arranges a meeting during which Guinevere kisses her knight for the first time. In Dante's version, the go-between meant to bring together Paolo and Francesca disappears in favor of the *Lancelot* book itself. Gallhehault, or Galeotto, is thus remodeled and becomes a synonym for helmsman ("galeotto" in Italian), a word used by Dante to describe Phlegyas when he ferries the poet and his guide across the Styx (*Inf.* VII. 17), and the angel helping the souls cross the sea to Purgatory (II. 27).[66] It is, as a result, this precise word that Francesca uses to describe both the object and author responsible for her damnation: "Galeotto fu il libro e chi lo scrisse"[67] (*Inf.* V. 137). Dante continues the parallel between the positive and negative consequences of reading by creating a mirror effect between his own situation in Hell and then in Heaven. Francesca and Paolo mention "solo un punto"[68] (*Inf.* V. 132) of *Lancelot* that overcame their resistance and made them succumb to temptation, while Dante refers to "[u]n punto solo" (*Par.* XXXIII. 94) that overpowered his memory. Dante is more than ever conscious of the danger represented by the compositions of courtly love poets, and in quoting the great names of this tradition (Dido, Cleopatra, Helen, Achilles . . .), he tries to save his audience from the trap that condemned Paolo and Francesca to Hell.

Dante henceforth attempts to lead his audience in the right direction by becoming helmsman himself:

> O voi che siete in piccioletta barca,
>   desiderosi d'ascoltar, seguìti,
> dietro al mio legno che cantando varca,
>   tornate a riveder li vostri liti!

---

[64] "the ancient ladies and the knights."
[65] "Love, that can quickly seize the gentle heart."
[66] Boccaccio himself named his most famous creation *Decameron, cognominato Prencipe Galeotto*, in reference to Prince Gallehault, a model of courtesy, who became thanks to Dante the symbol of go-betweens.
[67] "A Gallehault indeed, that book and he who wrote it."
[68] "one point alone."

> Non vi mettete in pelago, ché, forse,
> perdendo me rimareste smarriti.[69]
> (*Par.* II. 1–6)

This idea becomes central for Dante who worries about the effects of a possible misinterpretation of his work, and it is this obsession that further distances Chaucer from his Italian source. For despite its polyphonic aspects, the *Commedia*'s return to a speaking subject responsible for the enunciation tends to impose a precise meaning on our reading. The author's voice can be heard several times attempting to guide us on the right, moral path, the one he actually followed. Dante's will to influence the reader's reaction had of course little effect on Chaucer. Even though he shared the Florentine's religious convictions, Chaucer could not let himself be trapped by a monological vision of the world. His reprocessing of Boccaccio's treatment of *fin'amor* allowed him to reconnect with *Inferno* V and entertain an interdiscursive dialogue between three different visions of love: Boccaccio's, Dante's, and his own.

In the first lines of Book II, Chaucer uses the ancient and medieval topos that assimilates poetic composition with navigation. If Dante presented himself as a *galeotto* leading his audience's boat to Heaven, Chaucer operates once again a lowering of the sublime to describe himself as the helmsman of a skiff who has "swych travaylle, / Of my connyng, that unneth I it steere" (II. 3–4). Chaucer's alignment with *Inferno* V quickly becomes obvious. Just like the episode of Paolo and Francesca, his poem is composed by an author playing the mediator (with all that it entails in his objective-subjective, speaking-moral, positions) with his audience, and whose protagonists are equally brought together by a bookish go-between. Besides, if Troilus's behavior somehow reminds us of Lancelot—a great knight but slightly uncomfortable with love—it is precisely because Chaucer chooses to connect his romance with the tradition whose most famous representatives are condemned to Dante's Hell. Dido's character is here used as an anchorage point establishing a connection between Dante and Chaucer. Dante describes the second circle of Hell as "la schiera ov'è Dido"[70] (*Inf.* V. 85), thus generally identifying the sins of the lustful with Dido. Virgil likewise refers to Carthage's queen by mentioning her suicide, but also her betrayal of her dead husband, Sychaeus (*Inf.* V. 61–62). Dido's crime is not only her adultery (Criseyde) but also her attempt to find death because of an earthly love (Troilus).

---

[69] "O you who are within your little bark, / Eager to listen, following behind / My ship that, singing, crossed to deep seas, / Turn back to see your shores again: do not / Attempt to sail the seas I sail; you may, / by losing sight of me, be left astray."
[70] "the ranks where Dido suffers."

Resisting Closure and Refusing Judgment

TC also uses another traditional device of *fin'amor* in order to reinforce the link with *Inferno* V, namely the love potion. Although neither Criseyde nor Francesca end up like Isolde, Pandarus's niece cannot help but wonder "Who yaf me drynke?" (II. 651) when she sees Troilus passing in the street. But the narrator's comment on that declaration produces an interesting gap (666–86).

Indeed, not only is Criseyde a widow, but her father is a traitor and she thus cannot accept love so rapidly without arousing the audience's cynicism or provoking a scandal in Troy. The *inamoramento*, excused by a potion, cannot be resisted. Yet when Criseyde is touched, she reaches after long reflection the conclusion that nothing forces her to return Troilus's love:

> . . . Allas! Syn I am free,
> Sholde I now love, and put in jupartie
> My sikernesse, and thrallen libertee?
>   (II. 771–73)

We have here a capacity to resist that Francesca clearly did not have. "The narrator rejects the idea of her falling in love at first sight and emphasizes the gradual processes whereby she accepts Troilus's love in accordance with the ideal of a courtly lady."[71] In doing so, it seems she anticipates and answers any possible criticism, and the narrator defends her against our cynicism—he mentions "blissful Venus" (680) and divine intervention as an excuse for her sudden love. Yet Chaucer still leaves it to us to determine whether her love is gradual or instantaneous. Are we persuaded into "believing the narrator's evidence of the time-lag involved in her love?" Or are we more likely perceiving an "ironical ambiguity and sensing a gap between the narrator's comments and what Criseyde does?"[72] It all depends on our interpretation of events.

At this precise moment, *TC* and *Inferno* V differ and Chaucer's reception of Boethius becomes obvious. Criseyde falls in love as Troilus passes triumphantly underneath her window. Their love begins as natural love and is based on sight; Troilus falls in love when he sees her (272), and so does Criseyde (II. 1265–68). However, whereas Boccaccio turned this scene into an anecdotal episode (II. st. 82–83), Chaucer doubles and reinforces this sequence: Troilus passes twice, once by accident as he comes back from the battlefield (II. 610–51), and a second time because he follows Pandarus's advice

---

71 Nakao, *The Structure of Chaucer's Ambiguity*, 81.
72 Ibid.

(II. 1247–74). By emphasizing this double meeting, Chaucer can establish a parallel between human influence and fortune. And if the second passage confirms Criseyde's feelings, it is actually the first one that makes her feel she has drunk a love potion. It is besides by accident that Criseyde hears Antigone singing a song confirming all her fears (II. 899–903). Pandarus is, in effect, here one of fortune's instruments, and not the real instigator of the romance. This notion of fate and providence that apparently deprives characters of their freedom is fundamentally Boethian: in *Consolatio Philosophiae*, Philosophy explains that fate is but the manifestation of the ordinance of all things by an atemporal providence. Since human beings are by nature temporal, they only possess a truncated vision of the course of events, which leads them to believe their freedom of action is limited, or non-existent.

In reality, Boethius states that destiny must not be understood as the imposition of a divine will; on the contrary, the "future is 'necessary' only in the sense that it exists (not pre-exists) in the a-temporal vision of divine providence, which beholds past, present, and future in the timelessness of the eternal moment."[73] In other words, things only become obvious at the moment they happen, when partial glimpses of providence are perceived by the human observer. Chance or fortune is just a matter of perspective: Troilus has probably passed dozens of times in that very street, but this particular occurrence, produced by chance, is different because it brings together Pandarus's revelation to Criseyde, her reflection, and Troilus's triumphant return from the battlefield, and it thus contributes to the elaboration of a chronotope shared by the future lovers. The contrast between providence and destiny gives the audience the feeling that the story might evolve in different directions at any moment, thus creating suspense and a sense of verisimilitude.

Chaucer, therefore, develops his story in parallel with *Inferno* V to the point where all those correlations end up counterweighing the *Commedia*. But he follows a different perspective from the one offered by Dante and does not see eye to eye with the Thomist doctrine that animates the Italian's poem and presents a definitive vision of souls and complete knowledge of the moral state of the world. Saint Thomas Aquinas believed that after death, souls immediately reach a pre-defined position in accord with their merits (except for those heading to Purgatory). For the blessed and damned, the Last Judgment is nothing but the accentuation of their initial state for by reuniting with their bodies they will be able to revel or suffer with greater intensity.[74]

---

[73] Mann, "Chance and Destiny in *Troilus and Criseyde* and the Knight's Tale," 79.
[74] Auerbach, *Studi su Dante*, 79.

But Chaucer has always refused the absolute of closure and rather prefers the dynamic of openness. He bases his work on the uncertainty of a moving world: for example, Criseyde is traditionally defined by her sin—an absolute close to Dantean judgment.[75] Chaucer thus decides to envelop his Criseyde in a cloud of blurry uncertainty: the narrator does not give us her age, and we do not know if she has children or not. The very nature of her betrayal remains obscure. The poet accordingly does not change the story he has read in *Il Filostrato* but systematically underscores each doubt and leaves us with elements that are sufficiently confused to provoke a sense of ambiguity preventing us from judging and condemning Criseyde.

And this is a major evolution in the history of literature. Indeed, the *Commedia*, just like the *Roman* or even *Piers Plowman*, is an eminently symbolic work. The poem is constructed as a vision that may be interpreted in different ways (despite Dante's desire that we follow his interpretation) and in which time seems excluded from the action. The vision itself, in the case of Dante's pilgrimage, is relatively brief but its memory is atemporal and provokes both the spiritual awakening of the conversion of the pilgrim and the writing of the poem. Bakhtin remarks that the real time of vision and its coincidence with a precise biographic and historical time (the time of human life) is purely symbolic.[76]

The *Commedia* thus proposes a critical synthesis of a now closed era, hence the need to extend a vision of the world along a vertical axis connecting the circles of Hell, Purgatory, and Heaven: the temporal logic of this vertical world is in effect the pure simultaneity of all things or the coexistence of all things in eternity.[77] Everything that is consequently separated on earth by our temporality coexists, whether it is body, light, or voice. Dante thus reduces our world to a single chronotope in order to see and understand it as a whole, making it exist in a single place and time. Nonetheless, despite this existential verticality, all the spirits encountered by Dante seem to define themselves by their historicity and their belonging to the past. The integration of this vertical hierarchy into the Dantean conception of History and of politics forces the figures inhabiting this world to place themselves on what Bakhtin defines as the historically productive horizontal, to reach forward and not upward.[78] The story of Paolo and Francesca, for example, betrays a desire to move temporally within an atemporal axis, which explains the inherent tension of the world visited by Dante.

---

75 Criseyde is actually worried about what posterity will think of her (V. 1054–64).
76 Bakhtin, *Esthétique et théorie du roman*, 302.
77 Ibid., 303.
78 Ibid., 303–4.

Chaucer is quite willing to escape this verticality and offers, in *Troilus and Criseyde*, to move in a different direction, to increase a freedom already perceptible in the liberation of the characters' voices. By presenting us, for instance, with a double enunciation and therefore an ambiguous choice between two narrative levels, he illustrates the influence of conventions on the reading experience and does not validate any particular interpretation. The chronotope of the road thus becomes one of the structuring elements of this horizontal narration and unsurprisingly is later found at the heart of the *Canterbury Tales*. This refusal of closure, this temporal mutability, increases the characters' freedom but also gives them a relatively brief life cycle. When the Trojan parliament takes the decision to exchange Criseyde for the traitor Antenor in Book IV, Troilus remains speechless and is compared with a tree stripped by the passing of seasons:

> And as in wynter leves ben biraft,
> Ech after other, til the tree be bare,
> So that ther nys but bark and braunche ilaft,
> Lith Troilus, byraft of ech welfare.
> (225–28)

Chaucer borrows this image from *Inferno* XIII, where Dante describes Pier della Vigna's punishment. The soul is transformed into a plant (37) and Dante only notices this metamorphosis when he picks one of his branches. Deprived of their human form, the suicides are equally unable to communicate like human beings. Their language itself is deformed and seems to be mingled with the blood running from the wound inflicted by Dante (40–45).

Chaucer assimilates this image, but in Troilus's case the theological dimension of the *contrapasso* is ignored. Troilus is compared with a tree and loses the ability to speak ("His speche hym refer; unnethes myghte he seye"; IV. 249), even though he eventually overcomes his grief. Chaucer thus puts at the center of his story the idea that only death makes change impossible. Francesca was condemned to Hell because of her misdirected desire for transcendence; just like her, Troilus considers Criseyde as his means of access to the divine,[79] which turns Book III and its many references to *Inferno* V and Guinizelli into a representation of an idealized love supposedly leading to salvation. As a result, this use of Dantean references in a story taking place in antiquity "embodies a commentary on the *Commedia*, and it is in this respect that the utterly different surfaces of the two works, Christian and pagan, become important."[80] Chaucer emphasizes the

---

[79] Lines 1261–67 from Book III are adapted from *Par.* XXXIII. 13–18.
[80] Taylor, *Chaucer Reads "The Divine Comedy,"* 72.

historical dimension of his narrative frame but does not share Boccaccio's desire to underscore the pagan aspects of this world. His reprocessing of Boccaccio's treatment of *fin'amor* allows him to restore some of its glory to human love, for though it can lead to damnation, it remains an element essential to spiritual elevation. Courtly love operates on an axis between Christian love and natural love and is subject to their pressures. The love between Troilus and Criseyde follows the codes of *fin'amor* and is accordingly against the morality of their time. Criseyde insists for example on the fact that she fell in love because of Troilus's moral qualities, not through lust (IV. 1667–73), and it is this love that awakens in Troilus the following values:

> For he bicom the frendlieste wight,
> The gentilest, and ek the mooste fre,
> The thriftiest, and oon the beste knight
> That in his tyme was or myghte be.
> (I. 1079–82)

The pagan frame gives Chaucer the opportunity to save his conception of human love, which he presents as being moral but limited. Paolo and Francesca have sinned by putting at the heart of their relation human love while living in a Christian world; by contrast, Troilus and Criseyde inhabit a world dominated by natural law. Living before the Incarnation, they have no knowledge of God and therefore turn their love into the path to eternal bliss. The parallel with Dido continues until the end of the poem, even if the roles are suddenly reversed: Criseyde leaves town and betrays the man she had promised to love, while Troilus looks for and finds death on the battlefield. However, love ennobles Troilus; he breaks out of the limits of time and space and ends up being separated from this ancient life—unlike Paolo and Francesca who remain united even in Hell—and though his transfer to "the holughnesse of the eighthe spere" (V. 1809) remains uncertain, he is never associated with Dido's fate, who gave her name to the sins of the second circle.

Of all the authors Chaucer might have adapted, Dante is unquestionably the most formidable. The authority of the *Commedia* is indeed overwhelming. Whereas he might have found elements to improve in Boccaccio, what he found in Dante was an utterly different vision of the world and of literature. He consequently developed that triple dialogue between *Il Filostrato*, Dante, and himself so as to present once again a vision of the past as seen through the prism of reading and its echo in the human mind. As J.D. Burnely writes, "the meaning of a piece of literature is notoriously Janus-like, since it may be considered to possess the meaning intended by its author as well as a possibly quite different meaning attributed by its reader."[81] The relationship between the double enunciation and the narrative allows Chaucer to highlight all the ambiguity of the *Commedia*: the historical perspective supposed to lend credibility to the story becomes increasingly embarrassing in the last Books because of the emotional involvement of the modal subject. This discrepancy between intentions and actions is at the heart of the poem and creates ironical ambiguity caused by the gap between the actions of the characters and the narrator's comments. The objective narrator promises to faithfully transcribe his *auctour* while lingering on the love story between his protagonists and defending Criseyde. In doing so, he fails both as a historian (objective speaking subject) and as an imaginative witness (subjective modal subject), but this failure, orchestrated by Chaucer, is there to underline that the desires of the narrator are bound to alter the integrity of his message. *TC* is a work based on memory, like the *Commedia*. Yet no man has the capacity to render so faithfully so much material, an issue Dante acknowledges several times but which he manages to overcome at the end of the *Purgatorio* by obtaining the language and spiritual purity necessary to the transcription of his journey. His role as *scriba Dei* gives him the necessary legitimacy so that "una favilla sol della tua gloria / possa leasciare alla futura gente"[82] (*Par.* XXXIII. 71–72). Chaucer on the other hand questions the veracity of such an experience transcribed by fiction and suggests we should be careful when a narrator's desires are so clearly stated.

In the end, the shift from a dream vision to a pseudo-historical mode of representation gives Chaucer the opportunity to present a different vision of *fin'amor* and to stress the moral effects of reading. Dante had established a clear distinction between two forms of love, one leading to perdition (Paolo and Francesca), the other to salvation (Beatrice). That is why he insisted on his role of *galeotto* so that his audience not lose sight of the true message of his poem. In contrast, the pagan environment in *TC* allows Chaucer to distance his subject from his audience and present a still moving world, both freer and more didactic. In other words, Chaucer turns the *Commedia* into the *galeotto* of *TC*, for Dante's work gives him the necessary tools to achieve his own literary transcendence. It is consequently this dialogic intensification, made possible by the interdiscursive dialogue between Dante, Boccaccio, and Chaucer, together with the double enunciation developed by the English poet, to conjure the vision of a perpetually moving world, that turns Chaucer's poem into such a "modern" work. By connecting the very origins of the novelistic genre with several centuries of European cultural and literary evolution, he participated in the

---

[81] Burnley, *A Guide to Chaucer's Language*, 222.
[82] "I may leave to people of the future one gleam of the glory that is Yours."

progressive development of the historical novel as we know it today. As Boitani remarks, Chaucer seems ready to transform *Il Filostrato* into a Verdi or Bellini opera; the liberation of the characters' voices prefigures the polyphony of the novel that would appear in the following centuries:

> le complesse reazioni femminili, i dibattiti interiori di Criseida son quasi un'anticipazione di Pamela e Clarissa, o addirittura di Virginia Woolf; le brillanti scene di dialogo fra Pandaro e Criseida paiono adombrare Jane Austen; l'indecisione, la paralisi, il monologo filosofico ed esistenziale di Troilo preannunciano l'eroe moderno per eccelenza, Amleto.[83]

By proclaiming himself "sesto tra cotanto senno"[84] (*Inf.* IV. 102) at the end of *TC*, Chaucer makes us understand that he is no longer the young poet navigating in an ocean of literary influences. He is now able to steer the course of his own skiff and is more than ever intent on showing his talents as compiler and innovator by abandoning the lyricism of the *fin'amor* allegorical model. *The Legend of Good Women* thus represents a new step in Chaucer's career, one that would take him on a journey from the Tabard to Canterbury.

---

[83] "Criseyde's complex feminine reactions, her inner debates, almost prefigure Pamela and Clarissa, or even Virginia Woolf; the brilliant dialogue scenes between Pandarus and Criseyde might foreshadow Jane Austen; Troilus's indecision, paralysis, his philosophical and existential monologue anticipate the modern hero par excellence, Hamlet." Boitani, *Letteratura europea e Medioevo volgare*, 328.
[84] "sixth was I, 'mid so much wit."

Chapter 5
Hybridization and the Legend of Chaucer's Inventiveness

The Legend of Good Women has often been considered one of the least successful of Chaucer's poems, the "ugly duckling of the Chaucer canon":[1] it is repetitive, incomplete, and the poet himself seems to get gradually bored by his own narratives. Indeed, references to the poem in other late medieval texts are rare, which suggests that it was not the most well-known or loved work among fifteenth-century readers.[2] It has survived in ten manuscripts, and while this would usually be a proof of a work's popularity, the "close textual connections among witnesses to the *Legend* suggest it never circulated that widely, although the existence of several manuscripts produced outside of London points toward some provincial dissemination."[3]

Nonetheless, *LGW* remains Chaucer's third-longest poem, after *Troilus and Criseyde* and *The Canterbury Tales*, and the existence of two different versions of the Prologue (the F[4] was probably written in 1386 and the G[5] in 1394) seems to indicate that the poet's interest in this particular creation had not quite disappeared.

Setting aside the pseudo-historical mode of representation borrowed from Boccaccio's *Filostrato* and used in *Troilus and Criseyde*, Chaucer goes back, in the Prologue, to the more familiar dream vision of courtly love. In the first few lines, he thus describes himself as someone who loves to read above all else, except perhaps to see daisies freed by the sun when the month of May has come. But one night, he goes home to rest and as he falls asleep, he dreams of seeing the god of Love and his queen walking towards him. The author-narrator then sees his entire literary career criticized by a deity who is not particularly fond of his treatment of women and of love in *TC*, for instance. The narrator, however, avoids divine punishment thanks to the intervention of queen Alceste who offers him the chance to make amends: she asks him to spend his days writing about the virtues of women scorned and betrayed by men. The narrator accepts, of course, but is from the start fully aware of the

---

1 McCormick et al., "Introduction: Looking Forward, Looking Back," 3.
2 Cook, "Author, Text, and Paratext," 124.
3 Ibid., 130. See also Seymour, *A Catalogue of Chaucer Manuscripts*, 79.
4 Oxford, Bodleian Library, Fairfax 16.
5 Cambridge University Library, Gg.4.27.

https://doi.org/10.1515/9781501514364-006

difficulty of portraying "a woman whose suffering enthralls without coming to resemble those men who either cause or desire women's pain."[6] He nonetheless goes back to his books, ready to start writing about Cleopatra.

Although Chaucer seems to follow the conventions of courtly love in his Prologue, the true purpose of this collection of legends is, in fact, quite different from what we are invited to believe. Indeed, even though *LGW* was seemingly written as a palinode of *TC* with which it shares a "metaplot of love and betrayal,"[7] it is not just another dream poem and is much more innovative than we might think. The end of the 1380s was, in effect, a difficult time for Chaucer and would lead him to a creative revival: listing most of his literary creations in the Prologue, the poet sums up his career, turns a page, and shows his determination to work at something new and different. His use of the dream vision in *PF* was remarkable, but Chaucer seemed to have reached the limits of this particular mode of representation and abandoned it for another poetical experience in *TC*.

Its return in the Prologue of *LGW*, just as Chaucer was developing his abilities as a narrative poet, could accordingly be perceived as a critique of the conventions whose grip he is now trying to escape. As a result, "[t]he unfinished condition of the poem as it has come down to us is no more an indication that Chaucer abandoned it in distaste than is the unfinished state of *The House of Fame* or, for that matter, of *The Canterbury Tales*."[8] For the idea of associating the incomplete state of *LGW* with these other two poems would imply that its unexpected conclusion was not quite what Chaucer had planned. The existence of the G version of the Prologue, however, indicates that neither time nor weariness could possibly be considered as the causes of this abandonment. The narrator's boredom could, thus, be revealing of Chaucer's own narrative posture in the poem. For the poet clearly does not respect the sentence Alceste imposed in the Prologue, which gives him both a theme and a structure: as McGerr writes, the discrepancy between that sentence and "the *sentence* that emerges from the poem as a whole suggests that a major portion of the poem's significance arises from the tension between the monologic discourse of the tales and the poem's ultimate resistance to traditional forms of closure."[9]

The Legend of Good Women is, in that regard, representative of Chaucer's artistic maturity and desire to play with different approaches to literature. The most important evolution one may perceive here is not only his refinement of

---

6 Dumitrescu, "Beautiful Suffering and the Culpable Narrator," 108.
7 Collette, "Chaucer's Poetics and Purposes," 18.
8 Chaucer, *The Riverside Chaucer*, 587.
9 McGerr, *Chaucer's Open Books*, 123.

the short narrative but the duplication of dialogism. For although Chaucer continues to entertain an interdiscursive dialogue with his intertext, he introduces a form of external dialogue, a hybridization—or association of genres, close to Chrétien's *conjointure*—whose polyphonic richness depends on the linking of short narratives, each producing a different tone and effect. Chaucer starts to extract himself from the diegesis, and although he has not yet reached the level of extradiegetic dialogue implemented in the *Canterbury Tales*, he manages to produce a collection whose guiding and unifying thread would no longer be a unique narrative but a linguistic structure juxtaposing various elements of language. The ScaPoLinE[10] theory developed by Henning Nølke, Kjersti Fløttum, and Coco Norén makes a precise distinction between internal and external polyphony and remarks that polyphony is internal when the different enunciative roles associated with voice and points of view bring into play different images of the speaker, within a particular unit of meaning (the text, for instance), but without associating external enunciative instances to the actual enunciation.[11] On the other hand, external polyphony is when enunciative roles are associated with discursive instances foreign to the speaker.[12] In effect, Chaucer's interdiscursive dialogues have always been internal to the enunciation and implicated elements of the diegesis: the speaker interacts with others' discourse about a specific discursive object within the narration. The introduction of this hybridization allows Chaucer, however, to double the discursive interaction by adding a second layer outside of the unit of meaning that is the text, and thus move from intertextuality to metatextuality, by connecting a text "à un autre texte dont il parle, sans nécessairement le citer (le convoquer), voire à la limite, sans le nommer."[13] Chaucer produces, in other words, a dialogue between the narratives themselves, each one representing a genre commenting on the others, and accordingly, offers a critical look at the "vanité dangereuse de la littérature."[14] The poem as a whole serves to critique single-voiced discourse.[15]

---

10 "Théorie SCAndinave de la POLyphonie LINguistiquE."
11 See Nølke, Fløttum, and Norén, *ScaPoLinE: La théorie scandinave de la polyphonie linguistique*.
12 Perrin, "La voix et le point de vue comme formes polyphoniques externes," 66.
13 "with another text it is referring to, without necessarily quoting (summoning it), and even without naming it." Genette, *Palimpsestes*, 10.
14 "dangerous vanity of literature." Chaucer, *Les Contes de Canterbury et autres œuvres*, 12.
15 There is a strong consensus around this idea. See for instance Delany, *The Naked Text*, 235; Strohm, *Social Chaucer*, 171; and Dinshaw, *Chaucer's Sexual Poetics*, 87.

Dream Vision and Narrative Poetry

Chaucer's return to a world whose conventions had long guided his personal creative evolution is, without a doubt, the key to understanding the Prologue and the legends following it.

As we have seen, the fact that he chose to again write within the confines of the allegory of love is no coincidence and should invite us to read the Prologue with that particularity in mind. It is indeed an introduction, not a creation independent of the rest of the poem. One is in fact easily astonished by the difference between the introduction and the rest of the collection, and this astonishment is undoubtedly created by the "écart entre le texte qu'il découvre et l'horizon d'attente que la matrice littéraire lui avait fait imaginer."[16] For Chaucer leaves the dream vision as soon as *The Legend of Cleopatra* starts and almost never again uses the codes of *fin'amor*. This sudden break is not accidental. On the contrary, it is an effect deliberately produced by Chaucer in order to announce and justify his literary evolution.

The conventional dimension of the Prologue indicates Chaucer's will to change course. Nevertheless, one should always remember to be wary of Chaucer when he seems to be going straight to the point. The poet who started writing this Prologue is far from being the inexperienced young man who was trying to assimilate the influence of courtly love poetry in *BD*. It is thus particularly suspect to see so many elements borrowed from the *Roman de la Rose*, from Froissart, Machaut, and Deschamps in such a short number of lines. Even Guillaume de Lorris and Jean de Meun's revolutionary work is quite clearly at the heart of the Prologue, not only because of its courtly atmosphere but because of its translation, which partly causes the god of Love's wrath. The reference to allegorical figures in the *Roman*, during the flight of birds, reinforces the conventional aspect of the Prologue: whereas the company of fowls had chosen Danger as their master,

> . . . Pitee, thurgh his stronge gentil myght,
> Forgaf, and made Mercy passen Ryght,
> Thurgh innocence and ruled Curtesye.
> (F. 161–63)

The narrator's worship of daisies, which he can contemplate all day long, is an additional way for Chaucer to reinforce this conventional atmosphere, for the flower imagery is central to courtly love literature. Poets like Machaut (*Dit de la*

---

[16] "gap between the text he discovers and the horizon of aspiration that the literary matrix had made him imagine." Chaucer, *Les Contes de Canterbury et autres œuvres*, 1353.

marguerite, *Dit de la fleur de lis et de la marguerite*), Froissart (*Dittié de la flour de la marguerite*, *Paradis d'amour*), or Deschamps (*Lai de Franchise*) all contributed to the development of this particular poetical imagery. But it might also be considered as a "farewell performance," for as R.W. Frank, Jr. remarks:

> He would never use the vision form again; he would never write courtly poetry or treat courtly love seriously again. The sequence is reminiscent of some of the most delightful moments in the *Parliament of Birds* and might suggest that he is still preoccupied with the phenomenon of courtly love, however amused his attention may be.[17]

The sequence of the confrontation of leaves and flowers (F. 69–72; G. 61–75) is, for this reason, emblematic of an increasingly parodic approach to the genre. Richard II's courtiers and knights used to take as an emblem the Flower or the Leaf and would face each other in May, but Chaucer here entreats us to consider his own interest in daisies as separate from this particular tradition. Nonetheless, his refusal to be associated with any of these cults flirts with mockery, for "[i]f his plea avoids the necessity of taking sides, it also denies involvement."[18] And although this tradition was associated with a form of courtly love and thus with a particular set of values, the narrator's worship of the flower seems to be an end in itself. Unlike the rose in the *Roman* or the daisy of most French poets, Chaucer's flower is clearly not an allegorical representation of a Lady.

All the conventions and codes he is playing with here and all the emotions connected with *fin'amor* and with the use of these codes are called upon for a daisy, not for the object of love. And when one considers the hyperbolic nature of the language used in the sequence, it becomes obvious that Chaucer's true purpose is not to develop a proper dream vision but to play with the codes and mock those conventions. The narrator, for instance, wakes up at dawn to see "she that is of alle floures flour" (F. 53; G. 55) rise towards the sun. Its vision is enough to ease his pains (F. 50–51) and constantly renews his love (F. 56), which causes him to complain about the poor quality of his English: "Allas, that I ne had Englyssh, ryme or prose, / Suffisant this flour to preyse aryght!" (F. 66–67 or G. 59–60). Thus, whereas Guillaume de Lorris gradually allegorized his rose, which shifted from a representation of his Lady to a simple flower, and from a flower to the symbol of his quest, Chaucer merely puts his abilities as a lyrical poet to the service of a daisy, which "keep[s] the narrator within an area cleanly removed from the experience of courtly love"[19] and produces a dialogue with the tradition.

---

[17] Frank, *Chaucer and The Legend of Good Women*, 21.
[18] Ibid.
[19] Ibid., 22.

Indeed, if his devotion to the flower had been transferred to Alceste when the dream vision finally started, then the sequence would have been safeguarded from this parodic filter. But it is not the case. The flower is used to get the plot moving as soon as it is replaced by Alceste, but the relationship between the narrator and the queen is quite formal, and her description lacks the passion we witnessed in the daisy sequence:

> The god of Love, and in his hand a quene,
> And she was clad in real habit grene.
> A fret of gold she hadde next her heer,
> And upon that a whit corowne she beer
> With flourouns smale, and I shal nat lye;
> For al the world, ryght as a dayesye
> Ycorouned ys with white leves lyte,
> So were the flowrouns of hire coroune white.
> (F. 213–20)

He does refer to her beauty and composes a ballad in her honor (F. 249–69; G. 203–23), but only realizes who she really is hundreds of lines later, which allows Chaucer to establish a pictorial equivalence and not an emotional one between the daisy and Alceste.

Chaucer has always shown great respect for books; he transforms and consecrates them as the "key and integrating element of the dream experience—one of the fundamental activities of the human psyche—and of the creative process itself."[20] He questions the authority of books in the first lines of the Prologue, but he concedes that we must not believe what is only in front of our eyes and that we should believe in the teachings of books (F. 27–28). We know for instance what sorts of pains and joys await us in Hell and Heaven, although no living man ever visited those places: "Bernard the monk ne saugh nat all, pardee!" (F. 16). And in defending books in such a way, Chaucer develops a literary sub-structure whose purpose is to support his creation. The good women he is writing about only exist in these "olde appreved stories" (F and G. 21), which makes of *The Legend of Good Women* a powerful act of cultural transmission. There is no irony here. The poet is as devoted to the poetry of antiquity in *LGW* as he was in the conclusion of *Troilus and Criseyde* (V. 1789–92). In other words, the book is, for Chaucer, a fallible object, yes, but worthy of the greatest respect, for the transmission of our History depends on the stories they tell: "if that olde bokes were aweye, / Yloren were of remembraunce the keye" (F. 25–26). It conserves and saves our past while

---

[20] Boitani, "Old Books Brought to Life in Dreams," 41.

stimulating the artistic creations of future generations (see *HF* or more precisely, *PF*. 24–25).

It is consequently far from being surprising that books are both the source of the narrator's sins against Love in *LGW* and the object of his penitence since he is supposed to find in "sixty bokes olde and newe" (G. 273) the stories he is to write about. Nonetheless, unlike Boccaccio who merely turned his *De Casibus Virorum Illustrium* and *De Claris Mulieribus* into encyclopedic and didactic works with limited artistic interest, Chaucer seizes the very substance of the stories told by poets such as Virgil and Ovid, instills his own voice in their narratives, and makes their respective genres interact.

The dream vision is, in effect, one of Chaucer's most paradoxical creations. He puts remarkable energy into the elaboration of a world respecting the codes of courtly love poetry, but without ever achieving the emotional contemplation that one is expecting from such a sequence. He reproduces, with the dream vision, what he accomplished with the daisy sequence. All the traditional elements are present (the god of Love, his lovely queen, the ballad composed specifically for the occasion . . .), yet the conclusion of this moment of grace is nothing more than a literary discussion between the representatives of *fin'amor* and the poet, which lets this creation "go to waste, like an elegant wedding cake left melting in the hot sun."[21] He reminds us of the literariness of these elements so as to enable the discursive interaction between literary forms outside of the narration. It is all just literature. This discussion thus allows the legend to get started since it is during this discussion that Love accuses the narrator of having composed heretical poems (F. 330; G. 256) that have led people to mistrust women. It gradually becomes obvious that Chaucer has set a trap for his audience and leads us to believe that *LGW* will effectively take place in the familiar and comforting world of *fin'amor*. But when we start reading the legends themselves, we quickly realize that Chaucer's narratives speak of cynical seduction, torture, rape, despair, and violence, themes that have little to do with the codes of the genre. Chaucer, in fact, guides us through the garden of Déduit and once he has presented to us some of its most notorious inhabitants, jumps over the wall of the garden and forces us to march towards Canterbury.

Chaucer feels responsible for the transmission of our History and of our culture but does not necessarily wish to be hindered by its weight. By the time he started writing *LGW*, Chaucer had reached a certain artistic maturity and was able to free himself from the influence of courtly love poetry and to show,

---

21 Frank, *Chaucer and The Legend of Good Women*, 26.

notably with the ballad of the Prologue, how some traditions can "figer le vécu réel . . . autour d'un cliché et le transformer en stéréotype."[22] The fact that Love accuses him of heresy is essential, since the very notion of heresy questions one's freedom of speech, a subject as sensitive and problematical today as it was in the 1380s. And although Alceste supports the narrator, her defense is not really complimentary: she states that he is foolish and probably acted without malice (F. 362–63; G. 340–41), that he was asked to write those poems or that he was just translating without really thinking "of what matere he take" (F. 365; G. 343).

The question of the relationship between the medieval writer and his sources—that is to say, the texts forming the corpus he adapted or translated—is thus brought back to the foreground. The medieval writer or "author" (in the etymological sense of the word, namely "one who adds, increases") was, first and foremost, a transmitter. Writing and translating were considered as one single artistic activity whose purpose was to help the transmission of our culture and History: Alceste says, for instance, that Chaucer "maad the lyf also of Seynt Cecile" (F. 426; G. 416), while the Second Nun will later say that it is a "translacioun" (VIII. 25). Frank explains that "[t]he act of finding material involves not merely the poet's learning or the act of discovery through reading but the act of selecting, the act of choice. What this becomes, finally, is an act of intense imaginative response."[23] The *grand translateur* that is Chaucer accepts his penance while knowing that every single creative evolution will inevitably be met with some kind of resistance from his audience.

The god of Love is the perfect example of this reactionary resistance to evolution: his judgment of *Troilus and Criseyde* shows that he has misinterpreted the poem. In fact, his critique is "rooted in the belief that what a text says can change the way its readers act in the world, in this case by making men less trustful of women."[24] His comments suggest that Chaucer himself was negatively influenced by hiw own acts of reading. His reaction is thus dangerously close to extremism, something that queen Alceste notices when she tells him not to be "lyk tirauntz of Lumbardye, / That han no reward but at tyrannye" (F. 374–75; G. 354–55). The writer's task is thus quite complex since he must bear in mind this aversion to change, and it is easy to imagine Chaucer wondering how his creation will later be perceived, and if he will have the right to reply.

---

[22] "freeze the real experience . . . around a cliché and transform it into a stereotype." Chaucer, *Les Contes de Canterbury et autres œuvres*, 1358.
[23] Frank, *Chaucer and The Legend of Good Women*, 32.
[24] Cook, "Author, Text, and Paratext," 127.

For what is at the heart of the Prologue and of this dream vision is, in the end, Chaucer's elaboration of an excuse to innovate.

The persistence of this apparently foolish persona is revealing of Chaucer's posture in the Prologue. The idea of keeping up appearances is here central: the poet develops an introduction respecting the aesthetic conventions of courtly love poetry but does not get involved emotionally—he remains an objective speaking subject. But this first-person narrative is also superficially connected to the "I" of *fin'amor*. Indeed, literary conventions traditionally put at the heart of courtly poems an inexperienced young man facing love for the first time, but it is here obvious that this description no longer fits Chaucer. It might have worked in *BD*, but not twenty years later. Even though Chaucer's persona has always been a foolish potbellied character who describes himself as incompetent in both matters of love and literature, his age had never been an issue. But when Chaucer writes *LGW*, he is twice as old as Guillaume de Lorris's hero. And even if Gower referred to Chaucer as one of the servants of Venus in his *Confessio Amantis*, he cannot help but allude to their respective ages. Venus thus says in Book VIII:

> "Lo," thus sche seide, "John Gower,
>   Now thou art ate laste cast,
>   This have I for thin ese cast,
> That thou no more of love sieche.
> Bot my will is that thou besieche
>   And preie hierafter for the pes,
>   And that thou make a plein reles
> To love, which takth litel hiede
> Of olde men upon the need."
>   (VIII. 2908–16)

When Chaucer rewrote his Prologue, he accordingly added a remark that could very well be an answer to Gower's playful insinuations. Whereas he had first written "[f]or thogh thou reneyed hast my lay, / As other wrecches han doon many a day" (F. 336–37), he specified a few years later, "[a]lthogh thow reneyed hast my lay, / As othere olde foles many a day" (G. 314–15). The narrator has consequently become too old to be the hero of a courtly love poem, which reinforces the gap existing in the dream vision between conventions and reality and definitely turns *LGW* towards a new literary horizon.

Chaucer, therefore, continues to wear the poetic mask used in his early poems, but unlike earlier, the voice of the narrator does not fade away to the benefit of a dialogical relation between the different characters of the dream vision. Chaucer does not use comedy to define his narrator; on the contrary, he stages a trial during which his career is examined by Love which allows him to justify the innovative nature of his next creation. He insists, for instance, in the G version of the Prologue, on the fact that the legends will stray far from the comforts of courtly love and apologizes for their violence and their pagan dimension, foreign to Christian morality. Chaucer is no longer, at this stage of the narrative, the passive narrator of *The House of Fame* or *The Parliament of Fowls*. He is a narrator-author, a speaking subject, who gives himself the liberty to write what he truly wishes to write: "Once freed, Chaucer could work with material yet more alien, material even richer in possibilities for an artist of his widely ranging interests and varied talents: secular legend, folk tale, beast fable, fabliau."[25] The first and most innovative aspect of *LGW* is in effect not just Chaucer's playfulness but the fact that he doubles the dialogism of his previous creations to the benefit of an experimental work whose polyphony and cacophony are made possible by the hybridization of various literary genres and voices.

The Legend of Good Women and Chaucer's Exercise in Style

The first legends we encounter in *LGW* are probably not Chaucer's strongest pieces. Yet if we focus solely on their weaknesses, we lose sight of the fact that they represent a pure exercise in style. The legends of *Cleopatra*, *Thisbe*, and *Dido* form a distinct group in which Chaucer tries to master the technique of short narrative poetry while attracting his audience into his web of legends. This first phase is consequently of great importance since it allows the poet to train his skills in this new mode of writing and its discursive possibilities.

Cleopatra's place in English literature owes much to Shakespeare's play, yet it is Chaucer's quill that first introduced her in England. But whereas the Bard contributes to the mythification of the Egyptian queen by giving her charm and greatness, Chaucer develops her story only briefly, and quickly summarizes the main stages of her romance with Antony. Her very presence in *LGW* is actually a surprise:[26] Cleopatra was never part of the courtly love repertoire, unlike the other women of the collection, and owes her fame to Dante, Petrarch, and Boccaccio, who introduced her into European literature. However, Chaucer's treatment of the queen is unique. He does not merely present a relatively unknown character; he de-demonizes her, and if she does not yet possess Shakespearian

---

25 Frank, *Chaucer and The Legend of Good Women*, 35.
26 The fact that Love says "At Cleopatre I wol that thou begynne" (F. 566 and G. 452) is probably Chaucer's excuse to write about a character he has obviously liked since the days of the *Parliament of Fowls* (291).

greatness, neither does she have the defects attributed to her by the Italians. Portrayed as a cynical and perverse seducer in *Claris Mulieribus* (Chap. 86) and the *Inferno* (V), she remains here faithful to Antony until her death. It is therefore probable that our poet drew from Vincent de Beauvais's *Speculum historiale* (VI, 5) for this first legend. Boccaccio's treatment is indeed so unflattering that Chaucer would have been forced to cut through his text to reach its understructure, while Vincent offered a much more neutral portrayal, which was furthermore barely developed beyond a synopsis.

Chaucer composes this legend out of the few elements he has been able to gather and is accordingly forced to improvise in order to connect the different aspects of the narrative. He thus compresses all the expected components of the story—the conflict between Rome and Egypt, romance, exoticism—in only 125 lines and confesses that lingering on every single detail might overload his boat (621). Indeed, Chaucer finds himself trapped by the fear of being prolix, and it is significant that he spends eight lines justifying the absence of details:

> The weddynge and the feste to devyse,
> To me, that have ytake swich empryse
>   Of so many a story for to make,
>   It were to longe, lest that I shulde slake
> Of thyng that bereth more effect and charge;
>   (616–20)

Deprived of the *fin'amor* frame, Chaucer must find a new mode of representation for his characters. Their role cannot be the one prescribed by courtly love, yet it is still necessary to retain some traces of the tradition to lure the audience deeper into the collection. Chaucer presents certain similarities with *fin'amor* but does not go into details: the "ful worthy gentil werreyour" (597) that is Antony almost looks like one of Chrétien's knights, his passion for Cleopatra is such that "al the world he sette at no value" (602). Cleopatra herself seems to be smitten by the Roman general for perfectly conventional and appropriate reasons; she loves this "knyght . . . [t]hourgh his desert, and for his chyvalrye" (607–8). But Chaucer simply alludes to the codes of courtly love and does not transform the narrative into a story of love and chivalry. Antony remains far from the true courtly lover since he has both betrayed Rome and disloyally abandoned Octavia (591–95). The way in which Chaucer presents the situation even absolves Cleopatra. He does not condemn her—Chaucer is far too resistant to closure and monologism to condemn anyone—and just follows the historical progress of the narrative, using the battle of Actium (31 BC) as a catalyst. Unlike his treatment of war in *Troilus and Criseyde*, he actually depicts a naval battle sequence in which Antony is nowhere close to being the hero. In doing so, he refuses to reinforce his knightlihood, to justify his title of "werreyour," and rather brings to the fore an anonymous sailor, a "He" in the midst of the tempest. The values of chivalry never guide the action and give way, due to a succession of simple, even monosyllabic, impactful lines, to lists and alliterations evoking the chaos of the battle:

> He styngeth hym upon his speres ord;
> He rent the seyl with hokes lyke a sithe;
> He bryngeth the cuppe and biddeth hem be blythe;
> He poureth pesen upon the haches slidere.
> (645–48)

Cleopatra's death follows this battle and Antony's suicide. Left alone to face the consequences of the defeat, and fully aware of Caesar's anger, she takes refuge "for drede and for destresse" (664) in Egypt and prepares her exit. And when Chaucer might finally have let love speak, he just reminds us of her faithfulness (665–68) and underlines the opulence and exoticism that seduced Antony. But in refusing to mention their encounter and to linger on their marriage, he keeps this exoticism for the end, with a sequence in which the queen has Antony's body embalmed, set in a shrine of precious stones, full of spices, before throwing herself naked into the adjoining pit full of snakes (671–80 and 696–701). This exoticism, not unmixed with eroticism, is powerfully juxtaposed to the previous battle scene: Chaucer in effect compares the exuberance and violence of war with the delicacy of Cleopatra's spices and rubies, contrasting the refinement of the queen with the masculinity and hardness of the world she is imprisoned in. Cleopatra thus becomes a spouse, betrayed by Antony, but also a woman trapped and broken by men.

The closing remark not only reinforces this notion but also produces an ambiguity that makes us wonder if the narrator truly intends to accomplish the task assigned to him in the Prologue. Indeed, the narrator suggests it is hard to find a man as faithful as Cleopatra and who would die for love, which implies of course that virtuous women are easier to find. The narrator concludes that his head would ache long before he could find such a man. In effect, he reverses the situation and his "search has become one for tales of true men instead and, by praying that 'our hedes' remain headache-free, he implicates us in that search as well."[27] In other words, Chaucer involves us and insists that reading is an active process: he might be the author and speaking subject, but his whole enterprise depends on our involvement. He needs the audience to

---

27 McGerr, *Chaucer's Open Books*, 121.

interpret his words and effectively notice the discrepancies between his penance, the theme, his attitude, what is being said and left unsaid. *LGW* is a highly ambiguous work requiring us to infer how the speaker observes and cognizes the elements he has himself read and interpreted. As Irina Dumetriscu observes, the narrator is faced with a dilemma right from the start: the treacherous men of the legends are all skilled rhetoricians who use their particular talent to deceive women; as a result, when the narrator "fulfils his task of describing the suffering women of the *Legend*, he becomes author of their woes and complicit in the aestheticization of female pain."[28] And since pity is often associated with desire in the poem, by depicting women's sorrow he "turns them into objects of predatory lust."[29] In effect, whatever the narrator does—pitying, or praising those women—makes him resemble the men who victimize those good women. In *Cleopatra*, however, Chaucer struggles at times with the nuances of short narrative poetry but slowly starts to unravel the web in which Alceste has trapped him.

The Legend of Thisbe is from the start a very different sort of story. Indeed, if Cleopatra's lack of fame had forced Chaucer to improvise, this romance was so popular during the Middle Ages that he had access to a whole corpus. Machaut, Boccaccio, Gower, Christine de Pizan, or even the *Ovide moralisé* all reinterpreted this episode from the *Metamorphoses*. Yet Chaucer's version remains very different.

Ovid gave Chaucer a narrative stability that would serve him throughout his career. But the Latin poet's work also reassured Chaucer about the capacities of this poetical mode for developing a plot based solely on the potential energy of the narrative, that is to say, the narrative strength stored by the story before being set into motion. Chaucer thus follows the *Metamorphoses* while supplementing his rendition of the narrative with elements borrowed from the highly popular *Ovide moralisé* and eventually proposes a legend whose form is still close to the original material; he merely ignores elements that do not fit the theme of *LGW*, such as the mytheme of the blood-stained fruit, and organizes the various episodes in order to produce narrative stability. For instance, he reduces to one line the image of Pyramus bleeding to death (852), adds a passage in direct speech in which Thisbe, then hidden in a cave, fears her lover will believe her to be false if he does not find her (855–57), and thus creates a sense of balance between each episode of the legend.

---

28 Dumitrescu, "Beautiful Suffering and the Culpable Narrator," 109.
29 Ibid.

Chaucer consequently exploits Ovid's narrative structure in order to offer a new treatment of the myth. He ignores the Ovidian moral and proposes to read this romance in a different way: whereas Ovid had turned the death of his heroes into the triumph of desire, Chaucer makes it the triumph of innocence. The dreadful fate of Pyramus and Thisbe becomes for him the very example of the constant contrast between innocence and desire that is specific to youth. This contrast is concretely represented in the narrative by the wall separating the houses of the lovers. Chaucer explains that

> This wal, which that bitwixe hem bothe stod,
> Was clove a-two, ryght from the cop adoun,
> Of olde tyme of his fundacioun;
> But yit this clyfte was so narw and lyte
> It nas nat sene, deere ynogh a myte.
> But what is that that love can nat espye?
> (737–42)

The wall is used, in other words, as a stage prop allowing Ovid and Chaucer to create movement: it is this wall, symbolizing the romance, that stores within itself the potential energy of the narrative before liberating a force allowing the poet to reach the end of his story without amplifications or additions. Pyramus and Thisbe indeed rapidly notice the crack in the wall that will allow them to communicate. Their fathers' refusal to accept the wedding increases for a while this separation but eventually provokes their flight ("As wry the glede and hotter is the fyr"; 735). Unfortunately, a chronotopic imbalance once again changes the situation: they set a meeting point, but Thisbe arrives early and there finds a lioness with a bloody mouth (805–8). Terrified, she takes refuge in a cave, leaving behind her veil. When Pyramus arrives and sees the fabric torn by the lioness, he believes his lady has been killed "[a]nd with that word he smot hym to the herte" (850). Thisbe comes back, finds Pyramus bleeding to death and decides to die too. Their relationship in the narrative is as a result developed around the initial separation/reunion sequence represented by the wall and repeated in an echo throughout the legend. This conflict between desire and innocence is kept moving by the chronotopic imbalance, by the lovers' incapacity to truly be in the same place at the same time.

That is how Chaucer's style differs from Ovid's and reinforces his own reading of the myth. In the *Metamorphoses*, as in *LGW*, the accent is put on the characters' feelings rather than on their characterization. All that matters is that Pyramus and Thisbe love each other, that "bothe in love ylyke sore they brente" (737), which dictates their actions. But the specificity of the Chaucerian reading is that it becomes necessary to replace this lack of characterization by a change of tonality in order to humanize the characters and give a sense of shared innocence. To do so, Chaucer operates an important space-time transformation and moves Semiramis's Babylon to medieval England. The description of the city (706–14) strangely reminds us of fourteenth-century cities and as Dor remarks, "L'intégration de détails de la réalité quotidienne anglaise à l'exotisme oriental vient en effet s'ajouter à l'harmonieuse insertion d'éléments contemporains dans le contexte général d'un passé lointain."[30] This proximity is reinforced by Chaucer's language. His style is, indeed, once again quite conversational and avoids the rigidity of Latin formulas. Even if he shows his ability to follow Ovid with the rhetoric of the final sequence, he keeps this capacity to be both conversational and familiar, a tone that remains dominant despite the emotional charge of the last lines.[31] Line 893 even borders on comedy. When Thisbe takes Pyramus's sword and considers suicide, Chaucer juxtaposes her death with her doubts: her love, she says, will give her the strength to kill herself, before pausing at the rhyme "I gesse," which paints the picture of a character not particularly looking forward to piercing her chest with a sword. And if Chaucer clearly does not intend to lower the register to the grotesque—as he will often do in the *Canterbury Tales*—what this casualness does emphasize is an innocence preserved until the end.

The Legend of Thisbe consequently gives Chaucer the opportunity to exercise his skills in short narrative writing. This second legend thus proposes a new reading of the myth, but also represents a strong act of insubordination. For there is clearly no way out of his dilemma, since "writing of unfaithful women such as Criseyde leads him to his condemnation; writing of good ones implicates him in their abuse."[32] The terms of Chaucer's penance were clear in the Prologue: he had been asked to follow his books and produce narratives describing virtuous ladies betrayed by men. Yet *Thisbe* clearly does not adhere to these terms. Besides his transformation of the myth, Chaucer also presents a heroine who has nothing to do with the theme of the collection since Pyramus's sole crime has been to be a few minutes late. The narrator seems to play with this very idea: when Thisbe leaves her home, he tells us that she also abandons her friends, before noting "allas, and that is routhe / That evere woman wolde ben so trewe / To truste man, but she the bet hym knewe" (799–801). What a strange idea then to trust a man without knowing him! He does not even bother to hide a hint of sexism in the

---

30 "The inclusion of details from English daily life into the oriental exoticism indeed adds to the harmonious insertion of contemporary elements in the general context of a distant past." Chaucer, *Les Contes de Canterbury et autres œuvres*, 1360.
31 See lines 855–57, 860–61, and 890–93.
32 Dumitrescu, "Beautiful Suffering and the Culpable Narrator," 121.

final moralizing speech. Thisbe implores fathers to "lat no gentil woman hyre assure / To putten hire in swich an aventure" (908–9) and tries to prove by her suicide that a woman can be as faithful in love as a man (910–11)! This is a supreme irony for a narrative bearing only Thisbe's name and set in a collection supposed to defend female virtue. Chaucer continues to break the codes set in the Prologue and lets *Thisbe* answer *Cleopatra* with a typically Chaucerian tone and effect.

The exercise in style that defines the first three legends of *LGW* could not have ended without the intervention of a character as popular as Dido. The queen of Carthage indeed was considered an emblem of the passions during the Middle Ages and became, with Dante's text, the representative of a form of immoral and forbidden love. Nevertheless, if her name was synonymous with lust in the *Commedia* (*Inf.* V. 85), it is also linked with the very origins of the novelistic genre. Her role in the *Roman de Troie* and *Roman d'Énéas* was in effect essential to the development of European vernacular literature. It is accordingly not surprising that Chaucer seizes on the myth a second time to offer a narrative that goes further than the bivocal narration of *The House of Fame*.

Dido's first appearance in Chaucerian poetry owed much to Virgil, and this time is no different. Chaucer draws from the first four books of the *Aeneid*, but also from Ovid's *Heroides*, the details of the romance between Dido and Aeneas, which he then transcribes narratively. He thus entirely reworks the thousands of lines[33] composing his source corpus into a narrative of 143 lines that keeps on ignoring the Mantuan poet's guiding lantern. For if Chaucer devotes an invocation to Virgil (924–29), it is only to quickly disregard his influence to the benefit of a different narrative structure and interpretation of the legend. Chaucer has no intention of composing an epic poem, but rather a narrative of feelings.

Between *HF* and *The Legend of Dido*, Chaucer has gained experience. The sequence in the Temple of Venus allowed him to play with the concept of *visibile parlare* via a bivocal narration; by establishing a link between visible speech and the fallibility of the human mind, he offered a contrast to Dantean philosophy. To do so, Chaucer had to distance himself from Virgil: the bivocal narration was followed by a transformation of the myth of Dido, which suddenly illustrated both the notion of fame (Aeneas was then perceived as a polygamist who "wolde have fame / In magnyfyinge of hys name"; I. 305–6) and the frailty of the human transmission of history (Chaucer added details to the

---

33 Virgil devotes at least 1,300 lines out of the some 3,000 of the *Aeneid*'s first four books to the love story between the two characters, that is if we ignore the first 156 lines describing the tempest in Book I, and Books II and III in which Aeneas tells the story of his adventures. We should add to this account the 200 lines from the seventh epistle in the *Heroides*.

legend for which "[n]on other auctour alegge I"; I. 314). Things are now different with *Dido*. While he barely proposed any narrative content in *HF*, preferring moral comments, complaints, and abstracts, he manages this time to organize his story so as to reach his objective. He reminds us that "I coude folwe, word for word, Virgile, / But it wolde lasten al longe while" (1002–3), so he has to do things his way and sums up the fall of Troy (930) and the arrival of the survivors at Carthage (1001) in only sixty-six lines,[34] announces the themes of the narrative (love, treason, death, and destruction) in his incipit (930–45), and marches on until Aeneas "laft Dido in wo and pyne, / And wedded ther a lady hyghte Lavyne" (1330–31).

Chaucer thus stages, in this legend, an emotion dramatized by narration, and transforms the relationship between the two protagonists. In order to underline the emotional imbalance of the romance and to stimulate our sympathy for Dido, he must present the *inamoramento* that he had avoided in *HF* with the excuse that "[h]yt wol not be; / I kan not of that faculte" (I. 247–48). Virgil himself showed little interest in this crucial episode, preferring to linger on the consequences of their love, rather than on its origins. But Chaucer manages to get rid of the simple Olympian manipulation mentioned in the *Aeneid* and presents the instability of the romance in only a few lines. When Aeneas enters Carthage, for instance, he walks straight to the great temple of the city, where he meets the queen, but whereas Virgil insisted on the political dimension of this encounter (I. 494–506), Chaucer describes a young queen "fayrer . . . than is the bryghte sonne" (1006), praying, and praised by the whole world for her nobility (1008–10). In doing so, he suggests an innocence that the bold Trojan will soon exploit. Likewise, while Aeneas's companions in adversity were met with hostility by the Carthaginians in the ancient version of the myth (I. 539–43), in *LGW* they are attracted to the city by the legendary kindness of the queen (1053–54).

But presenting the origins of this love story in a few lines posed a problem of temporality for Chaucer. Dido had to fall in love quickly enough to prevent the story from getting stuck, but with enough resistance to keep the audience's empathy. She could not yield to the charms of Aeneas too rapidly, which usually implies the use of the love potion imagery or the atemporality of the Greek novel of chivalry. Yet Chaucer is here engaging in a narrative exercise and has accordingly no liberty to linger on the details of the love story, or to fall once again into the codes of *fin'amor*:

> What Chaucer does, therefore, is to create a kind of double time. He creates the impression that Dido falls in love almost at once, though it is not the blinding lightning flash

---

[34] Or seventy-one if we count the *occupatio* of lines 953–57.

that smites Troilus. . . . Contrariwise, however, Chaucer also creates the impression that her love evolved gradually though powerfully and that we move rather slowly before we come to the scene in the cave.[35]

To do so, Chaucer gives us the opportunity to perceive Aeneas through the eyes of Dido (1061–79), and produces this first contact by anaphora, giving us the feeling that each new quality detailed slowly increases, one line at a time, Dido's love:

> The queen saugh that they dide hym swych honour,
>   And hadde her ofte of Eneas er tho,
>   And in hire herte she hadde routhe and wo
>   . . .
>   And saw the man, that he was lyk a knyght,
>   And suffisaunt of persone and of myght,
>   And lyk to been a verray gentil man . . .
>   (1061–68)

By repeating this "And" structure twelve times, Chaucer shows that Dido remarks at first glance the qualities a lady should notice in a man. She has mercy on his sufferings, even if it is not the courtly mercy a lady grants a suffering lover, but a sincere compassion on which the poet insists (1078–81). Love thus seems inevitable; however, the narrator goes back to the objective storytelling, and gives us the feeling that some time has passed while the temporal deictic markers indicate that only forty-eight hours have passed between the temple scene and Dido's surrender in the cave.[36]

Several scenes take place during this temporal hiatus, which give Chaucer the opportunity to develop his plot. One of the most significant sequences, in this regard, is the gift episode. Whereas Virgil gave Aeneas the occasion to shine in Book I by illustrating his generosity (I. 643–54), Chaucer reverses the situation and highlights Dido with a new anaphora that echoes the temple scene. The poet tells us that there were

> Ne stede, for the justing wel to gon,
> Ne large palfrey, esy for the nones,
> Ne jewel, fretted ful of ryche stones,
> Ne sakkes ful of gold, of large wyghte
>   . . .
>   That Dido ne hath it Eneas ysent;
>   (1115–24)

---

[35] Frank, *Chaucer and The Legend of Good Women*, 1972, 65.
[36] See lines 1092, 1112, 1154, 1164, and 1188.

The queen shows her generosity and greatness with magnificent presents, revealing her emotional attachment, while Aeneas just gives her "[b]othe sceptre, clothes, borches, and ek rynges" (1131). The contrast between the two becomes increasingly obvious in this purely narrative sequence, and leads to the revival of amorous feelings (1150–59). As soon as Dido stops resisting and acknowledges her love, things accelerate to the point that the final tragedy can no longer be avoided. The conclusion is even concretely represented by a scene with courtly love characteristics: during the hunt, Dido, dressed in gold and precious stones, is the ultimate gift she has to offer Aeneas who controls his horse "as himself hath wold" (1209).

The Trojan is, in other words, master of his horse and of the situation while Dido is conquered and disarmed. Thus, through scenes that might otherwise have been simple amplifications, Chaucer manages to get his plot moving while delaying the consummation of the romance and simultaneously tending the fire of Dido's love. The cavern scene is in effect the logical conclusion of what we have seen up to that point.[37] Dido is in love and has confessed to her sister that she would gladly marry Aeneas (1179), yet when the moment comes she is engulfed by a passion described by Chaucer as the "firste morwe / Of hire gladnesse, and gynning of hire sorwe" (1230–31). The poet not only transforms the characters of the legend but also manages to present Dido's love and despair through brief comments and notes. While the rumor of their affair starts to spread in Carthage, Dido remains discrete until the moment her knight decides to take Trojan leave. She understands that something is wrong and questions Aeneas and his "false teres" (1301) when he announces his departure. Chaucer here makes us feel the violence of her pain by listing verbs betraying the queen's turmoil ("She seketh halwes and doth sacryfise; / She kneleth, cryeth, that routhe is to devyse"; 1310–15), and ending with an even more violent final supplication in direct speech (1316–24). She implores Aeneas twice to have pity and to take her with him, she shows her isolation in a world hostile to women in her condition, and announces she is ready to die as a wife and future mother of their child. Nonetheless, "al this thing avayleth hire ryght nought" (1325); Aeneas remains impervious and refuses to change his mind.

Despite the tragic ending of this romance, Chaucer does little to inspire an emotion more violent than antipathy for Aeneas. Unlike Virgil, he never gives us cause to feel the pity and sadness that Dido feels for him, and rapidly turns him into a scoundrel. To this end, he retains the temple scene in which the

---

37 The idea of "seeing" is quite important in short narratives of this sort since their picturality produces picture effects giving the audience an immediate perception of the scene.

Trojan bursts into tears upon seeing a fresco illustrating the fall of his city, but while Virgil made him cry for the sorrows of the world, Chaucer makes him regret the Trojans' shame and destitution (1027–32). He even insists on the debt he owes his hostess since his arrival in Carthage (1277–80) and begs women not to give their trust to men so easily (1254–56). This image of the false lover throwing himself at the feet of his lady in the cave "as a fals lovere so wel can pleyne" (1236) is entirely new and was not present in the original source material. Chaucer uses it to increase our animosity towards this character, laughing "at anothers wo" (1251). He is a villain, yes, but the narrator seems to murmur that the world cannot end for each scorned woman. The name "Sely Dido" (1157) is, in the end, not accidental given the word's polysemy. This qualifier meaning "happy," "saint," "weak," and "ridiculous" describes the evolution of Dido throughout the different stages of the romance and reveals the ambiguity of the poet's enterprise in *LGW*.

The legends of *Cleopatra*, *Thisbe*, and *Dido* constitute an exercise in style that allowed Chaucer to try his hand at a new stylistic line. For what opposes *LGW* to the rest of the Chaucerian corpus is truly this hybridization of effects and tones. Even if the first legends can be set apart because of their experimental nature, it is clear that each of these narratives addresses the unifying theme of the collection in a different manner. Cleopatra never manages to get heard, but the contrast between the battle and the tomb evokes masculinity and the hardness of the world; *Thisbe* invites us, on the contrary, to think about the recklessness and innocence of youth, while *Dido* paints the portrait a woman betrayed but who can only blame herself. These first legends not only comment on each other but also dialogue with the Prologue and its sentence, for the goodness of these women is set in direct contradiction to the behavior of other Chaucerian female characters and to the theme of the collection. But as Nakao remarks, this dichotomy of false men and good women is too arbitrary and absolute for Chaucer: "While dealing with positive feminine virtues, he comes gradually to touch upon feminine weaknesses hidden behind those virtues, and the double coherent structure of positive and negative values becomes prominent."[38] As the narrator gradually rejects the terms of his penance, he produces legends that not only contradict Love's sentence but also contradict themselves, which becomes all the more obvious with the genre changes of the following stories.[39]

---

[38] Nakao, *The Structure of Chaucer's Ambiguity*, 40.
[39] A complete analysis of each legend would be impossible here. We will illustrate the idea of hybridization with a look at some of the legends, starting with the development of the concept in the exercise of style represented by the first texts, then moving to the most striking narratives.

Counterbalancing Pathos with Comedy

The Legend of Hypsipyle and Medea is without a doubt a poem whose position in the collection exemplifies the ambiguity of Chaucer's enterprise. Read independently from the rest of *LGW*, it seems to give us an incredible account of the tribulations of Jason in Colchide; yet its dialogical interaction with *Dido* and with the emotional intensity of *Lucretia* cannot be ignored.

The first legends have shown Chaucer's keen interest in painting the lives of the women through the spectrum of the masculinity of these "telle of false men" (F. 486). He thus draws from Guido delle Colonne's *Historia destructionis Troiae*, the *Metamorphoses* (Book VII), the *Heroides* (sixth and twelfth epistles), Valerius Flaccus's *Argonautica*, and chapters fifteen and sixteen of *De Claris Mulieribus*, the material necessary to the composition of two stories depicting two different women, but unified around the notion of "false lovers" (1368) represented by Jason. Besides Chaucer's interest in this character, his decision to turn him into the focal point of the legend also comes from the nature of his material. Indeed, the *Argonautica* describes the rescue of his father by Hypsipyle while the Lemnian women joyfully slaughter all the men of the island because of their supposed infidelity—something that would have been difficult to put in a collection about *good* women! Guido also describes Medea as a sly and monstrous creature, whereas Ovid juxtaposes the tale of her life with its negative—Hypsipyle's story. Chaucer was accordingly forced to reduce the legend of these two women to the bare minimum and to get rid of everything that did not fit his theme (Lemnian women, Medea's infanticide . . .). In doing so, he extracted a stripped version of the plot. Hypsipyle and Medea here become two women whose lives differ completely, excepting the sole point of their encounter with Jason. In other words, Chaucer produces a diptych that focuses our attention on the Greek hero and not on his victims.

The narrator does not wait to display his fascination with Jason and starts his double legend with a twenty-seven-line introductive address in which he condemns his actions. Nonetheless, it rapidly becomes obvious that Chaucer's vehemence in this introduction is not the result of true indignation but rather a narrative pose. How would we otherwise read the attack launched at line 1383? "Have at thee, Jason! Now thyn horn is blowe!," Chaucer seems to cry out, waving his quill. In effect, both the images and language used participate in the implementation of a comical tone. By getting rid of the most sordid episodes of the lives of Hypsipyle and Medea, Chaucer gives himself the opportunity to characterize his protagonists in an entirely different way. Prefiguring his *mise-en-scène* of the fabliaux in the *Canterbury Tales*,[40] he produces an analogy between Jason's crimes and those of a fox in a farmyard and definitely destroys any chance of a tragic treatment of the myth. He gives us, for instance, the image of a "sly devourere" (1369), lover of these "tendre creatures" (1370) that are noble women, and especially appreciating their flesh once stuffed—"farced" (1373)—by his sweet words.

This carnivalesque representation of woman as stuffed poultry will then be used as a mirror by Chaucer to reflect both the misadventures of Hypsipyle and Medea and Jason's successes. Indeed, the word used in this animal analogy to define the victims is none other than "capoun" (1389 and 1392). The reasons that prompted Chaucer to speak of a capon rather than of a hen can seem obscure but remain perfectly congruent with the tone of the introductory address. The meat of the capon has, in fact, been particularly appreciated for centuries, which echoes the image of the "farced" poultry of the previous lines, yet its flavor results from the castration of the animal. Chaucer accordingly plays with the image of a castrated rooster to blur the boundaries between virility and femininity: Jason is, given the rest of the legend, as worthy of being called a "capoun" as are Hypsipyle and Medea.

Chaucer thus apparently remains faithful to his theme in the *Legend of Hypsipyle* and applies to his material the rigor of short narrative writing. He invokes Guido, invites us to read Flaccus to learn more about the Argonauts, but keeps the tonal gap that prevents the narrative from reaching an epic dimension. Jason has consequently no opportunity to make us forget the original presentation that is made of him and retains this comical aspect throughout the legend. Pelias's plot to get rid of Jason is presented, for instance, in such a way as to avoid horror, and the dangers surrounding the Golden Fleece barely produce a sense of wonder. In addition to the dragon protecting the famous ram, Chaucer notes that there are two fire-spitting bronze bulls and "moche thyng . . . up and doun" (1433, 1431). Pelias's invitation to take the road in spite of danger is so un-dramatic that it becomes comical: "Lat sen now, darst thow take this viage?" (1450).

It is accordingly difficult to picture Jason as a hero from antiquity accomplishing one of the most important mythological quests of the European cultural tradition. Especially when Chaucer accentuates his effect by producing, on the arrival of the Argonauts on Hypsipyle's lands, an imbalance between the conventions of *fin'amor* and our global, aesthetic vision of the hero's role in the legend.[41]

---

40 See *The Nun's Priest's Tale*.
41 See Bakhtin, *Esthétique de la création verbale*, 44.

Chaucer enjoys this gap: Jason has, after all, the qualities of a courtly lover, just like Aeneas. He knows how to be eloquent, is known as a "famous knyght of gentilesse, / Of fredom, and of strenghte and lustynesse" (1404–5), and remains, despite his sea journey, immediately recognizable as a gentleman of noble birth (1504–6). Besides, just like his famous predecessors of the courtly love tradition, Jason is accompanied by a go-between easing his amorous conquests.

However, whereas Pandarus exercised great subtlety in *Troilus and Criseyde*, Hercules does not seem to be able to act with finesse. Even if his intervention is successful, his description of Jason is messy and contradictory. Not only does he possess the qualities of a great courtly lover, which contradicts the introduction, but also of a possible king: he is both "hardy, secre" (1528), and is more dynamic than anyone alive or dead (1531), and yet this "lusty knyght" (1542) is so shy that he would rather kill himself than be seen in an amorous situation. In other words, Hercules seems to throw at Hypsipyle all the clichés that pass through his mind to facilitate the execution of their plan. The Jason described by Chaucer as a sly predator has here nothing of the fox but, being "as coy as is a mayde" (1548), rather looks like a capon. He eventually reaches his objective, a conclusion Chaucer dispatches like no one else: "And upon hire begat he children two, / And drogh his sayl and saw hir nevere mo" (1562–63).

After having used Hypsipyle, Jason gets back on the road and arrives in Colchide, where his appetite leads him to look for other women. King Aeetes allows him to try his luck with the Golden Fleece and asks his daughter Medea to keep him company during the festivities. But if he easily manages to seduce her, the roles quickly reverse, which makes the situation look rather antiheroic. Indeed, aware of the danger surrounding the Fleece, Medea takes charge and offers to tell the hero how to fulfil his quest, under the condition that Jason swears to marry her afterward (1629–42). Playing once more with the image of the castrated rooster, Chaucer here pictures a hero who owes his fame to the talents of a lady who saved both "his lyf and his honour" (1648). And since the first part of this declaration is true, the other part must be false. Chaucer then puts him in the bed of his victim, with so much promptness that he rymes "bedde" with "spedde" (1644, 1645), and, playing with what is left unsaid about Medea's monstrous acts, sends Jason towards a new adventure, named Creuse.

Consequently, despite the ambiguity of the situations, Jason remains for Chaucer the symbol of incredible luck. He tells us straight away that he is an unfaithful lover, yet whereas the audience might rightfully expect some sort of justice intervening to punish his actions, he just carries on with disturbing ease and, passing from one woman to the other ("There othere falsen oon, thow falsest two!"; 1377), ends up by succeeding in winning the Golden Fleece. While other lovers work hard to obtain the favors of a lady, at the risk of receiving "in armes many a blody box" (1388), Jason takes advantage of his lucky star and enjoys his loot,

> For evere as tendre a capoun et the fox,
> Thow he be fals and hath the foul betrayed,
> As shal the good-man that therfore hath payed.
> Al have he to the capoun skille and ryght,
> The false fox wol have his part at nyght.
> (1389–95)

As we can see, Chaucer presents here a first alternative to the tragic or courtly treatment of amorous passion. Sometimes prefiguring *The Miller's Tale*, he treats realistically the few *fin'amor* elements that survived the transfiguration of his material in order to show the complexity of these feelings when they are freed from the conventionalism of the tradition. After having promised the god of Love to strictly follow his source material, Chaucer actually frees himself from the conditions of his penance to question the authority of literature in the face of reality. Jasons's fortune and his constant success, made possible by treachery and plots, give a certain bitterness to the comical tone used by the poet.

Following the bitter lightness of *The Legend of Hypsipyle and Medea*, Chaucer tries with *Lucretia* to implicate his audience in an entirely different manner and passes from a comical tone to a reinforced use of pathos in order to present a new aspect of amorous passion. For if the treason or abandonment of Jason, Antony, and Pyramus had tragic consequences, Chaucer had always made sure to show that their crimes were despicable but not necessarily hateful, especially for Pyramus, who can hardly be accused of anything. With *The Legend of Lucretia*, the poet confronts us with the rape of a young girl and the tarnishing of her reputation, both within the narrative and in the global frame of the European literary tradition.

Chaucer mainly uses Ovid's *Fasti* for the narrative dimension of this legend but enlists Livy and Augustine in "a dialogue on feminine virtue."[42] He remains faithful to the passage concerning Tarquinius (II. 685–864) but remodels his text in order to focus on the feminine theme. Chaucer accordingly introduces Roman imperialism in the first lines of the legend, credits Livy and Ovid, then "rejects it entirely in favour of providing us with an account of Lucrece's wifely virtue."[43] In effect, he ignores the political dimension of the story and quickly sets up the plot. He mentions, for instance, the force and violence of the Romans

---

42 Schwebel, "Livy and Augustine as Negative Models," 32.
43 Ibid.

(1695), along with Tarquinius's eloquence (1699), before insisting on the idleness subsequent to the siege of Ardea and its consequences on the men. He remarks that "[n]o man dide there no more than his wif" (1701), which allows him to develop the woman theme via a game in which each man must praise his wife (1702–4).

Chaucer here fixes our attention on Lucretia, and in only a few lines describes a character whose virtue and humility are only matched by her innocence and honesty. To do so, he modifies Ovid's text and leads us gradually to the rape sequence, while continuing to emphasize the devotion and vulnerability of his heroine. As a result, when her husband Collatinus takes Tarquinius to Rome so that he may witness Lucretia's beauty, Chaucer brings together all the narrative components enabling the rape. Both men sneak into the house and secretly walk into her bedroom, where Tarquinius discovers a young woman "[d]ischevele, for no malyce she ne thoughte" (1720). Chaucer, therefore, prepares Tarquinius's return by showing us that he is capable of finding the way to Lucretia's bed without being noticed, and proves how vulnerable and fragile she actually is.

With this exposition, Chaucer manages to develop a pathetic atmosphere with surprising stylistic simplicity. Though not used to the genre,[44] he produces pathos by a simple characterization and the sobriety of his narration, while continuing to float between verisimilitude and conventions. Drawing both from the Christian tradition, particularly the emotionalism connected with the Virgin Mary,[45] and the sentimentalism of the *fin'amor* complaint, Chaucer develops a pathetic narrative mode that was until then unknown in English. He was obviously influenced by the Ovidian exploration of pathos in the *Heroides*, but he transcends this influence and turns the victim into a paragon of innocence. Chaucerian pathos is indeed mainly marked by the suffering and helplessness of a woman or child hurt by a hostile world. This concentration of the narrative on such a fragile figure allows the poet to transform this constant suffering into the guarantor of the universality of feelings. It is therefore not surprising to see Tarquinius, last king of Rome, sneak in "ful thefly" (1781) into a house, for the accent is placed on the victim's vulnerability and not on her social condition.

Horror is one of the tools used by Chaucer to intensify our reaction during Tarquinius's second intrusion. Indeed, he reinforces the horrific dimension of his act by slightly modifying the scene: whereas Ovid notes that Tarquinius

---

[44] Chaucer is the author of several pathetic tales in the *Canterbury Tales*, and although the order of composition of his poems is not always clear *Lucretia* is probably one of his first experiments with the genre.
[45] Muscatine, *Chaucer and the French Tradition*, 193.

penetrates Collatinus's house as a guest but takes advantage of the night to commit his crime, Chaucer instead describes a wolf covertly creeping into the home. This dramatically reinforces the alternation between the rapist's and victim's points of view: the poet starts by placing us in the mind of the assailant and makes us feel "[h]is blynde lust" (1756) and his obsession by using direct speech. Tarquinius succumbs to temptation, violates the courtly code (1757–58) and tiptoes into Lucretia's bedroom.[46] The horror then develops in crescendo with this image of a monstrous creature watching a victim from the darkness, and reaches its climax when the subjective narration changes point of view and gives voice to Lucretia. That is where Chaucer distances himself from his source for Ovid only lets the victim speak during her confession; yet, her direct intervention here intensifies the atmosphere. Feeling the presence of a strange weight on her bed, she asks herself "[w]hat beste is that . . . that weyeth thus?" (1788) and although the narrator swiftly takes over, he continues to describe the scene as seen from Lucretia's eyes. The poet makes us feel her doubts and fears: trapped like a lamb before a wolf (1798), she wonders if she must scream or cry, how to break free, and imploring Tarquinius eventually faints. However, unlike Ovid, Chaucer places the rape after Tarquinius's threat to kill one of her servants and to accuse her of adultery. Fear and shame make her swoon (1814–18), which completely exonerates her from willingly taking part in the sexual transgression. The fact that she has fainted reinforces her innocence and the atrocity of the situation, but it also allows Chaucer to produce an interdiscursive dialogue with his sources.

Indeed, for Livy, the horrific rape and its consequences were mainly political and social. Lucretia's concerns were those of "a woman focused on how her life and its end will be read by others";[47] she embodied "the figure of violated Rome"[48] since the rape epitomized Tarquinius's tyranny. But although Chaucer names Livy, he refuses the political implications of Lucretia's assault: "Her plight is not a historical motif, linking her to the vestal virgin, the Sabines, and Verginia" explains Leah Schwebel, "but rather a personal calamity, which Chaucer suggests by isolating Lucrece's story from other Livian narratives of rape."[49] Chaucer is interested in her sorrow: his Lucretia is barely able to speak of what has happened, her pain is "impossible" to articulate according to the narrator (1834–39), while in Livy's political narrative she asks for revenge.

---

46 Shakespeare might have been influenced by Chaucer's treatment of the legend. When Macbeth is about to go into Duncan's bedroom to kill him, he walks "with his stealthy pace, / With Tarquin's ravishing strides, towards his design" (Act II, Scene I).
47 Edwards, *Death in Ancient Rome*, 182.
48 Donaldson, *The Rapes of Lucretia: A Myth and Its Transformations*, 9.
49 Schwebel, "Livy and Augustine as Negative Models," 35.

The reference to Augustinian compassion at the beginning of the legend (1690) is equally important and dialogic since it shows Chaucer deliberately transforming a well-known passage from *De Civitate Dei*. In this text, Augustine wonders why Lucretia deserves so much praise if she has committed adultery, and questions the reason for her death if she has remained chaste.[50] The dilemma posed by Lucretia's situation has been a topic of discussion in societies dominated by religion for centuries, and although Ovid does not accuse Lucretia of anything in his *Fasti*, his view of the matter is not as open in *Ars amatoria*. He alludes several times to female resistance as a façade hiding pleasure (I. 657–80), a remark that does not suit Chaucer who rejects it, decides to vindicate Lucretia and to synthesize these different traditions within a pathetic narrative poem questioning the contrast between written authority and the experience of the real world. It is after all Collatinus's need to see rather than trust words ("it is no nede / To trowen on the word, but on the dede"; 1706–7) that introduces the wolf into the sheepfold. And by suggesting at the end of the legend that Lucretia is a Christian saint, Chaucer addresses both Augustine and Livy, who is personally named by the poet as a witness to her martyrdom:

> . . . she was holden there
> A seynt, and ever hir day yhlwed dere
> As in hir lawe: and thus endeth Lucresse,
> The noble wyf, as Tytus bereth witnesse.
> (1870–73)

Chaucer deliberately misrepresents "the grete Austyn" by announcing that he has "gret compassioun / Of this Lucresse" (1690–91), but he also "rewrites the story of Lucretia so that it accords with Augustine's purported compassion, depriving Augustine of any legitimate reason for feeling anything but this sentiment."[51]

Lucretia's suicide, therefore, marks the logical conclusion of the legend by representing the triumph of pathetic virtue. The poet has consistently painted the portrait of a delicate and vulnerable woman, the very type of ladies that tradition and conventions would have placed under Tarquinius's protection. Instead of behaving as a protector, Tarquinius succumbs to his desires and breaks a sacred code. Lucretia, however, has remained faithful to those values and prefers death, which turns her into the symbol of literary pathos. Northrop Frye remarks

---

50 Saint Augustine, *De Civitate Dei*, 1:19.
51 Schwebel, "Livy and Augustine as Negative Models," 41.

that pathos in low-mimetic tragedies[52] shows the hero—often a woman or a child—as being isolated and weak, which inevitably attracts our sympathy. He/she must face a ruthless adversary who feeds on the virtues of a victim fallen under his power.[53] The passivity and helplessness of the victim reinforce the pathetic mode and turn Lucretia into the perfect representative of those good women. But more importantly, the end of the legend forces Chaucer's audience to be cautious of the multiplicity of authorial accounts of a story. He rejects Livy's and Augustine's versions, follows Ovid, but adds many elements to the legend. In doing so, he effectively defends the virtue of Lucretia, but also rewrites her story to match his mission in *LGW*. But can we not consider that it makes him once again guilty of resembling the men of the legends? His task is not only to praise women, but also to versify their betrayal. In the case of Lucretia, it is praise that leads to her rape. The need to distance himself from his penance is here getting stronger and will greatly accelerate the denouement of *LGW*.

With *The Legend of Hypsipyle and Medea* and *The Legend of Lucretia*, Chaucer has produced two completely different narratives and effects. He easily moves from comedy to pathos and shows his intent to compose a work in which each poem is endowed with a voice of its own. Though he apparently continues to respect the terms of his penance, in the next legends he shifts first to a parodic and then to an ironic vision of the lives of these scorned women, but also of the literary tradition from which they spring.

From Parody to Irony

After having involved us emotionally in *The Legend of Lucretia*, Chaucer had to lead us in an entirely new direction with the following legend. He thus opposes to the intensity of *Lucretia*, *The Legend of Ariadne* whose relationship with its sources explains both the tone of the poem and its approach to the collection's theme.

Chaucer's sources for this legend constitute a rare literary imbroglio. Even if he obviously draws from Book VII of the *Metamorphoses* and the tenth epistle of the *Heroides*, the rest of the poem takes elements from the *Ovide moralisé*,

---

52 Northrop Frye establishes in the first essay of his *Anatomy of Criticism* a theory of modes allowing a definition of a work of fiction based on the actions of its heroes. He proposes five distinct modes: mythic, romantic, high-mimetic, low-mimetic, and ironic. In the high-mimetic mode, the hero is superior to other men but not to his environment. It is the traditional mode used in tragedies and sagas. The low-mimetic mode, on the other hand, features a hero whose humanity we share, which often corresponds to comic and realistic fictions.
53 Frye, *Anatomy of Criticism*, 38–39.

the *Teseida*, Boccaccio's *Genealogia deorum gentilium*, the Italian translation by Filippo Ceffi of Ariadne's letter to Theseus in the *Heroides*, or even from the *Jugement dou Roy de Navarre* and the *Aeneid*, among others. This variety of influences shows Chaucer's will not to limit himself to a monologic vision of his subject, but to produce as much variety as possible.

He thus devotes the opening of the legend to a long exposition scene in which he sums up the mythological context of the narrative. He mentions the opposition between Minos and the Athenians (1894–901), the siege of Megara on the isthmus of Corinth (1902–7), Scylla's betrayal (1908–21), the Minotaur's sacrifices (1928–37), but also keeps on bringing into play what is left unsaid. Chaucer indeed ignores information that the other authors would have mentioned, which inevitably conditions our reading of the legend. The tone is apparently serious in this first part, and the narrator's words do not seem openly ironic or pathetic. On the contrary, he seems satisfied with giving us the background necessary to our understanding of the betrayal to come. Yet only someone having a global aesthetic view of Ariadne's myth might notice the gap between Chaucer's sources and the manipulation of facts in this exposition. The *Metamorphoses* and the *Ovide moralisé* took advantage, for instance, of that introductory sequence to present the characters of Ariadne and Theseus, yet Chaucer does things his own way. Unlike them, he plays with appearances. He thus turns Minos, the judge of souls, and his grandson Minos, king of Crete, into the same person (1886),[54] transforms Scylla into another scorned woman, and completely ignores the unholy love between Pasiphae and the white bull. But by modifying the betrayal by Scylla, who out of love for Minos caused the death of her father and the sack of Megara, Chaucer seems to want to prepare us for the return of the collection's theme, while his intertext and use of evasions urge us to read this transformation differently. Scylla, Ariadne, and Phaedra are consequently no longer women betrayed by their lover, but rather princesses who willingly betray their father and king and are eventually hit by the backwash.

Once this exposition is over, Chaucer starts to develop his narrative around dialogues. He obviously draws from the soliloquies in the *Ovide moralisé* here, and thus offers a much more open narrative. Nonetheless, this dialogic staging of discourse in the narrative contributes to the development of an increasingly ironic tone, based on the contrast between appearances, supported by speech, and reality. Chaucer accordingly dedicates 160 lines out of 341 to discursive interactions between the main protagonists.

---

[54] The confusion between the two is not specific to Chaucer and belongs to the mythological tradition, yet his decision to create one Minos is not accidental here.

In doing so, he accentuates the dramatic effect from the *Ovide moralisé*, which merely produced long monologues. In other words, Chaucer prefers here dialogic interactions rather than monologic ones. This exchange articulated around three distinct voices raises the possibility of creating much more dramatic scenes, but Chaucer never exploits this possibility. Whereas a real interaction between the characters would have been interesting narratively and emotionally, the poet lets the situation get stuck and distances himself from the novelistic dimension of the myth. Frank remarks that unlike what we might expect, Chaucer

> has made the dialogue curiously circumstantial and prosy. Further, the characters emerging in these speeches are inappropriate for the romantic situation in which they are cast. Finally, and most comprehensively, the tone of these speeches and of the whole middle section is wrong for our preconceptions.[55]

Phaedra describes, for example, her plan to save Theseus with so many details and such precision that killing the Minotaur and finding one's way in the labyrinth seem easy. Yet this quirky tone is generated by the context in which Ariadne and Phaedra hear Theseus's laments. Chaucer explains that

> The tour there as this Theseus is throwe
> Doun in the botom derk and wonder lowe,
> Was joynynge in the wal to a foreyne;
> And it was longynge to the doughtren tweyne
> Of Mynos, that in hire chaumbers grete
> Dwellten above, toward the mayster-strete
> (1960–65)

The word "foreyne" can be defined as "privy."[56] This notion of a toilet connecting via a single shaft Theseus's dungeon and the apartments of Ariadne and Phaedra is, besides, the only explanation for the fact that they can hear him (1967–71). It would be difficult even for Chaucer to produce a chivalric atmosphere out of a speech heard from the latrines. In effect, the situation is quite unsuitable within a narrative about love and defines the rest of the legend, almost prefiguring the shattering of the romance vision in *The Merchant's Tale*. Chaucer thus moves here to a complete parody of the chivalric novel.

Theseus is, after all, a male figure whose characteristics we now recognize. The image of the hero risking his life and saved by a lady he then takes advantage of before leaving her is a motif we have seen several times in *LGW*. But this time, Chaucer decides to insist on the selfishness at the heart of the relation

---

55 Frank, *Chaucer and The Legend of Good Women*, 115.
56 Chaucer, *The Riverside Chaucer*, 1250.

between a hero in danger and his lady. For what makes Theseus, Jason, or even Aeneas despicable is their ingratitude, their lack of respect for a convention of the chivalric novel, namely the *quid pro quo*. The good women portrayed by Chaucer give generously and accordingly have the right to expect something in return, whether it is marriage or a sign of love. This notion of exchange is central to this genre. *Sir Gawain and the Green Knight* turns it, for example, into the central element of the narrative. In the *Libeaus Desconus*, Gawain's son also accepts to kiss a monstrous creature who then turns into a rich and beautiful young girl. There are many examples of the convention in medieval literature and it is therefore not surprising to see Chaucer using it as well.

The relationship between Ariadne, Phaedra, and Theseus is thus essentially articulated around this notion of exchange and gives to their conversation a strangely interested and anti-romantic dimension. Both sisters have pity for Theseus, but we are far from the pity felt by Dido. They do not care that a stranger might be devoured by the Minotaur, but Theseus is a prince, and it would be a shame if he were to end like this (1974–84). Phaedra thus exposes her plan coldly, letting reason speak and not passion; she describes to her sister all the stages of the rescue with a precision evoking a thief about to rob a bank. And although this long description of her plan (1987–2024) then allows Chaucer to summarize the fight against the Minotaur in only six lines (2144–49), it also destroys Theseus's heroism: "There is no sharp edge to his actions, presented so prosily by a shrewd-minded lady: a ball of wax and tow, to stick in the monster's teeth. It might almost have come out of *Mrs. Beeton's Household Management*."[57] Besides, Theseus does very little to improve the situation and looks increasingly like the capon of *Hypsipyle and Medea*. Phaedra indeed repeats several times to Ariadne that she doubts his courage (1993–96, 2002, 2024) and when the jailer brings them Theseus, the hero acts in a surprising way. He drops to his knees and for forty-four lines swears to the sisters that he will renounce his heritage, will serve them "as a wreche unknowe" (2034), and will be a page until the end of his days if they save his life (2029–73). Humility is one thing, but falling so low to save one's life is a completely different matter and Ariadne accordingly refuses to accept that a prince might serve them in such a way. The conversation then takes an even more interested turn: since Theseus is ready for anything to survive, Ariadne offers to marry him. This would both avoid the death of a prince and profit Ariadne since "ye ben as gentil born as I, / And have a reaume, nat but faste by" (2090–91). Theseus begrudgingly

---

57 Frank, Chaucer and The Legend of Good Women, 121.

accepts the deal and delivers an even more ridiculous speech in which he pretends that he has secretly loved Ariadne for seven years although he had never seen her before (2114–22).

Chaucer thus distorts another aspect of the chivalric novel: love for a stranger living in a distant kingdom is a recurring element in the genre, but it does not seem sincere coming from Theseus, who has already shown us he is ready for anything to get out of prison. Ariadne then arranges a double marriage, asking her sister to marry Theseus's son. Chaucer here radically transforms the image of Ariadne and turns this mythological figure supposed to represent feminine virtue into a potential wife of Bath:

> . . . "Now syster myn," quod she,
> "Now be we duchesses, bothe I and ye,
> And sekered to the regals of Athenes,
> And bothe hereafter likly to ben queens."
> (2126–29)

In this second part of the legend, Chaucer therefore parodies the materialism at the heart of *quid pro quo*. Love is never considered by the protagonists, who are more interested in the reward than in a disinterested act of generosity. As a result, when Theseus slays the Minotaur and leaves his dungeon, he does not forget to take his wife's dowry (2150–51) but then makes a stop on his journey to abandon a sleeping Ariadne on a desert island. He prefers to elope with Phaedra who is much more beautiful than her sister, according to the narrator (2170–75). Yet, after a parodic central section, Chaucer concludes the legend with a distressing return of pathos: there is indeed nothing comical in Ariadne's cries of sadness, as she desperately attempts to call Theseus. Her screams are only echoed by the rocks: her isolation is total, her misery absolute, and the danger deadly (2164–207).

Chaucer's linking of parody with pathos was risky, but his desire to produce a polyvocal and pluristylistic work prevailed, at the expense of purely aesthetic concerns. Ariadne represents the very image of the young girl wishing to live the experience of a chivalric novel; the ambiguity of the legend stems from that desire. Chaucer has shown since the beginning of *LGW* the contrast between conventions and reality, between words and experience; Ariadne is no exception. The parody and pathos of the legend come from her will to experience this novelistic way of life while Chaucer has violently extracted her from the mythological context that would have permitted this realization. The knowledge inherited from these "olde appreved stories" (F and G. 21) spills out of the narrative frame of the legend and allows Chaucer to ridicule their conventions and to weep for the consequences of their illusoriness.

If the association of parodic and pathetic tones gave Chaucer the possibility to explore another aspect of his theme and question the authority of words in *The Legend of Ariadne*, with *Philomela* he attempts to transmit his message with a different voice.

The details of the legend were well known during the Middle Ages, yet Chaucer does not mention his sources. Even if the *Metamorphoses* are probably central, Chaucer transforms the myth of Philomela and Tereus to the point that it is unrecognizable. While the original myth is composed of three episodes (rape, infanticide, metamorphosis), the poet only includes the first event so as to make Philomela fit the template of his collection. To that end, he sums up Procne's abduction, her rape, and mutilation, but refuses to mention the sisters' revenge. Chaucer consequently dissects the narrative by abandoning or weakening the most horrific sequences: Tereus's passion is, for instance, presented in a trivial way (2292–93), the fact that he cuts off Procne's tongue is also summarized in a few words ("And with his swerd hire tonge of kerveth he"; 2334), while his hypocrisy with respect to Philomela is described in one sentence (2342–44). In addition, he remains discreet about the final passion leading to a vengeance he does not wish to mention.

The Legend of Philomela is thus a remarkable work showing Chaucer's abilities as a short narrative writer. Nonetheless, though Chaucer does not manage to involve us emotionally in the narrative, his cursory treatment of the myth implies a highly revealing irony. The silencing of Procne cannot but remind us of the narrator's own silence, as he confesses in the first lines of the legend that to look into the story of Philomela and Tereus infects us and darkens our eyes: "Yit last the venym of so longe ago, / That it enfecteth hym that wol beholde / The storye of Tereus, of which I tolde" (2241–43). He seems to refuse to assume his auctorial responsibility; yet Chaucer manages, just like Procne, to find a way to communicate. Silence is sometimes more eloquent than a long speech, and the irony arising from the gap between what is said and what intertextuality suggests turns *The Legend of Philomela* into a new questioning of the responsibility of expression and writing, of the influence of words and of reading.[58]

Let us take as an example the disappearance of the revenge episode. When Philomela learns her sister's fate, she pretends that is going on pilgrimage but instead saves Procne; and whereas tradition follows this with a particularly violent and horrific scene, namely Tereus's unknowingly eating his son, Chaucer only notes that "[t]he remenaunt is no charge for to telle" (2383). In doing so, he adheres to the Prologue's instructions and tells us at the same time that if

---

58 Chaucer, *Les Contes de Canterbury et autres œuvres*, 1370.

the sisters had not gone so far, their story would have been worthy of the greatest hagiographic narratives. But by ignoring this unnatural act, Chaucer shows that its telling would turn two saintly women into infanticides: it is the intertextual relationship between Chaucer's silence and the literary tradition that allows him to "say" without necessarily spreading that venom. He leaves it all to us. Just as Procne weaved a web to tell the horrors she endured, Chaucer weaves a web connecting his poem to a larger tradition and accordingly shows the corruption of this myth without ever assuming the responsibility of the enunciation.

Narrative Posture and Ironic Conclusion

At this stage of the collection, one may rightfully wonder if Chaucer will still be capable of surprising us with the rest of the legends. The pattern is after all clear: a man is usually saved by a woman whom he seduces before abandoning her. Yet, after having played with comedy, pathos, parody, and irony, Chaucer proposes with *The Legend of Phyllis* a narrative whose comedy does not depend on the characters' situation, but rather on the narrator's ambiguous posture.

The direction to give to this particular legend was obvious for Chaucer given the popularity of its character. Besides the second epistle of the *Heroides*, her love for Demophon is mentioned in the *Ars amatoria* (Book II), the *Roman de la Rose* (13211–14), John Gower's *Confessio amantis* (IV. 731–878), and of course *The Book of the Duchess* (728–31) and *The House of Fame* (I. 388–96). It is precisely this abundance of options that forces Chaucer to distance himself from his sources: he places the male character at the heart of the narrative and modifies the tone of the poem, just like in *Hypsipyle and Medea*. He draws a distinction, for example, between Demophon and Jason, and insists on the importance of inheritance; Demophon is indeed Theseus and Phaedra's son and represents for Chaucer the proof that "wiked fruit cometh of a wiked tre" (2395). Comedy here does not come from his behavior, but rather from the fact that he is his father's son, and Chaucer insists that it is in men's nature to be unfaithful in love (2448–51).

As a result, Chaucer produces a refined narrative in which he accumulates rhetorical figures meant to shorten the development of the story. He does not even try to turn Phyllis into a "good woman" and speedily describes the encounter, romance, and betrayal sequences in about thirty lines in which the young woman becomes a caricature. When Demophon's ship runs aground on Phyllis's lands (2427–37), he is welcomed with honor at the court, and while his inherited traits should be apparent to all ("lyk his fader of face and of stature, / And fals of love"; 2446–47), Phyllis has nothing better to do than fall in love with him.

Chaucer actually confesses with very little solemnity that "[t]his honurable Phillis doth hym chere; / Hire liketh wel his port and his manere" (2452–53). The legend's comedic dimension comes from her inability to see Demophon's true nature, a situation that greatly exasperates the narrator who is now "agorted herebyforn" (2454). He does not even develop Phyllis's character or her relationship with Demophon, and since Chaucer takes a shortcut that spares us the details of the romance, we find ourselves with the portrait of a rather silly woman offering no resistance to the charms of this stranger and who only starts to react after he is gone. Chaucer's mocking tone makes it difficult for the audience to have pity for Phyllis. Her suicide is in effect presented with little empathy and in just a few words: "She was hire owene deth ryght with a corde" (2485).

And yet, the legend does not end with Phyllis's death for although the narrator refuses to waste the ink of a quill to write about Demophon again, he does mention the letter that Phyllis addressed to him—a risky sequence that was highly pathetic in the *Heroides*. The narrator nonetheless chooses "[a] word or two, althogh it be but lyte" (2495) and just when the atmosphere is about to become too solemn, he interrupts Phyllis by saying that her letter is too long. But he does not miss the opportunity to ironically reinforce the connection with the rest of *LGW* by quoting the passage in which Phyllis mentions Theseus's lack of loyalty (2543–47).

Heedless of her honor, Phyllis has accordingly shown little resistance or good sense and understands her mistake too late. The narrator's exasperation—perceived by many critics as a sign of Chaucer's boredom—with Phyllis's inability to notice what everyone else can see produces a mocking irony that can only make us smile. This new betrayal even reinforces the idea that disloyalty is typical of men and that only a fool would still trust them. Yet the narrator wants to reassure women that he is different: if there is indeed one man on earth they can trust, it is him (2561). One may feel that he is particularly "eager to distance himself from the victimization of women and from his own poetic task."[59] More importantly, the interruption in which he states his boredom (2454–58) makes it clear that he wants to get the legends moving in the direction of "deliberately bad poetry: the narrator breaks off one tale ... but does so in repetitive, meandering lines that counteract any sense of speed."[60] Chaucer says he can be trusted, is getting tired of the dilemma in which he finds himself, and wants to get on with his task. The question would then be to know if one can really

---

[59] Dumitrescu, "Beautiful Suffering and the Culpable Narrator," 118.
[60] Ibid.

trust a narrator who has proved he can manipulate people, and who has already violated several times the terms of his penance.

Chaucer seems to give an answer to that question with the last narrative in an apparently unfinished collection, *The Legend of Hypermnestra*. This last attempt to paint the picture of a virtuous woman is in many ways representative of the collection's aim. *Hypermnestra* is in effect a gem of narrative brevity and inventiveness: although the author draws from the fourteenth epistle of the *Heroides*, known for its lyricism, and uses elements borrowed from Boccaccio and Hyginus, he definitely frees himself from the "sixty bokes olde and newe" (G. 273) supposed to form his corpus. He never mentions his influences, but entirely remodels the myth, not in order that his heroine might fit the pattern of *LGW* but to reinforce the plot.

To this end, Chaucer takes those elements that are at the heart of Ovid's version, such as the order to kill during the wedding night, the father's threat, Hypermnestra's reflection, but ignores everything that would broaden the frame of his poem. Whereas Ovid mentioned, for instance, the wedding of Aegyptus's fifty sons to the fifty daughters of his brother Danaus, Chaucer inverts the names of the brothers and focuses on Hypermnestra's marriage with her cousin Lynceus.[61] In doing so, he increases the intensity of his narrative: always ready to remind us that cheating is a male characteristic, the narrator does mention the numerous offspring of the two brothers (2562–72), but remarks that most of them are largely illegitimate. Hypermnestra is accordingly described as the "ryghte daughter" (2628) that Danaus had with "his ryghte wyf" (2573). Besides, the insistence on the characters' predestination gives the story a suspense that greatly galvanizes the narrative. The influence of the stars and gods here becomes a remarkable tool used to rapidly characterize Hypermnestra: we learn, for instance, that Venus granted her beauty, while Jove gave her "conscience, trouthe, and drede of shame, / And of hyre wifhod for to kepe hire name" (2586–87). Venus's strength however reduced Mars's power, which explains why Hypermnestra will later be incapable of using a knife for evil purposes. Chaucer manages here to motivate the future actions of his character while engaging our sympathies for a young woman whose tragic fate has been decided since the day of her birth.

The narration thus continues, and the two cousins are quickly married. And while everything seems to be fine, Aegyptus calls for Hypermnestra and makes a speech sounding at first like the words of a loving father on his daughter's

---

61 By reversing the roles (Aegyptus becomes Hypermnestra's father instead of Danaus), he shows once more that one man is no better than the other.

wedding night. After having confessed how much he loves her ("So nygh myn herte nevere thyng ne com"; 2631) he tells her he dreamt that one of his nephews would one day be his undoing and that she has to cut Lynceus's throat while he sleeps or she will never leave the palace alive (2641–46). The shock produced by this declaration is as violent for Hypermnestra, who starts to tremble, as it is for the audience since we suddenly realize that the tragic fate mentioned earlier is about to fall upon her. This desire to move by shock and horror is once again specific to Chaucer. His exposition scene becomes all the more important when connected to this speech, for Chaucer's tightening of the context around a single marriage makes Aegyptus's declaration even more dramatic. And as if it were not enough, Aegyptus illustrates the threat hanging over Hympermnestra's head, like the sword of Damocles, by presenting the blade "as rasour kene" (2654) with which she must kill Lynceus. Hypermnestra thus remains faithful to the role dictated to her by fate and despite her frailty and isolation (2680–83), refuses to carry out such a terrible deed. She chooses to remain faithful to her nature and husband and wakes him up so that he might escape Aegyptus's wrath.

Chaucer here opposes to the mocking tone of *Phyllis* a pseudo-pathetic narrative in which the characters are subjected to an omnipresent predestination. Hypermnestra is innocent, fragile, alone in a hostile world in which she is manipulated either by her father's authority or by fate. Yet, Chaucer nuances the pathos of the legend by sparing us the despair of his heroine. She is in a position of evident weakness, but acts bravely, something that distinguishes her from pathetic figures like Lucretia. As we have seen, Chaucer refuses to present his theme in the same way twice throughout *LGW*. As a result, his re-use of pathos accompanies a more realistic presentation of the events:

> We are given the illusion that this is something that happened, a real occasion, if you wish, in which considerations of reality operate. It is not a monstrous world in which passions are out of control or where miracles of virtue are performed.[62]

Nevertheless, although Hypermnestra is condemned by her father's madness—he perfectly fits the ruthless adversary describes by Frye[63]—Chaucer insists that it is Lynceus's selfishness that provokes her death. That is in fact not surprising: he is after all the son of a particularly unfaithful man and there is no reason why he would not reproduce a behavior inscribed in his genes. He is not however as clever or cunning as his predecessors in the collection. On the contrary, Chaucer

---

62 Frank, *Chaucer and The Legend of Good Women*, 167.
63 Frye, *Anatomy of Criticism*, 39.

draws a rather comical portrait of a man drugged during his wedding night, and who sees no shame in climbing out on the gutter and running away ("This Lyno swift was, and lyght of fote, / And from his wif he ran a ful good pas"; 2711–12), leaving his wife in the hands of murderers. Would the narrator really be the only man women can trust? Lynceus's flight seems to confirm he truly is an exception, and yet his own behavior is noticeably irresponsible. He leaves us in effect with an unfinished collection that ends with a narrative that lacks a real conclusion. As so often in Chaucer's poems, closure leads to irresolution.

The "conclusioun" of *LGW* thus directly echoes the *House of Fame* and reminds us of the poet's love for rhetorical games that "encourage us to re-examine our sense of how a poem's ending relates to its meaning."[64] The use of the word "conclusioun" at the end of *Hypermnestra* both concludes the tale and ironically the sentence imposed by Aegyptys ("Tak this to thee for ful conclusioun"; 2646). Since Chaucer ends the legend and the collection by repeating this word, he establishes a parallel between Hypermnestra and his own sentence. Chaucer's resistance to traditional closure, to the literary conventions of his time, and to the terms of his penance here turns this absence of resolution into a form of "anti-closure"[65] and evokes rather the finished incompletion of the human condition.[66] In fact, as Dor wonders, "[n]e s'agirait-il pas plutôt d'un jeu visant à créer cette impression, digne conclusion d'un légendaire qui a souligné la duplicité des apparences?"[67] This notion of game thus seems central in Chaucer's creative process, particularly in a work like *LGW* in which he obviously enjoys manipulating conventions and cheating his audience:

> In his writings, Chaucer often casts himself in the role of "jogelour," a word which, besides suggesting "trickster," is a variant of "jangler," or false speaker. . . . [L]ike the juggler who is able to keep in motion several objects simultaneously, Chaucer challenges the appearance of things.[68]

The poet tries to stimulate us, to force us to get involved in the reading process at the heart of his poems. And he increasingly does this by turning into a trickster. He invited us to get involved, yet now anyone who would impose meaning and closure on his text would become similar to the god of Love, condemned

---

64 McGerr, *Chaucer's Open Books*, 1.
65 Delany, *The Naked Text*, 236.
66 Rowe, *Through Nature to Eternity*, 108–23.
67 "[W]ould it not rather be a game aiming at creating this impression, worthy conclusion of a collection that underlined the duplicity of appearances?" Chaucer, *Les Contes de Canterbury et autres œuvres*, 1374.
68 Reiss, "Ambiguous Signs and Authorial Deceptions in Fourteenth-Century Fiction," 124–25.

for his tyranny, or any of the men of the collection who seek their own ends—Tarquinius claims for example "What ende that I make, it shal be so" (1774). With *LGW* Chaucer is engaging in *reductio ad absurdum* to defend his polyphonic vision of the world. After having assured us of his trustworthiness, the narrator, in fact, imitates Lynceus and runs away, leaving us bewildered with Hypermnestra whose wedding night clearly did not go as planned.

The Legend of Good Women consequently represents an entirely new literary experience for Chaucer. At first hesitant, he gradually gains confidence in the potential of short narrative writing. His decision to abandon his old literary ground and to exercise his hand at something new is remarkable, for although he had already been innovative in *TC*, he had reached the limits of what could be achieved with courtly love poetry. The ending of *Hypermnestra* is representative of *LGW*: apparently written as a palinode, the collection is in fact composed of different styles and genres, presenting the many faces of amorous passion and showing via this hybridization of elements the contrast between literary conventions and the real world. It is precisely this highlighting of hybridization as a vector of polyphony that led the way to the extradiegetic dialogue of the *Canterbury Tales*.

Chaucer's narration cannot accordingly escape this theme: he progressively departs from the instructions received in the Prologue and goes so far as to mock the fate of certain good women. Once again, Chaucer makes the game into the very heart of this hybridization. Pandarus's remark in *Troilus and Criseyde* ("Here bygynneth game"; I. 868) had already allowed us to connect the hunt, central in *fin'amor* poetry, with the game of love. But Chaucer accentuates this effect here by taking part in the game: his narrator feigns boredom, plays with the conventions and takes evident pleasure in modifying his legends so as to offer a whole range of sensations and reactions. The hybridization is thus carried forward by the poet's desire to play with his art: with each legend, Chaucer is learning how to develop this new type of writing and innovates in order to escape the rules of the poetical game. By jumping over the wall of Déduit's garden in the Prologue, he leaves *fin'amor* behind him and announces his desire to create situations in which his characters would progress beyond the limits of the courtly code. In doing so, he assumes a new independence driven by the potential of short narrative poetry and eventually becomes himself a representation of the disloyal lover. Having delivered his message, the narrator concludes his collection with a final narrative spin and, taking advantage of Lynceus's flight, disappears as well.

Chapter 6
Extradiegetic Dialogue in *The Canterbury Tales*

Chaucer's inventiveness and originality allowed him to transcend his literary influences in *The Legend of Good Women*. The collection remains, however, nothing more than a transition between the lyrical and rhetorical accomplishment that is *Troilus and Criseyde* and the poetical monument represented by the *Canterbury Tales*. Frank's allusion to Chaucer composing *LGW* with a hand tied behind his back is a pretty good depiction of the particular character of this work.[1] Indeed, with each new legend Chaucer learned how to restructure a story, where to cut and when to amplify, how to characterize an action or a character with a few strokes of the quill. All these skills later became essential: by forcing himself to compose short narrative poems that departed from the traditional conventions of courtly love poetry, Chaucer progressively acquired the artistic maturity that would be necessary for the creation of his "comedye" (*TC*. V. 1788).[2]

In the *Canterbury Tales*, Chaucer adapted the linguistic structure of *LGW* to the pilgrimage narrative frame. Critics have long established a connection between the *Canterbury Tales* and Boccaccio's *Decameron*. Frederick Biggs notes, for instance, that Chaucer learned a new way of writing from novellas 1, 2, and 10 of the Eighth Day. He would no longer retell a story, but create new narratives based on disparate elements. More importantly, Biggs notes that his "tales would stand in dialogue with each other just as Boccaccio's *novelle* develop a more complex discussion of the relationship between morality and class by telling the same story in different economic settings."[3] In addition to this very important notion for what I will call in this chapter an extradiegetic dialogue, both collections present some formal similarities. But they also remain quite different from one another. Chaucer, for instance, insists on inviting various social classes on his pilgrimage, which gives his company more variety than the group of aristocrats traveling in the *Decameron*. He also takes the time to present and describe each pilgrim, playing with the contrasts, nuances, and similarities between them and makes sure that the tales are told on the road, not during the stops.

---

1 Frank, *Chaucer and The Legend of Good Women*, 186.
2 Having completed his tragedy of Troilus, Chaucer hoped to turn his talents to comedy; the *Canterbury Tales* is the result of this "turn." Chaucer's use of the words *tragedie* and *comedie* is interesting since the medieval idea of what constituted these genres was not fixed. They were far from being common terms and Chaucer is considered to be the one who shaped our notions of the genres. See Kelly, *Chaucerian Tragedy*.
3 Biggs, *Chaucer's Decameron*, 107.

This characteristic is especially interesting since it gives the poet the opportunity to reinforce the structure of his creation, allowing his readers to pass from one motif to another through the unifying chronotope of the road. Chaucer has indeed shown, in his previous works, his intent to describe a multifarious and moving world, freed from the verticality and rigidity of a more conventional form of literature. The chronotope of the road is, as a result, Chaucer's most suitable tool to give his poem a narrative stability that *LGW* did not necessarily possess while expanding the horizontality and polyphony of his narration. For it is only on the road, at the same spatiotemporal juncture, that the paths of people belonging to different classes, situations, religions, nationalities, and ages can meet. As Bakhtin points out, people usually separated by social hierarchy or distance can meet each other on the road and create all sorts of contrasts. It is there that a variety of fates can collide or mingle.[4] Chaucer's stylistic variation and multiplication of vocalities in the *Canterbury Tales* may thus well be seen, as Strohm noticed, as a response to factionalism within his social experience, which turns the aesthetic project of his last work into a social one:

> Viewed in relation to this challenge, Chaucer's aesthetic enterprise of defining a literary space that permits free interaction of different forms and styles may be placed in reciprocal relation with the social enterprise of defining a public space hospitable to different social classes with diverse social impulses.[5]

The chronotope of the road is consequently a fundamental element in the development of the novelistic genre, and it is accordingly no surprise to see the Earl of Wicklow, in his 1950 introduction to *The Old Curiosity Shop*, describe Chaucer and Dickens as "kindred spirit[s]" and "artists of the road."[6] Whether one is thinking of the ancient novel of manners or travel literature, or of picaresque, romantic, historical, or chivalric novels, all make use of this particular chronotope. The road might sometimes be metaphorized, but it always remains the dynamic principle of the novel, whether its author is called Cervantes, Daniel Defoe, Henry Fielding, Walter Scott, or Alexander Pushkin. It might be dominated by fortune and chance, yet it rarely crosses the borders of the hero's country. Bakhtin makes clear that the exoticism of this chronotope is social, in contrast with travel narratives.[7] The hero does not cover long distances in exotic faraway lands but stays in his homeland and

---

4 Bakhtin, *Esthétique et théorie du roman*, 384–85.
5 Strohm, *Social Chaucer*, 164.
6 Dickens, *The Old Curiosity Shop*, 1:VII.
7 The road in travel narratives has a similar function but includes the notion of distance, which becomes a chronotope parallel to the road, with its own characteristics.

there discovers, due to his many meetings, the various socio-historical aspects of his country.

This vision of the world was already present in *TC* and is accordingly developed with a greater intensity during this pilgrimage, whose purpose is no longer to respond to Dante's poetical vision but to offer a literary and philosophical alternative to the *Commedia*. The *Canterbury Tales* follows the structure of Dante's journey "[n]el mezzo del cammin di nostra vita"[8] (*Inf.* I. 1) in order to give the pilgrimage a similar philosophical value. In both cases, readers are invited to follow a narrator during a journey whose destination switches from a fixed geographical place to a transfiguration of Canterbury into a "Jerusalem celestial" (*The Parson's Prologue*, 51). Dante's verses remain, however, highly eschatological; he is the poet of beatitude while Chaucer chooses to stay on earth among his fellow human beings. The souls Dante encounters during his journey through Hell, Purgatory, and Heaven no longer possess the capacity to change and can only endure their punishment or enjoy their rewards.

In Chaucer's case, however, one is faced with a resistance to closure and a refusal of monologism and of the conventions and codes that kept driving him further away from the absolute of a theological vision. His pilgrims are part of a completely different dynamic and belong to a temporality allowing even the most despicable of them to repent, should he or she feel the need to. Chaucer does not condemn, nor does he judge his characters, but becomes one of them so as to expose and emphasize the true plurality of the world and of literature. As Taylor remarks, "[w]hereas Dante had written a divine comedy, Chaucer writes an earthly comedy about people still in the process of becoming."[9]

Chaucer embraces the chronotope of the road as a way to lead his work in a new direction and thus transform his pilgrimage into a carnivalesque and liminal occasion. But he also embraces a popular world marked by a polemical representation of the body. Indeed, in medieval thought, the human body was often considered a corrupt vessel, but according to Bakhtin, in everyday life a vulgar and repulsive license actually reigned.[10] Popular texts that celebrate all the various activities linked to the human body, such as laughing, eating, drinking, reproducing, and dying, participate in the folkloric and carnivalesque culture that later became associated with François Rabelais, and they present a vision of a new world. Dante's world and his conception of morality, space, and

---

8 "In the middle of the journey of our life."
9 Taylor, *Chaucer Reads "The Divine Comedy,"* 2–3.
10 Bakhtin, *Esthétique et théorie du roman*, 316–17.

time then only exists because of the irony of poets expressing these views through what could now be defined as a Rabelaisian chronotope.

This is, in other words, how the *Canterbury Tales* compares to *LGW* while assimilating the artistic maturity of *Troilus and Criseyde*. The linguistic frame allowing the hybridization of *LGW* produces here a much more complex form of dialogism. Whereas Chaucer had once produced polyvocality by means of dialogism and carnivalesque laughter, he is now able to develop and enhance this effect by an extradiegetic dialogue inherited from the hybridization of *LGW*. This opposition between a diegetic and extradiegetic dialogue is central: Chaucer's fiction of the pilgrimage and characters actually talking to one another would be consummately diegetic, that is, grounded in real-time physical actions and effects, rather than extradiegetic and independent of the poem's real actions in time and space. It allows the constituent narratives of the tales to comment upon each other, across narrative and generic boundaries that would seem to separate them. The Host's remarks to the pilgrims along the road to Canterbury constitute, by definition, a diegetic dialogue, whereas the dialogic relationship between *The Knight's Tale* and *The Miller's Tale* is extradiegetic. This dimension manifests itself like the symphonic music accompanying a movie in which no orchestra appears: the music connects and enhances the narrative's different feelings and styles in the background, without being necessarily noticed.

The first lines of the *General Prologue* establish a connection with the conclusion of *Troilus and Criseyde*: Chaucer's description of the death of his eponymous hero and his travel to the hereafter provoked a movement from the particular to the infinite, but in the opening of the *Canterbury Tales*, the poet reverses the situation and leads his readers through an inverted movement taking us from a dreamlike description of spring to the interior of the Tabard, with the description of its clients and future pilgrims.

General Prologue: Characterization, Drama, and the Theatrical

When Dryden wrote in his Preface to *Fables, Ancient and Modern* that reading Chaucer's work made him feel like he was encountering his ancestors,[11] he led the way for several generations of critics to look at the "realism" of Chaucer's descriptions. In order to understand the mechanism of the extradiegetic dialogue at

---

[11] "'Tis sufficient to say, according to the proverb, that here is God's plenty. We have our forefathers and great-grandames all before us, as they were in Chaucer's days." Dryden, "Preface to Fables, Ancient and Modern," 7.

the heart of the *Canterbury Tales*, it thus seems necessary to clarify what is Chaucerian realism. In effect, Dryden's—and his followers'—aesthetics allow a dramatic reading of *CT* that is now not only obsolete but also incompatible with this chapter's approach.

According to M.W. Bloomfield, realism "used to refer to a work which reproduces . . . the details of the external reality of the subject, and (to a lesser extent) an objective, unbiased presentation of the inner reality of the human characters who people the story."[12] The way we perceive realism, however, tends to change with time. The Aristotelian definition of mimesis is, for instance, similar to Bloomfield's while giving to the notion a broader meaning. For Aristotle, the artist can represent reality the way it is, seems to be, or the way it should be, so as to imitate or sublimate Nature. This mimetic vision would get us closer to a representation of the world as perceived by the artist at a precise moment. The imitative nature of descriptions would thus be more closely associated with verisimilitude than with "reality," which was then more generally linked with History. Classical culture believed for centuries that the idea of reality could in no way contaminate the conjectural nature of verisimilitude.

Medieval realism,[13] however, differs from its modern or ancient classical counterparts due to its tendency to be more than a simple echo of the world. Curtius insisted that description in a medieval work of fiction is subject to no specific form of realism[14]—and most authors had indeed no trouble in describing lions or olive trees in Scandinavian countries—but rather relies on a discursive and unreferential verisimilitude. As Roland Barthes explains in "The Reality Effect," the only thing that mattered was the "constraint of the descriptive genre" since it was "the generic rules of discourse which lay down the law."[15] Its true purpose was more often to maintain the suspension of disbelief rather than to create a credible representation of the world: the use of a witness narrator or of a dream vision is a way to anchor fiction in verisimilitude. But the bourgeois tradition that developed at the time includes exaggerations and caricatures that turned this verisimilitude into a form of realism that could easily be seen as an imitation of life itself. Chaucer is no Émile Zola, of course, and the realism used in the *Canterbury Tales* could in no way be mistaken for the

---

12 Bloomfield, "Chaucerian Realism," 179.
13 This is not a reference to the philosophical doctrine made popular by Saint Thomas Aquinas's writings but to a literary form of realism.
14 See Curtius, *European Literature and the Latin Middle Ages*, Chapter X.
15 Barthes, "The Reality Effect," 144.

naturalism developed in the Rougon-Macquart series. For what we perceive as realism in *CT* is

> the style of speech appropriate to the interchanges of everyday life. In this sense, "realism" is not only found in the speech of lower-class characters; Pandarus and Criseyde and the Eagle in the *House of Fame* all speak in the style of everyday speech. Indeed, Chaucer suggests the perspectives, objects, sounds, and sights of everyday existence less by extensive description than by the inclusion of certain images and frames of reference in the speech of his characters. Food imagery, domestic imagery, animal imagery, all are found not as fixtures in the Chaucerian landscape, but as "sayings" in the mouths of his characters, usually as proverbs, oaths, or homespun metaphors.[16]

It is not the naturalistic description that is thus important, but rather the language of Chaucer's characters, which [i.e. the language] immerses us in a quotidian existence "embodied in forms of talk that keep us shifting from one plane of social life to another."[17]

In effect, none of the tales presented by Chaucer could be thought of as a realistic narrative taken independently from the rest of the work. Deprived of their narrative frame, these fabliaux, fables, romances, and hagiographies can no longer communicate with each other and collapse, reduced to mere literary experiments. For it is the richness of the world Chaucer invites us into that guarantees the authenticity of his narrative: after having played with dream visions and the pseudo-historical mode of representation, the poet takes here a closer look at the social world he knows so well. He commits himself to accompany us in this pilgrimage and in becoming our referent on the way reinforces the illusion of reality.

Nonetheless, even though Chaucer was capable of rapidly describing the motivations of his characters and of preparing his readers for the denouement—as shown in the use of predestination in *The Legend of Hypermnestra*—his vision of his characters was very different from ours today. Chaucerian characters' acts are defined by their functions, attributed to them by the narrative frame; Troilus and Pandarus accordingly behave like the courtly Amant and Ami. But the fact that we tend to lose sight of this specificity proves Chaucer's ability to create bigger-than-life characters: the social and linguistic realism he develops, and which Dickens later inherited, allows him to soften the outline of his creations and gives them more depth.[18] However, Chaucer's decision to move away from the strict rules of courtly love poetry implied finding a new way to structure his work. Indeed, since

---

16 Ganim, *Chaucerian Theatricality*, 125.
17 Ibid.
18 Chaucer and Dickens shared the same theatricality, the same ability to reproduce realistically the voices of their characters.

his characters no longer corresponded to the conventional literary and familiar types known by his readers, it became necessary to establish, upstream of the beginning of *CT*, an introductory segment that would give us an idea of the pilgrims' functions.[19] This strategy allowed Chaucer to avoid disturbing the delicate balance of his short narratives with long descriptions and even gave him the opportunity to make his characters interact without having to present them again. Dialogism is, as a result, greatly facilitated by an apparently natural cacophony, which is in fact orchestrated by the poet.

GP is often used as an argument supposed to prove the validity of a dramatic reading[20] of the *Canterbury Tales*. And it is true that Chaucer's tendency to have his pilgrims parade before us and to present them like a playwright would with his stage directions tends to reinforce our feeling of verisimilitude. Yet, although establishing a connection between each tale and pilgrim offers pedagogical shortcuts to the teaching of this work, it does not give credibility to the dramatic theory. Indeed, the latter is mainly based on two assumptions: the first is that the connection between the pilgrims and the narrative links provided by the conclusions, prologues, and interruptions is consistent, while the second is that the relation between pilgrim and tale is significant. But as lively as the portraits of the pilgrims may be, they remain only portraits, that is to say, a partial representation of reality and not reality itself, as René Magritte would put it in *La Trahison des images*.

In the end, what we see of the pilgrims and what they tell us about the tales is nothing compared with what the poetics of the tales themselves reveal. And although we can easily picture the pilgrims as living characters, we must not let ourselves be fooled by appearances. Freed from the allegory of love and the courtly love code, Chaucer describes types and functions that may establish a connection between each tale and storyteller. And as Muscatine reminds us, "[n]o medieval poet would have sacrificed all the rich technical means at his disposal merely to make a story sound as if such and such a character were actually telling it."[21] Chaucer thus undertakes to give us "the condicioun / Of ech of hem, so as it semed me, / And whiche they weren, and of what degree" (*GP*. 38–40), focusing mainly on their social or professional functions. Each is a model of efficiency in his/her particular trade and possesses most of its vices or virtues—something inspired by medieval estates satire.

---

[19] Different "real seeming" character types, with exaggerated characteristics, offer Chaucer a basis for polyphony, for a heightened degree of difference and dissonance among characters that leads to radically different speech patterns and styles of utterance.

[20] The idea behind a dramatic reading of *CT* is that pilgrims interact as "personalities," whereas this chapter suggests that they interact polyphonically as different dictions and expressivities and genres.

[21] Muscatine, *Chaucer and the French Tradition*, 172.

The Knight is, for example, an almost idealized representation of his order: he is described as an admirable, noble, and courtly man, a defender of the values of chivalry and always ready to serve his lord (*GP*. 43–47). Although the references to the military campaigns in which he fought allow Chaucer to single him out and to give him a back-story, his military curriculum is actually far too impressive to be believable. He is supposed to have fought with Peter of Cyprus in Alexandria and Turkey (*GP*. 51, 58–59, 64–66), with the Teutonic Knights in Prussia (52–55), and would even have defended the Church, driving back Muslim armies in Spain and North Africa (56–57, 60–63). It thus seems more like a composite portrait gathering the deeds of several different knights, but this description is suddenly rendered more credible by the appearance of his son and squire, who turns out to be the perfect avatar of the courtly lover.

And the same is true for the Friar, who becomes the symbol of corruption and hypocrisy within the Church. Chaucer thus tells us that this merry fellow knew how to be lenient in giving penance when he received silver and was loved by and familiar with "frankeleyns over al in his contree / And eek with worthy wommen of the toun" (*GP*. 216–17). Lepers and beggars were not, according to Chaucer, worthy of his time for there is little honor and profit "[f]or to deelen with no swich poraille" (247)—a rather paradoxical declaration for a Friar! By contrast, he loved to work with rich landowners, or even "selleres of vitaille" (248). And if the descriptions of his greed were not enough, Chaucer explains that this Friar also excelled in the domain of lust:

> In alle the ordres foure is noon that kan
> So muchel of daliaunce and fair langage.
> He hadde maad ful many a mariage
> Of yonge wommen at his owene cost.
> Unto his ordre he was a noble post.
> (210–14)

Nevertheless, this rather typical portrait of a hypocrite at the same time presents Friar Huberd as charismatic, given to harp playing, and affecting a lisp "[t]o make his Englissh sweete upon his tonge" (265). Chaucer thus apparently proposes several generic portraits that are however marked by a characterization reinforcing the verisimilitude of his descriptions. Whether it is the fighting Miller and his unhealthy habit of breaking or heaving doors off their hinges with his head, his wart upon which stood a "toft of herys, / Reed as the brustles of a sowes erys" (555–56), or Prioress Eglentyne's compassion and tears whenever faced with a dead mouse or dog, all these characters come to life before us.

It is therefore not surprising that critics have tried, in the past, to establish a connection between Chaucer's pilgrims and his contemporaries. After all, if the poet has included in his group of fictitious characters real people like himself, Harry Bailly, Roger Knight de Ware—easily recognized by his first name (I. 4345–46) and by the fact that this "Knight" falls off his horse ("This was a fair chyvachee of a cook!"; IX. 50)—he might have done the same with the other pilgrims. And yet, if some characters do seem larger than life there is no doubt that they are actually defined according to characteristics and expectations known to a medieval audience.

The tour de force of Chaucerian realism stands on its ability to mingle "the actual and the ideal, with each lending its qualities to the other, so that the real Harry Bailly becomes a literary creation and the idealized Parson gains a measure of actuality."[22] In other words, Chaucer produces enough concrete details in his description so as to develop what Barthes called a referential illusion: "eliminated from the realist speech-act as a signified of denotation, the 'real' returns to it as a signified of connotations; for just when these details are reputed to *denote* the real directly, all they do—without saying so—is *signify* it."[23] Chaucerian realism produces a reality effect—"the basis of that unavowed verisimilitude which forms the aesthetic of all the standard works of modernity"[24]—that helps those conventional portraits take concrete shape.

Any dramatic reading of *GP*, or of the *Canterbury Tales* as a whole, would, as a result, have to face the fact that those pilgrims are essentially character types and that the scraps of information supposed to individualize them never allow us to understand their personal history and motivations in a modern way. As Benson reminds us, Chaucer's "method is to provide lots of smoke with no certainty that there is a real fire."[25] Each pilgrim is consequently one piece of a larger puzzle and tells us relatively little in the absence of the other elements which, once put together, offer a global vision of the work. Even if certain characters like the Wife of Bath or the Canon's Yeoman contribute to the success of the *Canterbury Tales* by the intensity of their dramatic intervention, they remain in the end dependent on the poem's narrative frame. Indeed, when the Canon and his Yeoman meet the pilgrims on the road, they start talking but after having described his master as a wise and remarkable man (VIII. 599–626), the Yeoman's tone suddenly changes as he starts condemning the Canon's actions (640–50). The interest of this scene does not come from the motivation of the Yeoman or the absence of logic in his words, but from the fact that he rapidly starts getting things off his chest and confesses everything to Harry Bailly. Chaucer has, therefore, no interest whatsoever in the

---

22 Chaucer, *The Riverside Chaucer*, 6.
23 Barthes, "The Reality Effect," 148.
24 Ibid.
25 Benson, *Chaucer's Drama of Style*, 8.

psychological realism of his characters, whether it is in *GP* or in *CT*, but merely creates situations allowing the plot to move on. In this case, he wishes to talk to us about the madness of alchemy and not of one particular alchemist. The situation is thus articulated so as to refer back to the craft itself and its vices, namely deception, and illusion.

A dramatic reading of the *Canterbury Tales* would consequently be as illusory and deceptive as alchemy itself. Despite G.L. Kittredge's belief that the tales are "only speeches that are somewhat longer than common,"[26] the impossibility of reading them as soliloquies, that is to say as the expression of a character's psyche, has to lead us to a different approach. And since the link between tale and storyteller is not always obvious—*The Shipman's Tale* might have been intended for the Wife of Bath, while *MerT* could have been attributed to the Friar according to IV. 1251—it becomes necessary to question the true nature of these short narrative poems. If we recontextualize the *Canterbury Tales*, we quickly understand that it has no stylistic unity. By turning himself into one of the pilgrims on the way to Canterbury—and therefore ceding his role as authoritative *auctor* and speaking subject—the poet makes sure that his voice does not dominate the debate and gives free rein to literary diversity, polyvocality, and polyphony. He moves effortlessly from the rhetoric of the *MerT* to the elegant simplicity of *The Clerk's Tale*, from hagiography to the obscenity and vulgarity of the fabliau and the animal fable. Chaucer puts at the heart of his work the literary unity represented by each tale and not the individuality and depth of his characters: "Chaucer has done nothing less than create a complete and original poetic for each tale. . . . *The Canterbury Tales* is not a dramatic clash of different pilgrims but a literary contest among different poets."[27] Benson thus explains that if Shakespeare changes genres between certain plays, his style remains, however, instantly recognizable. Yet moving from one Chaucer tale to the other is like moving from Shakespeare to Henry James. The possibility of attributing a tale to a particular pilgrim almost becomes immaterial to their stylistic differentiation.

As I mentioned at the beginning of this book, the notion of theatricality proposed by Ganim would be far more suitable than that of the drama. Chaucer's poetry in *CT* is much more dynamic and performative than a typical framed fiction such as the *Decameron*. The very presentation of the tales alters the narratives, which are not just framed but "reframed, reset"[28] by the linguistic structure of *CT*.

---

26 Kittredge, "Chaucer's Discussion of Marriage," 435.
27 Benson, *Chaucer's Drama of Style*, 20.
28 Ganim, *Chaucerian Theatricality*, 5.

A dramatic reading, as I said, would be incompatible with this chapter's approach; a theatrical one would on the contrary explain the dialogue between the tales:

> Given the fiction of the *Canterbury Tales* as talk, as recorded speech, I would stress the illusion of multivocality in Chaucer, not only in the fluctuating relations between teller and tale, but between tale and tale, and between Chaucer and his sources.[29]

Looking at *CT* as a social performance articulated around a linguistic, rather than Gothic, structure gives us the analytical tools necessary to the description of the extradiegetic dialogue.

Dialogism in *The Canterbury Tales* and the Chaucer Pilgrim

Chaucer's persona in the *Canterbury Tales* occupies a special place in his career and although we have discussed the nature of his different poetical incarnations in the previous chapters, the role of the Chaucer pilgrim is too important to be ignored here.

But when considering the role of the Chaucer persona one has to be especially cautious to avoid confusing the two senses of the word "narrator." For Chaucer is the narrator of *CT*, and each of the tales is, in effect, reported speech. But then there is the other Chaucer, the one who orchestrates the whole show. For A.C. Spearing, the word "narrator" "means both the person in the real world who tells a story and the agent within a narrative text by whom its story is told."[30] Of course, every oral narrative must have a narrator, someone who delivers the story, but that person "is not a part of the narrative itself; he or she stands outside it, as the origin of its spoken words. The narrator in this sense, as the performer of an oral narrative, has a real life outside the tale."[31] One may perceive in this definition how the Chaucer of *CT* is both poet and persona: the author at the origin of the spoken words is distinct from a flexible "I" on the road to Canterbury who narrates the events and quotes his traveling companions.

Whereas Chaucer's persona had until now allowed some experimentation with dialogism, the Chaucer pilgrim gives the poet the opportunity to reinforce the connection between his voice and those of his characters. As I mentioned earlier, his role as referent in the poem heightens the reality effect, but also lends credibility to the story and connects the various tales and genres in a much more

---

29 Ganim, Chaucerian Theatricality, 5.
30 Spearing, *Textual Subjectivity*, 18.
31 Ibid.

efficient and lively way than, for instance, in *LGW*. His mere presence guarantees that the author will not impose on us one single vision of the world, one interpretation of his work. And since debate is essential in a polyphonic narrative, he does not offer a narrator seeking to close off debate; on the contrary, as McGerr remarked, he "offers a narrator who is himself explicitly involved in the debate— and who inscribes us in that debate by challenging us to choose which tales we think we should read."[32] The very fact that one is able to read *CT* dramatically proves Chaucer's success: in becoming a pilgrim, the poet invited us to believe in his journey and brought to life a dialogue that would not necessarily capture our attention, for it remains essentially exterior to the diegesis.

This strange character describing his fellow pilgrims in *GP* and who later reappears to tell us *The Tale of Sir Thopas* and *The Tale of Melibee* thus exposes the limits of any dramatic reading while illustrating the literary variety that is at the heart of Chaucer's poetry. For although he constitutes an important anchorage for his audience, we know nothing about him and the rare fragments of information we may glean only come from his contradictory comments and actions. Just as in the other pilgrims' case, the interest of the character lies not so much in his psychological development but rather in his function since Chaucer never intended to turn his persona into a proper novelistic character. On the contrary, "the various portraits of the pilgrims are held loosely together by a nonspecific and flexible 'I' who is capable of adopting many perspectives, even contradictory ones."[33]

He is, as a result, one of the most fascinating characters of the group, for his inconsistency makes him as difficult to define for us as he is for his companions. After having told us that he has easily become a member of the group (*GP*. 30–32), he suddenly moves aside and merely describes and listens to the other travelers. Harry Bailly himself only seems to accidentally notice his presence after *The Prioress's Tale* and says: "'What man artow?' . . . 'Thou lookest as thou woldest fynde an hare, / For evere upon the ground I se thee stare'" (VIII. 695–97). We barely know what to think about this apparently shy fellow whose *naïveté* is reinforced by his admiration for pilgrims whose sins and faults are in complete disagreement with medieval ethics. His portrait of the Pardoner is, for example, especially revealing. The narrator describes him as the best of his order, walking around with relics supposed to make his fortune:

> But with thise relikes, whan that he fond
>   A povre person dwellynge upon lond,
>   Upon a day he gat hym moore moneye

---

[32] McGerr, *Chaucer's Open Books*, 150.
[33] Benson, *Chaucer's Drama of Style*, 27.

>   Than that the person gat in monthes tweye;
>   And thus, with feyned flaterye and japes,
>   He made the person and the peple his apes.
>   (*GP*. 701–6)

There is no doubt that Chaucer, the poet, would have condemned the actions of a man using the Church to make money, but it does not change the fact that those kinds of actions were as widespread as political corruption is today. Nonetheless, whereas one might expect the narrator to simply list the sins of this pilgrim (final judgment being still completely foreign to the Chaucerian philosophy), he adds: "But trewely to tellen atte laste, / He was in chirche a noble ecclesiaste" (*GP*. 707–8).

This relation between an apparently naive and foolish character and a group of people whose morality is often doubtful is another major characteristic of the novelistic genre which Chaucer uses here with more vividness than in his previous poems. Since he could not include a self-portrait in the *GP*, he waits until the end of *PrT* to give us a rather carnivalesque description of himself that reminds us of the portrait of Geffrey and his other incarnations in previous works. Harry Bailly thus tells us he is rather fat ("Now war yow, sires, and lat this man have place! / He in the waast is shape as wel as I"; VII. 699–700), that he would look ridiculous in the arms of a woman ("This were a popet in an arm t'enbrace / For any womman, smal and fair of face"; 701–2), and also that he looks mysterious ("He seemeth elvyssh by his contenaunce"; 703). Even if Chaucer had always used the humility topos and grotesque lowering as a way to lessen the force of his persona, he had until now retained a connection with courtly values. He was never before interested in crooks or thieves, yet we are suddenly faced with four in a row. This association of a foolish character with the social plurality of a group of pilgrims is therefore not accidental. The history of the novelistic genre has shown the importance of the fool or knave figure as a vector of incomprehension that exemplifies linguistic variety in a work of fiction. Bakhtin writes that it is precisely

> sur une petite échelle (dans les menus genres inférieurs, sur les tréteaux de foire, sur les marchés, dans les chansons et les historiettes de la rue) que s'élaborent les procédés de structure permettant de représenter le langage, de l'associer à la figure du locuteur, de le "montrer" objectivement en même temps que l'homme, non point comme un langage universel, impersonnel, mais caractéristique ou socialement typique d'une personne donnée— prêtre, chevalier, marchant, paysan, juriste. . . .[34]

---

[34] "on a small scale (in the lesser genres, at the stalls of fairs, in the markets, in street songs and anecdotes) that are developed the structural processes which make it possible to represent

The Chaucerian persona used in the courtly love poems was often described as a fool unfamiliar with the values of *fin'amor* and not understanding its rules. As a result, he took refuge in his books and eventually learned nothing from his adventures. Now freed from the conventions of courtly love, Chaucer places his narrative persona in a context that allows him to engage with the different classes of fourteenth-century English society and, through medieval estates satire,[35] with hypocrisy, lies, and other forms of language use. This incomprehension is thus fundamentally a dialogic characteristic and that is why it is always connected, in the novel, to discourse:

> [À] sa base se trouve l'incompréhension polémique du discours d'autrui, du mensonge pathétique d'autrui, qui a embrouillé le monde en prétendant l'interpréter, l'incompréhension polémique des langages usuels, canonisés, mensongers, avec les noms pompeux qu'ils donnent aux choses et aux événements—langage poétique, pédantesquement savant, religieux, politique, juridique, et ainsi de suite.[36]

The position of the Chaucer pilgrim gives the poet the opportunity to question the different visions of the world represented by the tales and pilgrims, for the fool is always in a dialogical opposition to a religious, political, or poetical discourse whose nuances he does not entirely understand. It allows the poet to represent different perspectives through the eyes of this character and because he does not comprehend what is obvious to everyone else, it gives the author the chance to externalize and to put those different social languages and their structural logic into perspective. In other words, in turning the *Canterbury Tales* into a comprehensive and multiform reflection of his time, Chaucer set up a linguistic microcosm fulfilling one of the constitutive requirements of the novel genre.

---

language, to associate it to the speaker, to 'show' it objectively at the same time as the man, not as a universal, impersonal language but as being characteristic or socially typical of a given person—priest, knight, merchant, peasant, jurist . . . ." Bakhtin, *Esthétique et théorie du roman*, 213.

35 Chaucer relies partly on the estates tradition; he also builds on and deepens established satirical tropes. He manipulates our reactions. Indeed, as Helen Phillips remarks, "he evokes uncertain, mixed moral signals, rather than the absolute moral abstractions common in estates satire, and creates an illusion of the pilgrims' own viewpoints and their self-presentation" ("Morality in the *Canterbury Tales*, Chaucer's lyrics and the *Legend of Good Women*," 166). See also, Mann, *Chaucer and Medieval Estates Satire*, 89–90.

36 "It is based on the polemical incomprehension of the other's discourse, of the other's pathetic lie, which has confused the world by pretending to interpret it; on the polemical incomprehension of everyday, canonized, untruthful languages and the pompous names they give to things and events: poetical, pedantically learned, religious, political, legal languages, and so on." Bakhtin, *Esthétique et théorie du roman*, 215.

Extradiegetic Dialogue

Presenting all of the tales and the many interruptions, contradictions, and answers that constitute the extradiegetic dialogue of the *Canterbury Tales* would be somewhat redundant. We will thus focus here on a few elements especially revealing of Chaucer's undertaking, namely the tales of the first Fragment (*KnT* and its completing fabliaux), *The Man of Law's Tale*, *The Pardoner's Prologue and Tale* diptych, and the two tales told by the Chaucer pilgrim.

After the presentation of the different clients of the Tabard in *GP*, Harry Bailly proposes to accompany the pilgrims to Canterbury and "to shorte with oure weye" (*GP*. 791) suggests that each member of the group tell two tales on the way. Bailly adds that the icing on the cake would be that the pilgrim having told the best tale would be invited to dinner by the other participants on their way back from Canterbury. The promise of a free meal and the Host's threat that whoever refuses to join in the game would have to pay for the travel expenses of the whole group rather unsurprisingly motivates the narrator's companions. Chance "or sort, or cas" (844) then gives the Knight the opportunity to start the game.

The Knight's Tale is one of the great classics of the Chaucerian canon and is far from being the poet's first attempt to adapt the subject matter of Thebes. *The House of Fame* had already borrowed several elements of its legend, but it is only with *Anelida and Arcite* that Chaucer tried for the first time to transpose this story into English. Although he was not, at the time, able to juggle the conventions of courtly love and the aesthetics of Boccaccio's *Teseida*, resulting in a poem lacking in coherence and narrative efficiency, he rewrote this story years later—he lists it in the Prologue to *LGW*[37]—and adapted the poem to the narrative device of the *Canterbury Tales*. The Knight thus remarks in his first *occupatio*:[38]

> The remenant of the tale is long ynough.
> I wol nat letten eek noon of this route;
> Lat every felawe telle his tale aboute,
> And lat se now who shal the soper wynne;
> (I. 888–91)

---

[37] "And al the love of Palamon and Arcite / Of Thebes, thogh the storye ys knowen lyte" (F. 420–21).
[38] *Occupatio* is a rhetorical device used, in theory, to bring up a subject by denying that it should even be mentioned. But it can also be used to amplify a story by listing all the details that the speaker promises not to mention: see, for instance, *KnT*, 2919–65.

When Boccaccio composed the *Teseida* between 1339 and 1341, he turned this legend into an epic worthy of figuring alongside classics from antiquity such as the *Aeneid* and the *Odyssey*. And it is precisely the epic dimension of the poem that troubled Chaucer for a long time since he did not necessarily share the ambition of his Italian counterpart. He thus tried, at first, to adapt Boccaccio's *ottava rima* in order to accentuate the narrative potential of his poem but despite the introduction of the rhyme royal he did not manage to turn *Anelida and Arcite* into a major narrative work. The situation changed, however, when he started to look at short narratives. Indeed, although *KnT* is one of the longest stories told during the pilgrimage, it is fundamentally marked by the poetical evolution that started with *LGW*.

Chaucer here succeeds in condensing the twelve books of the *Teseida* in 2,249 lines, which naturally implies cutting a few scenes from the original material. Thus, although he gets rid of several battles, whose narrative use was not obvious but which helped defined the epic character of Boccaccio's poem, Chaucer starts this tale by summarizing Theseus's exploits. At this stage of *KnT*, it becomes obvious that this version of Theseus is rather different from the grotesque and ungrateful character we met in *The Legend of Ariadne*. On the contrary, the Duke of Athens is described "[i]n al his wele and in his mooste pride" (I. 895) as the very flower of chivalry. His courage and honor are even illustrated when he swears to two widows that he would avenge the death of their husbands and kill the tyrant king of Thebes, Creon (957–64). Theseus then undertakes to track the Theban king and after having conquered his city, imprisons two young princes wounded in battle, Palamon and Arcite. From then on, the story focuses on the imprisonment of the two knights and on their falling in love with Theseus's sister, Emelye. Opposed by this shared love, Palamon and Arcite will not stop arguing and fighting "as dide the houndes for the boon" (1177). But once separated by Fortune (one is reprieved, the other escapes), they eventually meet again, decide to fight, and are discovered by Theseus, who tries to find a more chivalrous solution. He thus forgives them and organizes a tournament to settle the feud (1683–869). Mars, Venus, and Saturn are prayed to grant their support to each fighter, but while Mars grants victory to Arcite, Saturn is convinced by Venus to intervene and causes an accident that kills him (2209–478).

As we can see, Chaucer entirely remodels his material and transforms the Italian epic into a true philosophical romance. He keeps only the action sequences useful to the narrative and contributing to the characterization of his protagonists, while creating empathy for their respective fates. In other words, he reproduces the pattern already implemented in *TC* and which turned the romance between his characters into the heart of the narrative, deliberately neglecting the warlike aspect of Boccaccio's epic. Chaucer even demonstrates his new understanding of the short narrative by amplifying his descriptions and dialogues so as to give to *KnT* a distinctive dignity and regularity.

This tonality, accentuated by the use of rhyming couplets in iambic pentameter, is, besides, supported by the Boethian reinterpretation of the Italian poem. The meeting between Theseus and the widows, who were once kings' wives, and their reference to Fortune and its traitorous wheel[39] (I. 925), rapidly give the narrative a meditative and philosophical dimension unknown to Boccaccio's poem. Theseus's famous speech after the death of Arcite is accordingly the best example of this philosophical rewriting. Indeed, the Duke of Athens explains:

> The First Moevere of the cause above,
> Whan he first made the faire cheyne of love,
> Greet was th'effect, and heigh was his entente.
> Wel wiste he why, and what thereof he mente,
> For with that faire cheyne of love he bond
> The fyr, the eyr, the water, and the lond
> In certeyn boundes, that they may nat flee.
> (I. 2987–93)

Men, whether they are kings or pages, share a common mortality that could strike them down at a moment's notice. Theseus counsels his audience to make a virtue of necessity and not break the chain of love. But the hundred or so lines composing this speech are a direct reference to the lesson taught in Book II (Meter 8) of *The Consolation of Philosophy*. In that passage, Boethius writes about the constant changing of the world and about the perennial alliance, made possible by the love governing both the heavens and earth, connecting all the elements of Nature: Phœbus, the god of light, walks with dawn while the moon, awoken by the evening star, reigns over the nights, and the sea prevents the rising tide from flooding the earth.

The fact that Chaucer starts the *Canterbury Tales* with a chivalric romance, a genre that dominated European literature for nearly five hundred years, is no accident. Unlike the realist novel of the eighteenth and nineteenth centuries, the chivalric romance does not pretend to tell us an original story; on the contrary, the author joins in a long tradition and gives us a story based on older tales. The codes of the chivalric romance do not impose to the storyteller the need to create "realistic" (in the modern sense of the word) situations or characters, since the purpose of the work is to produce feelings matching the theme of the

---

[39] Fortune says in *The Consolation of Philosophy* (Book II, Prose II): "Richesses, honours, and swiche othere thinges ben of my right. My servauntz knowen me for hir lady; they comen with me, and departen whan I wende."

narrative. As Benson notes, "[t]here is little attempt at creating lifelike characters: the invariably noble heroes and heroines are more types than individuals, and their actions, manners, emotions, and speech represent an ideal of aristocratic conduct."[40] By beginning the *Canterbury Tales* with a chivalric romance, Chaucer indicates by a subtle *mis-en-abyme* that his pilgrims belong to the same diegetic plane of existence as Palamon, Arcite, or Theseus, but he also gives us the vision of an aristocratic world that would be used to trigger the extradiegetic dialogue.

Indeed, once the Knight has finished his tale, his companions expect another noble figure to follow up with a story. Harry Bailly thus invites the Monk to compete with this first tale, but he is rather quickly interrupted by the Miller who is so drunk he can barely sit on his horse (I. 3120–21). And it is precisely at this stage that the ambiguity and particularity of Chaucer's narrative device are revealed, in complete opposition to the one used in the *Decameron*.

The social diversity of the pilgrims and Chaucer's desire to have the story told on the road was a first revealing element, but the very order in which the first tales are told equally reinforces this opposition. Boccaccio uses a variation on the *Commedia*'s structure: the notion of spiritual journey (the characters flee the plague and then return to a Florence coming back to life) is not unknown to Dante and the diversity of stories echoes equally diverse human behaviors, whether it is treachery, Cepparello's patience, or Griselda's kindness. The plague thus gives Boccaccio and his characters the right to "use other words, to have another approach to life and to the world"[41] thanks to this condensed image of death that remains "the indispensable ingredient of the *Decameron*'s entire system of images, in which the regenerating material bodily stratum plays the leading role."[42] Nevertheless, despite this folkloric and carnivalesque aspect, Boccaccio seems to prefer to keep the cacophony and energy of the marketplace at a distance. He tells us in his introduction (Intr. 33–35) that decency and order have been swept away from Florentine life by the plague, so the members of his *brigata* refuse to give up on their values and to infringe the limits of reason (Intr. 52–75). They consequently elect a leader whose mission is to organize their journey, but they keep an open mind, as shown by the fabliaux told by Dioneo.

The conclusion of the *Decameron*, however, strongly nuances this apparent flexibility and reveals Boccaccio's desire not to completely open the floor to the carnivalesque discourse and spirit. Dioneo is, for instance, portrayed throughout the poem as the avatar of grotesque realism and as the figure of anarchy in the

---

40 Chaucer, *The Riverside Chaucer*, 7.
41 Bakhtin, *Rabelais and His World*, 272.
42 Ibid., 273.

brigata. And yet it is he who concludes the *Decameron* with the tale of Griselda. Besides, while the other members of the group agree that their stories should follow a specific theme, Dioneo asks for an exemption "di spezial grazia,"[43] praising the importance of values and of "ordine"[44] and wishing not to proceed "secondo la proposta data"[45] (First Day, Conclusion, 12–13). In other words, Boccaccio presents us with a rather strange character who asks the permission of his companions before rejecting the established order and who, as a result, turns the *Decameron* into the Italian "high point of grotesque realism but in its poorer, petty form."[46]

The Knight's Tale and its vision of a chivalric world endowed with aristocratic values could then lead us to think that Chaucer intended to keep up this tone throughout *CT*. But the Miller's interruption is evidence to the contrary. Harry Bailly himself, leader of the group and figure of authority, tries in vain to restore order ("Abyd, Robyn, my leeve brother; / Som bettre man shal telle us first another"; I. 3129–30) before throwing in the towel and just letting the Miller say whatever he wants to say. The Miller thus decides to answer the Knight's tale with a story designed as an attack against the Reeve, who does not ease the tension when he interrupts the Miller with a rather courteous "[s]tynt thy clappe!" (I. 3144). With this cacophony, Chaucer gives us the feeling that we are, if not in an actual tavern, at least in the marketplace. The Chaucer pilgrim is even forced to encourage his audience to turn the leaf and choose another tale. He refuses to be considered as responsible for the vulgarity of the Miller, the Reeve, or the other pilgrims ("Blameth nat me if that ye chese amys"; I. 3181) but has to move on with the next tale.

We do not know for certain what are Chaucer's sources for *MilT* but the elements composing it are typical of the fabliau. A young man named Nicholas falls in love with Alison, the wife of the old carpenter with whom he lives. In order to consummate his love, he convinces his host that the Flood is near and that it would be a good idea to hang three tubs loaded with provisions and an axe from the roof of his barn (I. 3513–600). In the meantime, Absolon, Nicholas's unhappy rival, tries to seduce Alison but to no avail. One night, however, while the carpenter is sleeping in his tub and Nicholas is sleeping with Alison, Absolon comes and begs her to kiss him and is consequently humiliated (3730–43). Determined to take revenge, he burns Nicholas's backside with a red-hot coulter, so that Nicholas cannot help but shout "Help! Water! Water!" (3815), thus waking up the carpenter who, believing the Flood has started, cuts the rope and crashes to the ground with the tub.

---

43 "of special grace."
44 "the order."
45 "according to the proposed plan."
46 Bakhtin, *Rabelais and His World*, 273.

Though Chaucer draws here from several fabliaux, he considerably broadens the scale of *MilT* by doubling its plot. Usually, a fabliau consists of a guiding theme around which the different characters interact. But in this particular case, Chaucer reinforces the narrative with a secondary plot and crosses the Flood story with the humiliated lover substory in the conclusion, which both provokes an increased laughter and follows the theme of *KnT*. For although the contrast between those first two tales is extreme, it produces a unique literary experience. By allowing the Miller (fabliau) to answer the Knight (romance) in that way, Chaucer uses the extradiegetic dialogue as a way to reveal the potential of a poetical art that may, on the one hand, serve a specific cause and, on the other, just be used to entertain an audience.

The art developed in *MilT* is in no way a corruption of what is offered in *KnT*, as has been suggested in the past. On the contrary, each narrative presents a certain vision of the world. The many vagaries of a fabliau (deception, farce, beatings . . .) are never the result of mere chance but answer to a form of justice specific to the genre. It would never come to the mind of a romance author to punish old age, sluggishness, or a character's desire not to be cheated on by his wife, because the internal logic of the fabliau reverses society's expectations and values. This reversal is one of the main principles of grotesque realism and puts carnivalesque culture at the heart of the fabliau. Just like the carnival King, who is crowned and then beaten up by the crowd at the end of his relatively short reign, the heroes of the fabliau join in this reversal between a material, physical, and topographical "high" and "low." The most respected members of society (hard workers, prosperous merchants, and chaste women) thus become the victims of lecherous friars and penniless clerks, which turns the fabliau into

> a light-hearted thumbing of the nose at the dictates of religion, the solid virtues of the citizenry, and the idealistic pretensions of the aristocracy and its courtly literature, which the fabliaux frequently parody, though just as frequently they parody lower-class attempts to adopt courtly behavior.[47]

Because of its tendency to parody courtly attitudes, *MilT* accordingly becomes an almost perfect answer to *KnT*. Pandarus remarked in *TC* that "[b]y his contrarie is every thyng declared" (I. 637), which marvelously describes Chaucer's project here. Indeed, the poet opposes to the balance and dignity of *KnT*, a narrative whose lyricism systematically conceals a rather ambiguous vision of love. The musicality of its poetry covers up several ribald puns that contribute to the grotesque lowering. For instance, Chaucer describes Nicholas as a passionate astronomer

---

47 Chaucer, *The Riverside Chaucer*, 8.

(I. 3208–11) who loves to taste the pleasures of furtive love trysts. But he also tells us that he has a psaltery "[o]n which he made a-nyghtes melodie / So swetely that all the chambre rong" (3214–15). It seems obvious that such an adventurous young man would use his skill as a musician to court young ladies, as any good lover would. But Chaucer rapidly reverses the situation by giving this courtly "melodie" a brand-new meaning. When Nicholas is about to lie with Alison, the narrator remarks:

> Whan Nicholas had doon thys everideel
> And thakked hire aboute the lendes weel,
> He kiste hire sweete and taketh his sawtrie,
> And pleyeth faste, and maketh melodie.
> (3303–6)

The romance aspect of the lover wooing his lady with a serenade is as a result swept aside by Chaucer who gives the scene, without being vulgar, an openly sexual connotation.

The same is true of Alison's description which, while remaining faithful to the conventions of the chivalric romance, also falls victim to grotesque lowering. She is presented to us shortly after we get a glimpse of her husband, in a portrait that follows the conventions: she is described from head to toe, from her white smock and cap to her arched, plucked eyebrows as "blake as any sloo" (3246); from her apron as white as morning milk to her shoes; and her song is as loud and lively as that of a swallow sitting on a barn. Yet in the midst of this delicate description appears the image of the drunken Miller we saw in *MilP*. It is more unpleasant than difficult to imagine him salivating at the thought of Alison's collar, which is as "brood as is the boos of a bokeler" (3266), especially since he describes her as a "prymerole, a piggesnye, / For any lord to leggen in his bedde" (3268–69).

But having doubled the plot of his fabliau, Chaucer adds to the tale another lover who not only lacks Nicholas's good fortune but is also humiliated. Chaucer is used to incompetent lovers in his poems, his own persona being a wonderful example. Yet he had until now spared us the details of this incompetence. Chaucer describes Absolon as a rather attractive young man, full of qualities that local barmaids seem to love, such as the ability to draw blood, cut hair and shave, and even make "a chartre of lond or acquitaunce" (3327). He also possesses notable musical abilities since he can play songs on a small fiddle and on a guitar, to which he sometimes sings in a loud high treble (3332).[48] And as Derek Pearsall remarks about Absolon, he "has had some success with the flighty local barmaids, but he is a deal too circumspect for your true courtly lover."[49] Indeed, no reader of a chivalric romance would expect a courtly lover to take a nap to get ready for a night of love (3685–86), nor would he imagine him chewing cardamom and licorice "[t]o smellen sweete" (3691). Not to mention that calling a woman "lemman" (3700, 3705) and telling her that his love makes him "swelte and swete" (3703) is not really appropriate in these circumstances.

Chaucer thus systematically parodies the courtly attitudes of chivalric romances but does not merely laugh at the conventions. Carnivalesque and folkloric parody is very different from modern parody, which has been greatly deprived of its regenerative value. The ambivalence of carnivalesque laughter allows the poet to connect parody with an artistic renewal, which is especially obvious in the conclusion of *MilT*. After his serenade, Absolon becomes the victim of a farce whose conclusion joins the two plots in a cacophonic explosion. Alison promises him a kiss and taking advantage of darkness, she exposes her naked backside (3730–35). Absolon, however, quickly realizes he has been fooled:

> Abak he stirte, and thoughte it was amys,
> For wel he wiste a womman hath no berd.
> He felte a thyng al rough and long yherd,
> And seyde, "Fy! allas! what have I do?"
> (3736–39)

Following this, Nicholas tries to trick Absolon again but ends up with his own backside burned, which provokes the fall of the carpenter who thinks the Flood has started.

This opening of the heavens expected by the carpenter is actually a rereading of the conclusion of *KnT*, in which the gods intervene and deprive mortals of control. The divine movement from top to bottom is thus echoed in *MilT* and reinterpreted so as to fit carnivalesque logic. Indeed, Bakhtin explains that this movement to the lower strata, to "the depths of the earth, the depths of the body,"[50] is the central axis of the Rabelaisian, or in our case, the Chaucerian world. All of the images and metaphors of this grotesque universe are in fact oriented towards the nether world, be it terrestrial or corporal. Pantagruel and

---

[48] This characteristic is revealing of the contrast between the two rivals, especially when one looks at the true meaning of music in this tale. Nicholas is indeed a gifted musician and competent lover, while Absolon succeeds neither in *melodie* nor in love.
[49] Pearsall, "The Canterbury Tales II: Comedy," 131.
[50] Bakhtin, *Rabelais and His World*, 371.

the heroes of the Chaucerian fabliau find themselves at the heart of a comical re-reading of Dante's *Commedia*. In getting down through the window to have her backside kissed by Absolon (a rather literal corporal bottom), Alison acts out a descent through Hell (topographical and philosophical bottom).

Although this might seem unlikely or inappropriate for a reader whose mind has been shaped by modern aesthetics, Chaucer's and Rabelais's contemporaries were perfectly aware that the substitution of top and bottom was associated with death and Hell.[51] Indeed, during the Middle Ages, several geological faults became very popular with pilgrims who thought these openings led straight to Hell. Saint Patrick's hole in Ireland was particularly famous since it was supposedly connected to Purgatory. And the human mind being what it is, it obviously did not take long before these pilgrimage sites took on more obscene connotations and Rabelais did not miss his chance to immortalize them in such a way.[52] This lowering thus led to Hell, but just like Dante, Chaucer allows us to get through it and to reach Heaven thanks to the ambivalence of grotesque imagery. The bottom becomes the top; the backside and the belly turn into allusions to reproductive organs that are themselves instruments of a constant renewal.

The fabliau allows Chaucer, as a result, to reveal the animalistic impulses that courtly conventions keep at a distance in *KnT*. The association of these two tales gives Chaucer the opportunity to show us that poetical truth can be found both in the idealism and nobility of the Knight and in the Miller's depravity. He also illustrates that human nature is made of needs and appetites whose legitimacy is no less important than that of chivalric sentimentalism. In other words, Chaucer plays with contrasts and gives us a glimpse of what we should expect of his *Canterbury Tales* while emphasizing the complexity and richness of human nature.

Chaucer is also surprisingly capable of sustaining the extradiegetic dialogue while continuing to compose within the limits of the same literary genre. Thus, although the company of pilgrims globally enjoyed the Miller's entertaining tale (I. 3855–58), Oswald the Reeve, who used to be a carpenter, feels insulted by the story and decides to get even: "by your leve, I shal hym quite anoon; / Right in his cherles termes wol I speke" (3916–17). We should accordingly be expecting a new iteration of the classic story of a husband cuckolded by a young man he

---

[51] The literary conventions of the past centuries have often considered public stage laughter as unworthy of a proper literary and mythological analysis, while Bakhtin thought this particular laughter was the only opposition to feudal and religion powers, both in the Middle Ages and the Renaissance.

[52] The sibyl's hole becomes synonymous with Hell once the Panzoust sibyl shows her backside to Panurge in *Le Tiers livre des faicts et dicts héroïques du bon Pantagruel*.

invited into his house. However, despite what the Reeve's words led us to think, his tale is far from being a pale imitation of *MilT*. On the contrary, Chaucer develops a world that is far different from the Miller's: whereas *MilT* answered *KnT* by making fun of chivalric idealism, *The Reeve's Tale* invites us into an even more somber world, marked by the complete absence of courtly conventions. Everything is done to help the Reeve get even with the Miller, which inevitably gives this tale a highly carnivalesque destructive power. While *MilT* opened with a description of Alison, *RvT* presents in its first few lines the miller Symkyn and portrays him as a legitimate target. He is described as a belligerent man, proud "as any pecok" (I. 3926), and quite ready to rob and scam his fellow man (3939–40). His wife is likewise portrayed with unabashed contempt: this parson's daughter fostered in a nunnery likes to be called a "dame" (3956) and seems to suffer from a deplorable excess of pride (3950). Their twenty-year-old daughter is, on the other hand, described without disdain but without affection or excitement either:

> This wenche thikke and wel ygrown was,
> With kamus nose and eyen greye as glas,
> With buttokes brode and brestes rounde and hye.
> But right fair was hire heer; I wol nat lye.
> (3973–76)

Symkyn thus seems to be a rather dangerous fellow and one who would be hard to deceive, which renders the conclusion of the tale all the more delightful. Indeed, after having scammed the University of Cambridge, the miller receives a visit from two penniless clerks called John and Alayn who thoroughly intentioned to trick Symkyn. Both clerks end up passing the night in the miller's house and decide to sleep with his wife and daughter (4116–248), but an incredible misunderstanding happens when Alayn goes back to sleep in the wrong bed and, thinking that he is lying next to John, confesses to Symkyn that he has enjoyed his daughter's hospitality. The miller then tries to kill the clerk, who defends himself. Symkyn is thus eventually beaten up by his guests and his wife—who thought she was knocking out one of the clerks (4273–306)—robbed (they get their flour back and do not pay for supper), and humiliated in the worst possible way, leaving the Reeve nothing to add in conclusion but "[h]ym thar nat wene wel that yvele dooth" (4320).

As a result, even though the adventures of *RvT* do seem similar to those of *MilT*, they are also revealing of the development of a unique poetic, completely different from the one Chaucer used in his second tale. In addition to the descriptions of the characters, which are not as flattering as in *MilT*, Chaucer articulates his fabliau around a less elaborate storyline that gives free rein to the characters' instincts. Nicholas had developed an elaborate scheme in order to sleep with Alison but John and Alayn do not think for a minute and just jump on their victims. When Symkyn's wife goes back to the wrong bed, John barely gives her the time to lie down before moving into action:

> Withinne a while this John the clerk up leep,
>   And on this goode wyf he leith on soore.
>   So myrie a fit ne hadde she nat ful yoore;
>   He priketh harde and depe as he were mad.
>   (I. 4328–31)

Chaucer also parodies the traditional dawn scene, during which the lovers are supposed to part after a night spent together,[53] and debases the atmosphere by telling us that John is exhausted, "[f]or he had swonken al the longe nyght" (4235).

The poet likewise switches to a much more popular register that takes us away from the parody and puns of *MilT*. To this end, Chaucer's has his clerks speak in the dialect of the north of England. But he does not merely imitate caricatural accents or comical grammatical forms; on the contrary, he reproduces with great care and precision a different variety of English, which shows that Chaucer thought and wrote as a nineteenth- and twentieth-century linguist.[54] He gives them, for example, a vocabulary that would have been completely foreign to the standard English spoken in London ("heythen," 4033; "ille," 4045; "ymel," 4171, etc.), which reinforces the contrast between the clerks and the miller. Such dialectical mimicry is truly unique in Middle English literature and shows the linguistic abilities of a poet capable of developing the comedy and polyphony of his narrative by playing with the varieties of English known to his readers and audience. In other words, "[f]or this one tale, and to define its special poetry, Chaucer created a remarkable and sophisticated literary device he was never to use again."[55]

He also reminds us by this use of contrast that the tale told by the Miller is just as idealized as the Knight's since the world is generally peopled by thieving millers and sex is often synonymous with power and domination. But, as destructive as this tale might be, its carnivalesque value lends it a particular philosophical dimension. Just like the final sequence in *MilT*, the concluding sequence of *RvT* once more gives Chaucer the opportunity to play with a substitution of top and

---

53 See *TC*, Book III, 1422–533.
54 See Tolkien, "Chaucer as a Philologist: The Reeve's Tale," 1–70, and Fruoco, "Chaucer as a Sociolinguist," 216–30.
55 Benson, *Chaucer's Drama of Style*, 99.

bottom. "The blows have here a broadened, symbolic, ambivalent meaning," according to Bakhtin, "they at once kill and regenerate, put an end to the old life and start the new."[56] As a result, now that he has Symkyn beaten up and considers himself even with "The Miller's Tale," the Reeve reverses the tone of the tale and brings us out of the depths of earth and up to the celestial throne with a benediction aimed at all the pilgrims, including the Miller: "And God, that sitteth heighe in magestee, / Save al this compaignye, grete and smale!" (4322–23).

The atmosphere of the *Canterbury Tales* and the peculiarity of this extradiegetic dialogue are therefore established as soon as the first Fragment of the poem. And although *The Cook's Tale* is unfinished, the few lines that compose it tend to show Chaucer's intention to thrust the first part of the pilgrimage deeper into the world of the fabliau. We do not know anything else about this tale, however, except that a bawdy apprentice is fired by his master and moves in with a friend whose wife "heeld for contenance / A shoppe, and swyved for hir sustenance" (I. 4421–22).

In the first lines of the second Fragment, the Host asks the Man of Law to respect his promise and tell them a tale of his own choosing. But the pilgrim answers that, just like the renowned author of love stories and of a treatise on good women that is Chaucer, he wishes to talk about beautiful and pleasant things, even though "I recche noght a bene / Though I come after hym with hawebacke" (II. 94–95). The Man of Law notes, however, that Chaucer, who has told every story known to man (51–52), has chosen to remain silent about the bad example of Canace's sinful romance with her brother, or about Antiochus's rape of his own daughter. Chaucer, adds the Man of Law, could never be the author of "swiche unkynde abhomynacions" (88)—a rather delightful comment considering the fabliaux Chaucer just told us. And although these few words might very well be an allusion to Gower, who does not hesitate to describe such *abhomynacions* in his *Confessio Amantis*, they also directly confront Chaucer the pilgrim with Chaucer the poet, in a dialogical opposition that negates the very reality of the literary world. The silence of the pilgrim after the Man of Law's compliments, which he obviously heard since he has written them down, distances the poet from his persona and returns to the foreground this notion of a dialogue fundamentally external to the narrative.

The Man of Law's Tale, an adaptation of Nicholas Trevit's Anglo-Norman chronicles and of the *Confessio Amantis*, thus tells the story of Constance, whose faith is continually tested by fate. She is successively victim of her stepmother's schemes, both in Syria and England, persecuted because of her religion, and betrayed and condemned to death twice by being set adrift on the sea

---

56 Bakhtin, *Rabelais and His World*, 205.

(the first time on her own, and then with her son). She eventually manages to go back to Rome where her son succeeds his grandfather as emperor. *MLT* is, in other words, a tale of pathos at the intersection of hagiography and romance and whose philosophical and poetical dimension contrasts sharply with the *MilT, RvT,* and *CkT*.

But it is also a highly ambivalent text in which the narrator's words clash with Constance's voice, decentring through dialogue the authoritative discourse of the narrative.[57] Indeed, unlike the romance told by the Knight, this story brings to the fore suffering, helplessness, and passivity, and not the feat of arms of a hero. The well-named Constance resorts to her faith and beliefs during each ordeal and God thus guides her steps and strikes down with His vengeful hand the infidels daring to slander or threaten the princess. As Dor remarked, "Constance's view is the traditional one. She is the voice of the poor, faithful woman who asks for God's assistance, and accepts whatever He decides should be her fate. She utters monological discourses without ever expecting a dialogue."[58] Her passivity and blind acceptance of what is to come is especially obvious in her first prayer and address to her father (ll. 274–87). This embryonic discourse, in which she "recomandeth" herself unto her father's grace, contains the seeds of all her future prayers, each time activated by a specific context. "The point here is that, although she actually quotes utterances from other contexts, she does not want the listener to hear them 'with quotation marks': she has totally submitted herself to the voice."[59]

The Man of Law's voice as a narrator, however, is quite different. He starts by creating a *mis-en-abyme*: the pilgrims are both actors and spectators during this journey and in this case, he invites his fellow-travelers to listen to a tale he heard from a merchant. As I mentioned earlier, he even complicates things further by a direct reference to Chaucer himself, who has told every tale known to man. In doing so, he covers his tracks since we are no longer able to distinguish who is responsible for what. This ambivalent reflection on the act of writing is extended by a reading of the text itself as if it belonged to the outside world.[60] Chaucer thus creates an interplay of multiple viewpoints in a tale whose theme is surprisingly polemical, namely the relationship with a monological God in the age of polysemy and polyphony. To do so, he plays with the pseudo-objectivity of the Man of Law who, as a good omniscient narrator, pretends to report opinions but actually distorts them. He balances Constance's Biblical creed with a creed of his own marked

---

57 Morson and Emerson, *Mikhail Bakhtin: Creation of a Prosaics*, 314.
58 Dor, "Dialogical Reading," 110.
59 Ibid., 113.
60 See Kristeva, *Sèméiotikè*, 170.

by untraditional views, such as rebellion against Providence for the lack of material happiness in this world.[61] He considers God as a provider of temporal assistance towards a better life right here and right now. And as Jill Mann noticed, he goes so far as to transform Constance's subjection to her father into a subjection to all males.[62]

The Man of Law gets even surprisingly close to blasphemy when he echoes Constance's embryonic prayer through a series of rhetorical questions. When she is chased away from Syria, the narrator asks one rhetorical question after the other and wonders where Constance found food and water during more than three years adrift at sea; who commanded the spirits of the storm to protect her skiff; who saved her from the schemes of her step-mother . . .

> . . . Who myghte hir body save?
> And I answere to that demande agayn,
> Who saved Danyel in the horrible cave
> Ther every wight save he, maister and knave,
> Was with the leon frete er he asterte?
> No wight but God that he bar in his herte.
> (II. 471–76)

These questions are later echoed by another series (932–945), which, as a whole, turn the expression of faith into an answer to rhetorical questions: "what he distorts is not only the prayer itself, but also the nature of the traditional superaddressee. God, the supreme listener, who would understand the utterance in just the right way, has been replaced by *men*."[63] The Man of Law gives, in effect, a pseudo-religious dialogic response to Constance's utterances and shows Chaucer's shift from the monologism of the genre here in play to the polysemous features of dialogism.

Chaucer consequently changes the tone of the *Canterbury Tales* by jumping from the fabliau to a Christian romance, but also opposes *MLT* to the chivalric romance that is *KnT*. Indeed, in the Knight's narrative, Chaucer used the surprise of the final peripeteia as a catalyst allowing for the Boethian philosophical meditation. And although the philosophical and renewing values of the carnivalesque culture are at the center of the following fabliaux, the role of Fortune in human affairs is no longer taken into account. Constance's misfortunes, however, give him the opportunity to showcase religion as a guide, while demonstrating the

---

[61] See Astell, "Apostrophe, Prayer and the Structure of Satire in *The Man of Laws's Tale*," 81–97.
[62] Mann, *Geoffrey Chaucer*, 134.
[63] Dor, "Dialogical Reading," 116.

influence of Providence on our lives. The intertextuality of the *MLT*, that is to say the Chaucerian re-reading of Trivet and Gower, is accordingly associated with the dialogue between *KnT* and the fabliaux and gives us the chance to check, as Hélène Dauby explains, "la profondeur des convictions religieuses de Chaucer et sa sympathie pour ceux que la société range parmi les faibles: les femmes, les enfants."[64]

Chaucer composed several memorable prologues, such as the Pardoner's and Wife of Bath's. Although both introductions are written as a confession in which the character boasts about his/her vices, the tone of *PardP* and its relationship with its *Tale* is particularly interesting. The Wife of Bath perfectly fits with her tale: she tells us she buried five husbands, but that she is very keen on finding a new man and then tells an Arthurian fairy tale whose moral is that a husband should obey his wife. The Pardoner's case is, however, quite different since Chaucer turns his character into the perfect representation of the false preacher, capable of telling "[a] moral tale" while being "a ful vicious man" (VI. 459–60).

At the end of *The Physician's Tale*, the Host urges the Pardoner to take over, which he accepts on condition of making a stop in a tavern. It is thus with one arm on the bar that he starts describing to his companions his function and the theme of his tale, namely that greed is the root of all evil ("My theme is alwey oon, and ever was— / *Radix malorum est Cupiditas*"; 333–34). He then continues with an account of his own depravity and of the different schemes used to take money from his flock: when he walks about, he shows the patent with his bishop's seal so as not to be bothered by members of the clergy and displays his false relics while spicing his sermons with a few Latin words "to stir hem to devocioun" (346). But his little speech does not really sound religious and, on the contrary, turns our Pardoner into a mountebank selling elixirs of dubious authenticity in an Old West medicine show. Waving one of the "relics," in this particular case a sheep shoulder bone, the Pardoner proclaims that once washed in a well, the water from that well can cure cow or calf or sheep of any disease. Likewise, if the farmer owning the stock drinks of this water regularly, his beasts will multiply; if a jealous husband uses that water to make his broth,

> . . . never shal he moore his wyf mystriste,
> Though he the soothe of hir defaute wiste,
>   Al had she taken prestes two or thre.
>   (369–71)

---

[64] "the depth of Chaucer's religious convictions and his sympathy for those whom society considers weak: women and children." Chaucer, *Les Contes de Canterbury et autres oeuvres*, 32.

He consequently makes sure to cast a wide net so as to gain as much money as possible. He is even rather proud of his little schemes and confesses that, by this trick, "have I wonne, yeer by yeer / An hundred mark sith I was pardoner" (389–90). Nevertheless, despite the comic dimension of this speech, Chaucer does not turn his Pardoner into a particularly attractive or likable character: the poet does not judge him either way. Although he certainly provides us with enough material to permit a judgment, he does not condemn him, and we have even observed that the Chaucer pilgrim thinks of him as a *noble ecclesiaste*. And yet, he gives him the means of his own destruction by emphasizing the pride he feels in his deeds and the scorn he feels for his victims. Many of the Pardoner's sermons are openly dishonest; some are even "for veyne glorie, and som for hate" (VI. 411). He is quite capable of stinging with his acerbic tongue and, under the cloak of holiness, of spitting venom in the face of his detractors. The Pardoner even sums up his ambitions by once more repeating his theme: greed is the subject of his sermons and he preaches "nothyng but for coveitise" (433). In the end, Chaucer does not use sarcasm or irony in this prologue, but he still manages to show us one thing while saying another. Indeed, by giving the Pardoner the freedom to present his mission and define his vices, he conditions our reaction, for as Coghill and Tolkien remarked, "[i]f he were going to Hell, we would open the door for him."[65]

Chaucer does not choose to present a despicable character for no reason. Pardoners were a disturbance well known to his contemporaries, even though their mission was originally commendable since they collected funds during religious festivities under the strict control of the clergy. A pardoner had accordingly neither the power to pardon sins nor to preach; he was only supposed to read official documents, approved by the pope himself or by the bishop supervising the collection. The practice degenerated quickly, and unsurprisingly, into large-scale fraud, forcing Pius IV to stop it during the Council of Trent in 1562. Chaucer's description of a particularly corrupt clergyman is thus clearly comical and grotesque since his contemporaries knew the social phenomenon in question. But he also produces a discrepancy between the vices of *PardP* and the Christian values of *PardT*. The notion of confession is accordingly at the heart of the diptych. According to the Church, pardon can only be granted after *contritio cordis* (contrition), *confessio oris* (confession to a priest), and *satisfactio operis* (accomplishment of the penance). But pardon is only granted by God when the words of absolution are said by the priest, who has himself no powers. Thus, although *PardP* is a literary confession, it is quite obvious that

---

65 Chaucer, *The Pardoner's Tale*, 21.

the Pardoner is far from being granted absolution, which is especially interesting when one considers the Christian moral of his tale.

It is not surprising that *PardT* is, in fact, an *exemplum*. A story without a moral or philosophical value was often looked at suspiciously during the Middle Ages, which explains why the pedagogical dimension of a text often took precedence over its artistic value. The Pardoner seems to be aware of this and remarks in his Prologue that he tells old stories to his victims "[f]or lewed peple loven tales olde; / Swiche thynges kan they wel reporte and holde" (VI. 437–38). Several of the *Canterbury Tales* even end on a note stressing that the story illustrates one truth or another (*RvT*. I. 4320–21; *MerT*. IV. 2410; *CYT*. VIII. 1476–79). But the relation between the Pardoner and the subject matter of his tale makes his performance suspicious since he has confessed to us that he uses stories to trick people, not teach them.

PardT remains, however, a remarkable narrative developed in two distinct parts, namely a sermon and its accompanying *exemplum*. Its first part accordingly consists of a denunciation of the abuses met in taverns, articulated around the Pardoner's favorite theme "*Radix malorum est Cupiditas*." Yet although the sermon's form shows great erudition (the Pardoner successively quotes Seneca, Innocent III, Saint Jerome, Matthew, Jeremy, and several other parts of the Bible[66]), its spiritual dimension is far less significant. Indeed, the three sins mentioned in this tale (gluttony, gambling, and swearing) are of little importance but can be quite easily made exciting by the Pardoner so that his audience might follow his commercial approach to religion. Gluttony is, for instance, a sin related to lust and whose link with the Fall is of essential importance in the Christian tradition, yet the Pardoner addresses the matter with a rhetorical excess unsuited to the situation:

> O glotonye, ful of cursednesse!
> O cause first of oure confusioun!
> O original of oure dampnacioun,
> Til Crist hadde boght us with his blood agayn!
> (VI. 498–501)

He gives in to sensationalism and exposes the dangers of alcohol in a rather grotesque way. The difference between the form and the substance thus gives his words a comical and carnivalesque dimension they should not have. He says, for

---

66 Lines 485–85 come from *De Miseria condicionis humane*, by Innocent III; Seneca's comment (492–97) is taken from his *Epistulae morales ad Lucilium* (letter 83); the allusion to Adam's gluttony (505–11) is borrowed from Saint Jerome's *Adversus Jovinanum*, etc.

example, that when a man drinks excessive quantities of red and white wine "of his throte he maketh his pryvee" (527). But he also mentions that such abuses provoke rather unpleasant noises:

> O wombe! O bely! O stynking cod,
> Fulfilled of dong and of corrupcioun!
> At either ende of thee foul is the soun.
>   (534–36)

In other words, the spiritual content of his preaching leaves something to be desired, especially since he successively shows signs of extravagance, grandiloquence, and even vulgarity. It is, as a result, not so much the intellectual aspect of the preaching that strikes his audience but the amount of energy he puts into it. And since the preacher's performance (which revolves around his own rhetorical excesses) absorbs our attention at the expense of the message, the Pardoner perpetrates the linguistic equivalent of the gluttony he condemns.

He manages, however, to go back to his tale and starts his *exemplum* with the description of three scoundrels in a tavern. As a funeral procession passes nearby, they learn that the deceased has been the victim of an aptly named bandit: "Ther cam a privee theef men clepeth Deeth, / That in this contree al the peple sleeth" (IV. 675). The three men then agree that they should find this villain and kill him before other people become his victims. Once on the road, they meet a pale and miserable old man who confesses that he is eagerly awaiting death but that despite his pleas, he cannot find eternal rest: "Ne Deeth, allas, ne wol nat han my lyf" (727). Nevertheless, even though he seemingly cannot die himself, the old man is able to show them the way to death, as they end up plotting and killing each other for gold.

Chaucer presents us in this *exemplum* a striking portrayal of death during the Middle Ages. What else could be said about this silent thief taking lives throughout the country? There is little doubt that his contemporaries saw in that description of "Deeth" a troubling personification of the Black Death. This particular threat is however not the real plague of the tale. The Pardoner has ceaselessly told us that greed is the root of all evil and it seems that upon discovering the gold, the three "riotoures" signed their death warrant. The old man, whose mysterious nature is never explained by Chaucer, seems to be the ideal witness to the fate of these scoundrels: his sheer presence transcends the mechanics of the tale and brings to this death quest an obvious philosophical depth.

The moral of *PardT* is, in other words, in accordance with the theme announced in its *Prologue*.[67] The Pardoner, however, does not give the pilgrims the chance to take in the moral of his tale and immediately tries to take advantage of the emotions caused by his conclusion. He turns to Harry Bailly who is, according to him, "moost enveluped in synne" (942) and offers him his relics to be kissed, which the Host vehemently refuses to do:

> "Thou woldest make me kisse thyn olde breech,
>   And swere it were a relyk of a seint,
>   Thought it were with thy fundement depeint!
>   . . .
>   I wolde I hadde thy coilons in myn hond
>   In stode of relikes or of seintuarie.
>   Lat kutte hem of, I wol thee helpe hem carie;
>   They shul be shryned in an hogges toord!"
>   (948–55)

In *PardP* and *PardT*, Chaucer thus questions the power of rhetoric and of literature, especially when they are associated with moral issues and corruption. Eloquence is not necessarily condemned by the Church. On the contrary, it is possible and even encouraged, to adorn a sermon and touch believers. Nonetheless, excess is condemnable when a preacher uses his eloquence for personal glory. The Pardoner is in a way the perfect representation of these extremes: his performance in the Prologue and the sermon preceding the *exemplum* show that this master of rhetoric knows all the tricks in the book that will drive his flock to give him money. And yet, the *exemplum* itself, without losing its rhetorical strength, possesses an authentic spiritual dimension that makes of this narrative one of Chaucer's finest compositions. The narrator remains modest and manages to produce a perfectly paced tale whose rhetoric is well suited to the subject matter.

Chaucer accordingly produces here a dialogue between the *PardP* and *PardT* through which he shows his understanding of what Christian poetry could be if fiction and doctrine were perfectly balanced. But a dialogical work of fiction possesses, by definition, an energy and a vitality allowing it to resist any form of doctrinal subordination. Spearing explains in this regard that "[t]he very details in the narrative that make it vivid and memorable may well diverge from the doctrine supposedly served and even make us question it."[68] The Pardoner's talent, associated with the vices mentioned in his Prologue, raises a

---
67 The possibility still exists that the Pardoner is trying to be jocular here but misjudges the mood and temper of his audience.
68 Spearing, "The Canterbury Tales IV: Exemplum and Fable," 160.

doubt about the real value of his *exemplum*—a doubt expressed by Harry Bailly at the conclusion of the tale. The Pardoner's ambiguity lies in this opposition, through which Chaucer illustrates an issue fundamentally external to the diegesis of the *Canterbury Tales*.

Chaucer's role as a pilgrim and his dialogical importance have been mentioned earlier in this chapter but without going into the details of his own tales. *The Tale of Sir Thopas* and *The Tale of Melibee* represent a genuine microcosm of the diversity and the extradiegetic dialogue Chaucer places at the heart of his *magnum opus*. When the Host notices Chaucer's presence, he invites him to take over and tell a "tale of myrthe" (VII. 706), but the pilgrim quickly replies that the only story he knows is a rhyming romance. *Th* is an entertaining tale, whose chivalric and novelistic nature borders on the comical. Indeed, when he asked this "popet" (701) to tell a story, Harry Bailly probably expected something less delicate and certainly did not imagine Chaucer turning into a minstrel. And yet, Chaucer seems to take malicious pleasure in putting in his own persona's mouth a parody of the most popular literary genre of his time. He tells us about this brave knight called Sir Thopas, a "doghty swayn" (724) loved and desired by all maids. But his virtue prevents him from marrying someone so unworthy of him and he accordingly falls in love with a fairy queen. Thopas then "priketh over stile and stoon" (798) until he finds Fairy-land and the giant protecting it. He challenges his adversary and goes back to fetch his armor and that is precisely when the narrative is brutally interrupted by Harry Bailly who can no longer tolerate Chaucer's incompetence.

The reasons for this failure are manifold and encompass both the poet's appeal for a poetic renewal and a new reflection on the power of literature. The tale is indeed conceived as a celebration of art for art's sake, with no other objective than to show off the storyteller's technical prowess. Chaucer, therefore, establishes a parallel between the poetic developed by his avatar in the poem and Thopas's own behavior. Whereas he should be getting ready for the fight ahead, the knight asks his minstrels to tell "tales . . . Of romances that been roiales, / Of popes and of cardinales" (VII. 846–49) while his servants fetch him sweet wine, mead, and other royal delicacies. Likewise, the Chaucer pilgrim loses sight of what is essential in the narrative and starts sacrificing his plot to sport, herb, bird, and armor lists (736–887). In doing so, he illustrates the worst things that medieval fiction had to offer, namely a mere succession of lines without any purpose or pedagogical value.

Nonetheless, as limited as *Th* may be, Bailly does not interrupt the narrator because of the subject matter of the narrative but because of its form. He clearly states that "also wisly God my soule blesse, / Myne eres aken of thy drasty speche" (922–23) and when the Chaucer pilgrim is understandably offended, Bailly retorts with his usual frankness and crudeness: "for pleynly, at a word, / Thy drasty rymyng is nat worth a toord!" (929–30). But although the Host notices the difference of style between this tale and the others, he makes the mistake of confusing extreme sophistication with incompetence for the simple reason that its versification is the polar opposite of Chaucer's customary simplicity. While the prologue of *Th* is in rhyme royal, the pilgrim quickly starts to imitate the poetical style of minstrel romances in the tale itself:

> Listeth, lordes, in good entent,
>   And I wol telle verrayment
>   Of myrthe and of solas,
> Al of knyght was fair and gent
> In bataille and in tourneyment;
>   His name was sire Thopas.
>   (VII. 712–17)

Even though short-line stanzas (trimeters and even diameters) were popular with Chaucer's contemporaries, it was never a favorite of his because its disjointed rhythm and demanding structure force the poet to use ready-made phrases and repetitions. In the first stanza of *Th* alone, the Chaucer pilgrim calls his audience—which includes knights, yes, but is mostly composed of all kinds of thieves and villains—"lordes"; the words "entent" and "verrayment" lose their –*e* suffixes, while "fair and gent" is only here because it rhymes with "tourneyment." It was likewise thought of as rather vulgar to use the title "sire," something that the Chaucer pilgrim does several times, even calling the giant "sire Olifaunt"[69] (807). For the poet this pastiche is in effect "par l'absurde, un manifeste en faveur d'une poétique nouvelle."[70]

The Host grants a second chance to Chaucer, however, who does not miss the opportunity to tell a moral tale but apologizes first if his version of the story is not exactly the same as other storytellers'. Whereas *The House of Fame* warned us against mistaking the difference between an event and its verbal echo, the Chaucer pilgrim claims that even if the words change, the meaning stays the same. Just as in the Gospels, where different versions of the same story "acorden as in hire sentence, / Al be ther in hir tellyng difference" (VII. 947–48). Since the poet is perfectly aware of the effect a new narration may have, his remark tends to diminish the narrator's credibility as a dramatic

---

[69] Burrow, "The Canterbury Tales I: Romance," 114.
[70] "by reduction to the absurd, a manifesto in favor of a new poetics." Chaucer, *Les Contes de Canterbury et autres oeuvres*, 31.

character and forces the informed reader to question the poet's real motivations. The *Canterbury Tales* is, after all, a work made up of stories that generally share the same narrative structure but this does not prevent them from being systematically characterized by a unique and distinctive poetics. Chaucer "precludes reducing 'sentence' to story alone, and stresses instead the difference wrought by style, teller, and the circumstances of telling; the effect of the discourse on the story."[71] His tales are the narrative representation of what the dreamer experiences in *The House of Fame* (III. 1073–83), namely a transformation of words into images: each tale takes, in the reader's mind, the shape of an entity in its own right, endowed with a voice of its own and which transcends the limits of the dialogue between characters trapped within the diegesis.

The Tale of Melibee is consequently a long moral treatise composed of quotes and proverbs whose philosophical dimension, content, and style contrast so radically with *Th* that it could very well be the work of a different poet. It is accordingly one of the least accessible texts in the *Canterbury Tales*, even though its theme is surprisingly modern.[72] Yet, besides the importance of the moral value of the tale, Chaucer shows once again with this juxtaposition of *Th* and *Mel* that literature must keep a sense of balance between content and form if it is to keep entertaining people.

Likewise, *Mel* has a particular connection with several other tales, but the Chaucer pilgrim does not communicate this to his companions. The debate on the influence of advisers is, for instance, a reference to *MerT*, with which *Mel* shares several lines (IV. 1363–74 and VII. 1098–101). The relation between Melibee and his wife, Prudence, is also an echo to the remarks made by the Wife of Bath, while the tale's understanding of nobility and of the influence of Christian doctrine refers directly to *KnT*. And even if the Host is quite satisfied with this new story, wishing that his wife could have heard it (VII. 1091–94), none of the pilgrims concerned react. The passage from *Th* to *Mel* is in fact crucial, for Chaucer abandons his pilgrims to literally foreground his tales as the true characters of his work: it is consequently not surprising that Alison does not comment on Melibee's decision to be guided by his wife, since the dialogue between *Mel* and the rest of the *Canterbury Tales* is, by definition, extradiegetic.

---

71 Taylor, *Chaucer Reads "The Divine Comedy,"* 112.

72 Benson notes about the themes of *Mel*: "They are problems of war and peace, of the maintenance of national honor and its relation to a policy of pacific disarmament, of how policy is made and of the proper roles of legislatures and advisers in formulating that policy." Chaucer, *The Riverside Chaucer*, 17.

There is, in the end, something fundamentally iconoclastic in the very structure of the *Canterbury Tales*. "Break the images, the forms! Spontaneous life surges in," writes Brewer.[73] But breaking the codes and staging this liberation requires a rhetorical discipline without which this cacophony, here orchestrated by Chaucer, would be sheer chaos. The dialogism of his *magnum opus* supports its narrative frame and gives the poet the opportunity to conceive a dialogue between literary genres. To this end, he superimposes narrative voices in an extradiegetic dialogue between the artistic motifs that are worked out throughout Chaucer's composition, as opposed to a dialogue between the features that are peculiar to his constituent narratives, with their own tellers and vocalities. What could be said about this narrator who is naive, shy yet sociable, and dominated by the Host? Should we ignore one of these voices, deconstruct the Chaucerian persona to find the very essence of the poet? Of, course not. On the contrary, all these voices resonate at the same time in perfect harmony. The Chaucer pilgrim possesses different sides, as shown by his two tales. And *Th* and *Mel* are the perfect representation of what the poet is doing in the *Canterbury Tales*:

> the totality of voices, all the layers of meaning together, is what gives the tang. Chaucer's poetry is in some ways like medieval polyphony—music in which a number of different voices are singing the same words to different melodic lines. Except that Chaucer's poetic line, until the mind is alerted, may seem deceptively simple, and the careless reader may notice only one of the voices.[74]

As we have seen, the pilgrims are not dramatic characters, which means that each tale represents a voice, a unique literary genre or a unique approach to this genre. According to Bakhtin, the novel is a microcosm of multilingualism, hence the importance of interpolated and non-literary genres to it. For by incorporating into the novel elements that are by nature not literary, the author greatly amplifies and diversifies the linguistic universe of his fiction.[75] And that is precisely what the dialogism of the *Canterbury Tales* reproduces: by this innovation and association of different voices, all singing the same song on different melodic lines, Chaucer manages to elaborate a dialogue that fully displays the plurality of the literary world and allows a reflection on the power of poetry.

Left unfinished, the *Canterbury Tales* ends on Chaucer's *Retraction* and underlines once more the importance of refusing closure. In fact, if Chaucer ever

---

73 Brewer, *An Introduction to Chaucer*, 170.
74 Ibid., 171.
75 Bakhtin, *Esthétique et théorie du roman*, 222–23.

had "a sense of closure and containment, he must have abandoned it as the tales themselves opened up a multiplicity of perspectives."[76] As Peter W. Travis noted, the *Retraction* is a literary *parergon*, a concept Jacques Derrida borrowed from Kant and that both delimits and foregrounds the aesthetic essence of the framed object.[77] It serves as both "a marginal gloss and an essential constituent of the tales."[78] For the voice behind this *Retraction* encourages us to associate it with Geoffrey Chaucer, the poet. He discusses not only *CT* but also his earliest works and prompts us to read it as a commentary on his career and on the ends of fiction. McGerr remarks that the word *retraccioun* refers to Saint Augustine's *Retractationes* and follows its lead in "reviewing a literary career, but his allusion helps to show how the whole of the *Canterbury Tales*, even in its 'unfinished' state, interrogates Augustine's arguments about the workings of memory, experience, and reading."[79] By concluding *CT* with such a coda, Chaucer makes sure that the debate remains open since the *Retraction* is essentially a moment for reevaluation:

> Looking back from the end of the work, we can see associations and significances that were not so readily evident during a first reading of the text. Only with the cumulative vision afforded by memory and the "retrospective structure" of the work do the individual elements take on the contexts that give them greater meaning.[80]

Indeed, this literary confession clearly breaks into two mutually exclusive assertions, one in which the poet humbly defends a work whose purpose is "in harmonious alignment with sacred Scripture,"[81] and another introduced by a "Wherefore" that condemns his poetry. This disjunctive conjunction is the last piece of a large heuristic puzzle, Chaucer's last *volte-face*, a proof that when logic fails in a writer's work we have reached the moment "of his deepest penetration into the actual nature of literary language, or of language as such."[82] The binary opposition between the parts, articulated around that "Wherefore," does not close *CT*, but encourages us to look back and question its structure, motifs and themes, to discuss Chaucer's utterances and ultimately join in the dialogue.

---

76 Ganim, *Chaucerian Theatricality*, 65–66.
77 See Derrida, "The Parergon," 3–40.
78 Travis, "Deconstructing Chaucer's Retraction," 136.
79 McGerr, *Chaucer's Open Books*, 133.
80 Ibid., 143.
81 Travis, "Deconstructing Chaucer's Retraction," 146.
82 Miller, "Stevens' Rock and Criticism as Cure," 338.

Conclusion

It would be rather counterproductive for me to write a definitive "conclusioun" after having written about open-ended narratives, refusal of closure, and polyphony for so long. I do not intend, here, to suggest that this polyphonic quest is over and that there is nothing left to say and write on the subject. Quite the contrary: I hope that my modest contribution to the field of Chaucerian dialogism will encourage others to explore it further. What I have attempted to show in *Chaucer's Polyphony* is the importance of Chaucer to the development of English polyphonic prose. The theory of the novel offers, in that respect, the best tools to systematically describe the narratological and linguistic framework in which dialogism can be perceived.

Indeed, this approach allows us to see the relationship between Chaucer and the novel. Their association is interesting because the "modern" novel is defined not just by a certain form of realism or naturalism, but rather by a linguistic freedom preventing the monological domination of the author. For Bakhtin, as soon as several meanings and foreign voices are integrated into poetical discourse, its linguistic frame is destroyed, and its content is transferred within a prose framework. That image is especially interesting in Chaucer's case since his narrative poetry gradually acquired a novelistic dimension, something motivated both by his literary influences and his multilingual discourse.

As we have seen, Chaucer's polyphonic practice was made possible by his own linguistic sensitivity. In his poetry, he translated the internationalism of his cultural and linguistic background. England had been conquered, converted, and administered by several different populations (Romans, Christians, Vikings, Normans, and French) throughout its history, which inevitably left marks on its linguistic DNA, as we have seen in the etymological analysis of the English lexicon in Chapter 1. Chaucer lived in a multilingual society, and his own speech absorbed that cultural diversity; consciously or not, in his writing he transcribed a stratification revelatory of literature's steps on the path to literary polyphony.

Then, as he started composing poetry in English, Chaucer encountered a European intertext that gradually enhanced his sensitivity to polyvocality. His assimilation and translation of *fin'amor* and later of the Italian *Dolce Stil Novo* were essential to his evolution as a poet. Chaucer developed his metrical and narrative abilities as his enunciation increasingly began expressing a more nuanced and complex polyvocal structure. While he presented a first alternative to the conventions of *fin'amor* in *The Book of the Duchess*, his later works, like *The House of Fame*, show how Dante, Petrarch, and Boccaccio transformed his poetry into a reflection on reading, an act of enunciating dialogically opposed to the voices heard in his intertext. With *The Parliament of Fowls*, Chaucer went even further, effectively incorporating the accents of different traditions, be they aristocratic and courtly, carnivalesque, or the richness of Trecento poetry. The passive witness who refuses to affirm authorial intent and is plunged into the final parliamentary cacophony is a wonderful example of Chaucer's progressive liberation from literary conventions.

With *Troilus and Criseyde*, Chaucer eventually reached new artistic and narratorial heights. The ambiguity at the heart of the poem, associated with the double enunciation staged by the poet, shows a new approach to dialogism. He favored a pseudo-historical mode of representation that distanced him from Boccaccio's aesthetic sensibility and brought him closer to the very origins of the novel genre, notably through a presentation of *fin'amor* in line with the doctrine developed by Chrétien de Troyes and Guillaume de Lorris. Chaucer was accordingly able to turn his translation of *Il Filostrato* into a reading experience in which the narrator becomes the fulcrum of a double enunciation shared between a witness and a historian offering an apparently objective vision of the romance punctuated with personal remarks. Chaucer willingly destroyed the narrative's authentication so as to show that the integrity of a story is necessarily altered by the will of its narrator. *TC* thus offered a surprisingly "modern" narrative in which the characters do not rely on the will of the author, and where no single voice dominates the debate.

Troilus and Criseyde consequently represented a transition between two different stages in Chaucer's career. Chapter 5 allowed us to see that with *The Legend of Good Women* Chaucer turned a page and left behind the lyricism and codes of *fin'amor* as he started composing a collection of short narratives illustrating polyvocality and his vision of literature. To justify the change in narrative structure, Chaucer presented *LGW* as a palinode of *TC*, as a penance imposed by the God of Love. But to accomplish this task, Chaucer needed to put himself forward as a poet, and no longer as a passive persona. He thus managed to produce polyvocality by way of hybridization: moving from pathos to comedy, from irony to parody, he showed the various dimensions of passionate love once it is freed from the conventionalism of the courtly love code. His aspiration to present the difference that exists between the world of literature and the real experience of love could thus be attained by this dialogue between effects and genres. Each legend is therefore endowed with its own voice, which allowed Chaucer to offer a unique vision of love and of its place in the world.

Resisting closure has always been part of Chaucer's game. In *LGW*, he illustrated the contrast between reality and literary conventions by becoming himself the avatar of the unfaithful lover and abandoning us with an unfinished work. In other words, even if Chaucer's persona never enters into a dialogic relationship with the elements of the collection, the author himself avoids monologism through a hybridization highlighting the ambiguity of his poem and allowing him to affirm his authority as an author without suppressing the work's polyphony.

The linguistic structure at the heart of *LGW* is representative of Chaucer's willingness to innovate and develop new narratological frameworks. *The Canterbury Tales* represents his tour de force. In that poem, Chaucer pushed the hybridization of *LGW* a step further and created an extradiegetic dialogue between the literary genres of the tales. Whereas his narrative strategy had once consisted in establishing dialogism between the narrator's voice and his characters (in the diegesis), at the end of his career he achieved polyphony in his work by creating a dialogue that escaped the limits of the narrative. *CT* is consequently a resolutely modern work since it gives dialogue the opportunity to take place both inside and outside of the narration.

In the Introduction, I asked if it was possible to consider that the intertextuality of Chaucer's poetical influences and the assimilation of their different voices allowed him to revolutionize his conception of literature, and thus sow the seeds in English of what Bakhtin would later define as literary polyphony. That is the question at the heart of *Chaucer's Polyphony*.

I do believe that Chaucer's contribution to English literature is not to be looked for in his transformation of the English language itself, nor in the fact that he was one of the first to start writing in English in post–Norman Conquest England. Chaucer was not writing novels, he was not a Renaissance man, nor was he really Early Modern for that matter. He was a man of his time and had no idea he was a medieval poet. And yet his influence on English literature cannot be ignored. What I have tried to accomplish with this book is to show that we might find in Chaucer's contribution to the English polyphonic prose an answer to the question: Why Chaucer?

But that is just one possible answer. And in academia just as in Chaucer's poetry, debate and dialogue are important; they will allow us to continue to find answers to that question as we introduce Chaucer to a new millennium.

Bibliography

Archival Sources

London, British Library, MS Harley 4866.
Paris, Bibliothèque Mazarine, MS Mazarine 177, fol. 92d.
Paris, Bibliothèque Nationale de France, MS fr. 840, fol. 62.
Paris, Bibliothèque Nationale de France, MS fr. 1792, fol. 2r.

Primary Sources

Alighieri, Dante. *The Divine Comedy*. Translated by Allen Mandelbaum. New York, London, Toronto: Everyman's Library, 1995.
Alighieri, Dante. *De vulgari eloquentia*. 5th ed. Milan: Garzanti Editore, 2005.
Alighieri, Dante. *La Divina Commedia*. Milan: Bur, 2008.
Alighieri, Dante. *Vita Nuova*. Edited by Manuela Colombo. 5th ed. Milan: Feltrinelli, 2010.
Augustine. *Les Confessions*. Translated by Joseph Trabucco. Vol. 1 [Livres I–VIII]. Paris: Garnier frères, 1950.
Augustine. *Les Confessions*. Translated by Joseph Trabucco. Vol. 2 [Livres IX–XIII]. Paris: Garnier frères, 1950.
Augustine. *Œuvres de Saint Augustin. 71, Homélies sur l'évangile de Saint Jean. I–XVI*. Translated by Marie-François Berrouard. Paris: Desclée de Brouwer, 1969.
Augustine. *Œuvres de Saint Augustin. 72, Homélies sur l'évangile de Saint Jean. XVII–XXXIII*. Translated by Marie-François Berrouard. Paris: Desclée de Brouwer, 1977.
Augustine. *De Civitate Dei*. Edited by Bertrand Olivier. Translated by Raoul de Presles. Vol. 1. Paris: Honoré Champion, 2013.
Blyth, Charles R., ed. *Thomas Hoccleve: The Regiment of Princes*. Kalamazoo: Medieval Institute Publications, 1999.
Boccaccio, Giovanni. *Teseida*. Edited by Salvatore Battaglia. Florence: G.C. Sansoni, 1938.
Boccaccio, Giovanni. *Filostrato*. Edited by Luigi Surdich. Milan: Ugo Mursia Editore, 1990.
Boccaccio, Giovanni. *Decameron*. Edited by Vittore Branca. 5th edition. Milan: Mondadori Editore, 1998.
Chaucer, Geoffrey. *The Pardoner's Tale*. Edited by Nevill Coghill and Christopher Tolkien. London: Harrap, 1958.
Chaucer, Geoffrey. *The Nun's Priest's Tale*. Edited by Nevill Coghill and Christopher Tolkien. London: Harrap, 1965.
Chaucer, Geoffrey. *The Riverside Chaucer*. Edited by L.D. Benson and F.N. Robinson. 3rd edition. Boston: Houghton Mifflin Company, 1987.
Chaucer, Geoffrey. *A Variorum Edition of The Works of Geoffrey Chaucer*. Edited by Malcolm Andrew, Daniel J. Ransom, et al. 2 vols. Norman, OK; London: University of Oklahoma Press, 1993.
Chaucer, Geoffrey. *Les Contes de Canterbury et autres œuvres*. Translated by André Crépin et al. Paris: Robert Laffont, 2010.

Dickens, Charles. *Nicholas Nickleby*. London: Heron Books, 1970.
Dickens, Charles. *The Old Curiosity Shop*. London: Heron Books, 1970.
Gower, John. *Confessio Amantis*. Edited by Russel A. Peck. Translated by Andrew Galloway. Kalamazoo: TEAMS, 2006.
Langland, William. *Piers the Plowman and Richard the Redeless*. Edited by W.W. Skeat. London: Oxford University Press, 1969.
Lorris, Guillaume de, and Jean de Meun. *Le Roman de la Rose*. Edited by Armand Strubel. Paris: Le Livre de poche, 1997.
Lydgate, John. *Lydgate's Fall of Princes*. Edited by Henry Bergen. 4 vols. Washington: Carnegie Institution of Washington, 1923.
Oxford Classical Texts: P. Ovidi Nasonis: Amores; Medicamina Faciei Femineae; Ars Amatoria; Remedia Amoris. Edited by Edward J. Kenney. Oxford: Oxford University Press, 1994.
Petrarca, Francesco. *Canzoniere*. Edited by Ugo Dotti. Rome: Donzelli Editore, 1996.
Petrarch, Francesco. *Letters on Familiar Matters (Rerum Familiarium Libri)*. Translated by Aldo S. Bernardo. 3 vols. New York: Italica Press, 2008.
Shakespeare, William. *The Oxford Shakespeare: The Complete Works*. Edited by Stanley Wells et al. Oxford: Oxford University Press, 2005.
Troyes, Chrétien de. *Le Chevalier au lion*. Edited by Michel Rousse. Paris: Éditions Flammarion, 1990.
Troyes, Chrétien de. *Érec et Énide*. Edited by Jean-Marie Fritz. Paris: Le Livre de Poche, 1992.
Troyes, Chrétien de. *Œuvres complètes*. Edited by Daniel Poirion et al. Paris: Éditions Gallimard, 1994.
Troyes, Chrétien de. *Le Chevalier de la charrette*. Edited by Catherine Croizy-Naquet. Paris: Honoré Champion, 2006.
Virgil. *L'Énéide*. Translated by Maurice Rat. Vol. 1. Paris: Éditions Garnier Frères, 1955.
Virgil. *L'Énéide*. Translated by Maurice Rat. Vol. 2. Paris: Éditions Garnier Frères, 1955.
Virgil. *Aeneid*. Translated by Frederick Ahl. Oxford: Oxford University Press, 2007.
Voltaire. *Candide ou l'optimisme*. Paris: Pocket, 1998.
Wilde, Oscar. *Oscar Wilde: Plays, Prose Writings and Poems*. New York, London, Toronto: Everyman's Library, 1991.

Secondary Sources

Aarne, Antti. *The Types of the Folktale: A Classification and Bibliography*. Helsinki: The Finnish Academy of Science and Letters, 1961.
Adams, Robert M. *Strains of Discord: Studies in Literary Openness*. Ithaca: Cornell University Press, 1958.
Astell, Ann W. "Apostrophe, Prayer and the Structure of Satire in *The Man of Laws's Tale*." *Studies in the Age of Chaucer* 13 (1991): 81–97.
Auerbach, Erich. *Studi su Dante*. Translated by Maria Luisa De Pieri Bonino and Dante della Terza. Milan: Feltrinelli, 2009.
Austin, John L. *How to Do Things With Words: The William James Lectures Delivered at Harvard University in 1955*. Oxford: Clarendon Press, 1962.
Authier-Revuz, Jacqueline. "Hétérogénéité montrée et hétérogénéité constitutive: éléments pour une approche de l'autre dans le discours." *DRLAV* 2 (1982): 91–151.

Authier-Revuz, Jacqueline. *Ces mots qui ne vont pas de soi. Boucles réflexives et non-coïncidences du dire*. 2 vols. Paris: Larousse, 1995.
Bakhtin, Mikhail M. *Esthétique et théorie du roman*. Translated by Daria Olivier. Paris: Éditions Gallimard, 1978.
Bakhtin, Mikhail M. *The Dialogic Imagination: Four Essays*. Edited by Michael Holquist. Translated by Caryl Emerson and Michael Holquist. Austin: University of Texas Press, 1981.
Bakhtin, Mikhail M. *Esthétique de la création verbale*. Translated by Alfreda Aucouturier. Paris: Éditions Gallimard, 1984.
Bakhtin, Mikhail M. *Problems of Dostoevsky's Poetics*. Translated by Caryl Emerson. Minneapolis: University of Minnesota Press, 1984.
Bakhtin, Mikhail M. *Rabelais and His World*. Translated by Helene Isowlsky. Bloomington: Indiana University Press, 1984.
Bakhtin, Mikhail M. *Speech Genres and Other Late Essays*. Edited by Caryl Emerson and Michael Holquist. Translated by Vern W. McGee. Austin: University of Texas Press, 1986.
Bakhtin, Mikhail M. *Toward a Philosophy of the Act*. Edited by Vadim Liapunov and Michael Holquist. Translated by Vadim Liapunov. Austin: University of Texas Press, 1999.
Bally Charles. *Linguistique générale et linguistique française*. Berne: Francke, 1932.
Barber, Bernard. *Social Stratification*. New York: Harcourt, Brace, Bernstein, 1957.
Barber, Charles. *The English Language: A Historical Introduction*. Cambridge: Cambridge University Press, 2000.
Barthes, Roland. "The Reality Effect." *The Rustle of Language*. Translated by Richard Howard. Berkeley: University of California Press, 1989, 141–8.
Bede. *The Ecclesiastical History of the English People*. Edited by Judith McClure and Roger Collins. Oxford: Oxford University Press, 2008.
Bennett, Jack A.W. "Chaucer, Dante and Boccaccio." *Chaucer and the Italian Trecento*. Edited by Piero Boitani. Cambridge: Cambridge University Press, 1985, 89–113.
Benson, C. David. *Chaucer's Drama of Style: Poetic Variety and Contrast in the Canterbury Tales*. Chapel Hill: University of North Carolina Press, 1986.
Benson, C. David. "*The Canterbury Tales*: Personal Drama or Experiments in Poetic Variety?" *The Cambridge Chaucer Companion*. Edited by Piero Boitani and Jill Mann. Cambridge: Cambridge University Press, 1988, 93–108.
Benveniste, Émile. *Problèmes de linguistique générale*. Paris: Gallimard, 1966.
Biggs, Frederick M. *Chaucer's Decameron and the Origin of the Canterbury Tales*. Cambridge: D.S. Brewer, 2017.
Bloemendal, Jan, Peter Eversmann, and Elsa Strietman. *Drama, Performance and Debate: Theatre and Public Opinion in the Early Modern Period*. Leyden: Brill, 2012.
Bloomfield, Morton W. "Chaucerian Realism." *The Cambridge Chaucer Companion*. Edited by Piero Boitani and Jill Mann. Cambridge: Cambridge University Press, 1986/1988, 179–93.
Boitani, Piero. "What Dante Meant to Chaucer." *Chaucer and the Italian Trecento*. Edited by Piero Boitani. Cambridge: Cambridge University Press, 1983, 115–39.
Boitani, Piero. *Chaucer and the Imaginary World of Fame*. Cambridge: D.S. Brewer, 1984.
Boitani, Piero. "Old Books Brought to Life in Dreams: The *Book of the Duchess*, the *House of Fame*, the *Parliament of Fowls*." *The Cambridge Chaucer Companion*. Edited by Piero Boitani and Jill Mann. Cambridge: Cambridge University Press, 1988, 39–57.
Boitani, Piero. *The European Tragedy of Troilus*. Oxford: Clarendon Press, 1989.

Boitani, Piero. *Letteratura europea e Medioevo volgare*. Bologna: Società editrice il Mulino, 2007.
Bres, Jacques, and Bertrand Verine. "Le bruissement des voix dans le discours: dialogisme et discours rapporté." *Faits de langues* 19 (2002): 159–69.
Bres, Jacques and Sylvie Mellet. "Une approche dialogique des faits grammaticaux." *Langue française* 163, no. 3 (2009): 3–20.
Brewer, D.S. "Images of Chaucer 1386–1900." *Chaucer and the Chaucerians: Critical Studies in Middle English Literature*. Edited by D.S. Brewer. London: Thomas Nelson and Sons Ltd., 1966, 243–46.
Brewer, D.S. "The Relationship of Chaucer to the English and European Traditions." *Chaucer and the Chaucerians: Critical Studies in Middle English Literature*. Edited by D.S. Brewer. London: Thomas Nelson and Sons Ltd., 1966, 1–38.
Brewer, D.S., ed. *Chaucer: The Critical Heritage. Vol. 1, 1385–1837*. London, Boston: Routledge and Kegan Paul, 1978.
Brewer, D.S., ed. *Chaucer: The Critical Heritage. Vol. 2, 1837–1933*. London, Boston: Routledge and Kegan Paul, 1978.
Brewer, D.S. *An Introduction to Chaucer*. London, New York: Longman Group, 1984.
Brewer, D.S. "Chaucer's Poetic Style." *The Cambridge Chaucer Companion*. Edited by Piero Boitani and Jill Mann. Cambridge: Cambridge University Press, 1988, 227–42.
Burger, Glenn. "'Pite rennet soone in gentil herte': Ugly Feelings and Gendered Conduct in Chaucer's *Legend of Good Women*." *Chaucer Review* 52, no. 1 (2017): 66–84.
Burnley, J.D. *A Guide to Chaucer's Language*. London: Macmillan, 1983.
Burrow, J.A. "The Canterbury Tales I: Romance." *The Cambridge Chaucer Companion*. Edited by Piero Boitani and Jill Mann. Cambridge: Cambridge University Press, 1986/1988, 109–24.
Butterfield, Ardis. *Poetry and Music in Medieval France: From Jean Renart to Guillaume de Machaut*. Cambridge: Cambridge University Press, 2002.
Butterfield, Ardis. "Chaucer and the Detritus of the City." *Chaucer and the City*. Edited by Ardis Butterfield. Cambridge: D.S. Brewer, 2006, 3–22.
Butterfield, Ardis. "Chaucerian Vernaculars." *Studies in the Age of Chaucer* 31 (2009): 25–51.
Butterfield, Ardis. *The Familiar Enemy: Chaucer, Language, and Nation in the Hundred Years War*. Oxford: Oxford University Press, 2009.
Cannon, Christopher. "The Myth of Origin and the Making of Chaucer's English." *Speculum* 71 (1996): 646–75.
Cannon, Christopher. *The Making of Chaucer's English*. Cambridge: Cambridge University Press, 1998.
Cannon, Christopher. "What Chaucer's Language Is." *Studies in the Age of Chaucer* 24 (2002): 301–8.
Chancellor, Philip the. *Motets and Prosulas*. Edited by Thomas B. Payne. Middleton, WI: A-R Editions, 2011.
Chateaubriand, François-René de. *Essai sur la littérature anglaise et considérations sur le génie des hommes, des temps et des révolutions (1836)*. Edited by Sébastien Baudoin. Société des Textes Français Modernes. Paris: Classiques Garnier, 2012.
Childs, Wendy. "Anglo-Italian Contacts in the Fourteenth Century." *Chaucer and the Italian Trecento*. Edited by Piero Boitani. Cambridge: Cambridge University Press, 1985, 65–87.
Clifford, James. "On Ethnographic Authority." *Representations* 1 (1983): 136–37.

Coates, Ruth. *Christianity in Bakhtin: God and the Exiled Author*. Cambridge: Cambridge University Press, 1998.

Coghill, Nevill. "Chaucer's Narrative art in *The Canterbury Tales*." *Chaucer and the Chaucerians: Critical Studies in Middle English Literature*. Edited by D.S. Brewer. London: Thomas Nelson and Sons Ltd., 1966, 114–39.

Cole, Andrew. "John Gower Copies Geoffrey Chaucer." *Chaucer Review* 52, no. 1 (2017): 46–65.

Collette, Carolyn P. "Chaucer's Poetics and Purposes in the *Legend of Good Women*." *Chaucer Review* 52, no. 1 (2017): 12–28.

Cook, Megan L. "Author, Text, and Paratext in Early Modern Editions of the *Legend of Good Women*." *Chaucer Review* 52, no. 1 (2017): 124–42.

Crépin, André. "Le plurilinguisme de l'Angleterre médiévale." *Carnets d'atelier de sociolinguistique* 2 (2007): 28–44.

Crow, Martin M., and Clair C. Olson. *Chaucer Life-Records*. Oxford: Oxford University Press, 1966.

Curtius, E.R. *European Literature and the Latin Middle Ages*. Translated by W.R. Trask. Princeton: Princeton University Press, 1990.

Dahmus, J.H. *The Prosecution of John Wyclif*. New Haven: Yale University Press, 1970.

Davidson, Mary Catherine. *Medievalism, Multilingualism, and Chaucer*. New York: Palgrave Macmillan, 2010.

Delany, Sheila. *The Naked Text: Chaucer's Legend of Good Women*. Berkeley: University of California Press, 1994.

Derrida, Jacques. "The Parergon." *October* 9 (1979): 3–40.

Dinshaw, Carolyn. *Chaucer's Sexual Poetics*. Madison: University of Wisconsin Press, 1989.

Donaldson, Ian. *The Rapes of Lucretia: A Myth and Its Transformations*. Oxford: Oxford University Press, 1982.

Dor, Juliette. "Dialogical Reading and the Biblical-Creed Narrative Prayers in Chaucer's 'Man of Law's Tale.'" *English Studies in Transition: Papers from the ESSE Inaugural Conference*. Edited by Robert Clark and Piero Boitani. London, New York: Routledge, 1993, 107–19.

Ducrot, Oswald. "La notion de sujet parlant." *Recherches philosophiques sur le langage: Cahier du groupe de recherche sur la philosophie du langage, université des sciences sociales de Grenoble* 2 (1982): 65–93.

Ducrot, Oswald. "Esquisse d'une théorie polyphonique de l'énonciation." *Le dire et le dit*. Paris: Editions de Minuit, 1984, 171–233.

Ducrot, Oswald. "Enonciation et polyphonie chez Charles Bally." *Logiques, structures, énonciations*. Paris: Minuit, 1989, 165–91.

Duméril, Edelestan. "La vie et les ouvrages de Wace." *Comptes rendus des séances de l'Académie des Inscriptions et Belles-Lettres* 1 (1857): 74–82.

Dumitrescu, Irina. "Beautiful Suffering and the Culpable Narrator in Chaucer's *Legend of Good Women*." *Chaucer Review* 52, no. 1 (2017): 106–23.

Dryden, John. "Preface to Fables, Ancient and Modern." *The Harvard Classics: Prefaces and Prologues to Famous Books*. Edited by Charles William Eliot. Vol. 39. New York: P.F. Collier & Son, 1909/2001.

Eco, Umberto. *The Open Work*. Translated by Anna Cancogni. Cambridge, MA: Harvard University Press, 1989.

Eliot, T.S. *To Criticize the Critic, and Other Writings*. New York: Farrar, Strauss and Giroux, 1965.

Engle, Lars. "Bakhtin, Chaucer, and Anti-Essentialist Humanism." *Exemplaria* 1 (1989): 489–97.
Engle, Lars. "Chaucer, Bakhtin, and Griselda." *Exemplaria* 1 (1989): 429–59.
Edwards, Catharine. *Death in Ancient Rome*. New Haven: Yale University Press, 2007.
Farrell, Thomas J., ed. *Bakhtin and Medieval Voices*. Gainesville: University of Florida Press, 1996.
Fleischman, Suzanne. *Tense and Narrativity: From Medieval Performance to Modern Fiction*. Austin: University of Texas Press, 1990.
Fourrier, Anthime. "Encore la chronologie des œuvres de Chrétien de Troyes." *Bulletin bibliographique de la société internationale arthurienne* (1950): 69–88.
Frank, R.W., Jr. *Chaucer and The Legend of Good Women*. Cambridge, MA: Harvard University Press, 1972.
Frank, R.W., Jr. "*The Canterbury Tales* III: Pathos." *The Cambridge Chaucer Companion*. Edited by Piero Boitani and Jill Mann. Cambridge: Cambridge University Press, 1988, 143–58.
Fruoco, Jonathan. "Chaucer as a Sociolinguist: Understanding the Role of Language in Chaucer's Internationalism." *Critical Insights: Geoffrey Chaucer*. Edited by James M. Dean. Ipswich, MA: Salem Press, 2017, 216–30.
Fumo, Jamie C. *Making Chaucer's Book of the Duchess: Textuality and Reception*. Cardiff: University of Wales Press, 2015.
Fumo, Jamie C. *Chaucer's Book of the Duchess: Contexts and Interpretations*. Cambridge: D.S. Brewer, 2018.
Frye, Northrop. *Anatomy of Criticism, Four Essays*. Princeton: Princeton University Press, 1973.
Fyler, J.M. *Language and the Declining World in Chaucer, Dante and Jean de Meun*. Cambridge: Cambridge University Press, 2010.
Gaignebet, Claude, and Jean-Dominique Lajoux. *Art profane et religion populaire au Moyen Age*. Paris: PUF, 1985.
Ganim, John M. *Chaucerian Theatricality*. Princeton: Princeton University Press, 1990.
Genette, Gérard. *Figures III*. Paris: Editions du Seuil, 1972.
Genette, Gérard. *Palimpsestes: La littérature au second degré*. Paris: Seuil, 1982.
Genette, Gérard. *Nouveau discours du récit*. Paris: Editions du Seuil, 1983.
Grudin, Michaela Paasche. *Chaucer and the Politics of Discourse*. Columbia: University of South Carolina Press, 1996.
Gushee, Marion S. "The Polyphonic Music of the Medieval Monastery, Cathedral and University." *Antiquity and the Middle Ages: From Ancient Greece to the 15th Century*. Edited by James McKinnon. London: Macmillan, 1990, 143–69.
Guthrie, Steve. "Dialogics and Prosody in Chaucer." *Bakhtin and Medieval Voices*. Edited by Thomas J. Farrel. Gainesville: University of Florida Press, 1996, 94–108.
Halàsz, Katalin. *Images d'auteur dans le roman médiéval (XIIe-XIIIe siècles)*. Debrecen: Kossuth Lajos Tudomanyegyetem, 1992.
Harding, Wendy. *Drama, Narrative and Poetry in the Canterbury Tales*. Toulouse: Presses universitaires du Mirail, 2003.
Hill, John M. *Chaucer's Neoplatonism: Varieties of Love, Friendship, and Community*. London: Lexington Books, 2018.
Hindley, Geoffrey. *A Brief History of the Anglo-Saxons*. London: Robinson, 2006.
Holquist, Michael. *Dialogism: Bakhtin and His World*. New York: Routledge, 1990.
Hsy, Jonathan. *Trading Tongues: Merchants, Multilingualism, and Medieval Literature*. Columbus: The Ohio State University Press, 2013.

Jefferson, Judith A., Ad Putter, and Amanda Hopkins, eds. *Multilingualism and Medieval Britain (c. 1066–1520): Sources and Analysis*. Turnhout: Brepols, 2013.
Jenaro-MacLennan, Luis. *The Trecento Commentaries on the "Divina Commedia" and the Epistle to Cangrande*. Oxford: Oxford University Press, 1974.
Joseph, Gerhard. "Chaucer's Coinage: Foreign Exchange and the Puns of The Shipman's Tale." *Chaucer Review* 17 (1983): 341–57.
Kane, George. *Chaucer*. Oxford: Oxford University Press, 1984.
Kelly, Henry Ansgar. *Chaucer and the Cult of St. Valentine*. Leiden: E.J. Brill, 1986.
Kelly, Henry Ansgar. *Chaucerian Tragedy*. Cambridge: D.S. Brewer, 1997.
Kermode, Frank. *The Sense of an Ending: Studies in the Theory of Fiction*. Oxford: Oxford University Press, 1986.
Kimmelman, Burt. "Ockham, Chaucer, and the Emergence of Modern Poetics." *The Rhetorical Poetics of the Middle Ages: Reconstructive Polyphony*. Edited by John M. Hill and Deborah M. Sinnreich-Levi. Madison, NJ and London: Fairleigh Dickinson University Press and Associated University Presses, 2000, 177–205.
Kirkpatrick, Robin. "The Wake of the *Commedia*: Chaucer's *Canterbury Tales* and Boccaccio's *Decameron*." *Chaucer and the Italian Trecento*. Edited by Piero Boitani. Cambridge: Cambridge University Press, 1985, 201–30.
Kittredge, G.L. "Chaucer's Discussion of Marriage." *Modern Philology* 9, no. 4 (1912): 435–67.
Kittredge, G.L. *Chaucer and His Poetry: Lectures Delivered in 1914 on the Percy Turnbull Memorial Foundation in the Johns Hopkins University*. Cambridge, MA: Harvard University Press, 1915.
Kleinhenz, Christopher, and Keith Busby, eds. *Medieval Multilingualism: The Francophone World and Its Neighbours*. Turnhout: Brepols, 2010.
Knapp, Peggy. *Chaucer and the Social Contest*. New York: Routledge, 1990.
Kristeva, Julia. "Le mot, le dialogue et le roman." *Séméiotiké. Recherches pour une sémanalyse*. Paris: Editions du Seuil, 1969, 82–112.
Labov, William. *Sociolinguistic Patterns*. Philadelphia: University of Pennsylvania Press, 1972.
Lambert, Mark. "Telling the Story in Troilus and Criseyde." *The Cambridge Chaucer Companion*. Edited by Piero Boitani and Jill Mann. Cambridge: Cambridge University Press, 1988, 59–73.
Larner, John. "Chaucer's Italy." *Chaucer and the Italian Trecento*. Edited by Piero Boitani. Cambridge: Cambridge University Press, 1985, 7–32.
Lawton, David. *Chaucer's Narrators*. Chaucer Studies 13. Cambridge: Brewer, 1985.
Le Goff, Jacques. *The Medieval Imagination*. Translated by Arthur Goldhammer. Chicago: University of Chicago Press, 1988.
Leith, Dick. *A Social History of English*. London: Routledge and Kegan Paul, 1983.
Lewis, C.S. *Oxford History of English Literature: English Literature in the Sixteenth Century Excluding Drama*. Edited by F.P. Wilson and Bonamy Dobrée. Oxford: Oxford University Press, 1954.
Lewis, C.S. *The Allegory of Love: A Study in Medieval Tradition*. Oxford: Oxford University Press, 1936/1959.
Lewis, C.S. "What Chaucer Really Did to 'Il Filostrato.'" *Selected Literary Essays*. Edited by Walter Hooper. Cambridge: Cambridge University Press, 1969, 27–44.
Mann, Jill. *Chaucer and Medieval Estates Satire: The Literature of Social Classes and the General Prologue to the Canterbury Tales*. Cambridge: Cambridge University Press, 1973.

Mann, Jill. "Chance and Destiny in *Troilus and Criseyde* and the Knight's Tale." *The Cambridge Chaucer Companion*. Edited by Piero Boitani and Jill Mann. Cambridge: Cambridge University Press, 1988, 75–92.

Mann, Jill. *Geoffrey Chaucer*. Hassocks: Harvester, 1991.

Martin, Ellen A. "The Interior Decoration of His Mind: Exegesis in *The House of Fame*." *The Rhetorical Poetics of the Middle Ages: Reconstructive Polyphony*. Edited by John M. Hill and Deborah M. Sinnreich-Levi. Madison, NJ and London: Fairleigh Dickinson University Press and Associated University Presses, 2000, 106–29.

McClellan, William. "Bakhtin's Theory of Dialogic Discourse, Medieval Rhetorical Theory, and the Multi-Voiced Structure of the Clerk's Tale." *Exemplaria* 1 (1989): 461–88.

McClellan, William. "Lars Engle—'Chaucer, Bakhtin, and Griselda': A Response." *Exemplaria* 1 (1989): 499–506.

McClellan, William. "'Me Thynketh It a Thyng Impertinent': Inaugurating Dialogic Discourse in the Prologue to the Clerk's Tale." *The Rhetorical Poetics of the Middle Ages: Reconstructive Polyphony*. Edited by John M. Hill and Deborah M. Sinnreich-Levi. Madison, NJ and London: Fairleigh Dickinson University Press and Associated University Presses, 2000, 149–63.

McCormick, Betsy, Leah Schwebel, and Lynn Shutters. "Introduction: Looking Forward, Looking Back on the *Legend of Good Women*." *Chaucer Review* 52, no. 1 (2017): 3–11.

McCrum, Robert, Robert MacNeil, and William Cran. *The Story of English*. London: Faber and Faber, 1986.

McGerr, Rosemarie. *Chaucer's Open Books*. Miami: University Press of Florida, 1998.

McKeon, Michael. *The Origins of the English Novel, 1600–1740*. Baltimore: Johns Hopkins University Press, 1987.

McMullan, Gordon, and David Matthews, eds. *Reading the Medieval in Early Modern England*. Cambridge: Cambridge University Press, 2007.

Mehl, Dieter. "Chaucer's Narrator: *Troilus and Criseyde* and the *Canterbury Tales*." *The Cambridge Chaucer Companion*. Edited by Piero Boitani and Jill Mann. Cambridge: Cambridge University Press, 1988, 213–26.

Mersand, Joseph. *Chaucer's Romance Vocabulary*. New York: Comet Press, 1939.

Miller, H. Hillis. "Stevens' Rock and Criticism as Cure." *Georgia Review* 30 (1976): 330–48.

Minnis, Alastair. *Translations of Authority in Medieval English Literature: Valuing the Vernacular*. Cambridge: Cambridge University Press, 2009.

Morson, Gary S., and Caryl Emerson. *Mikhail Bakhtin: Creation of a Prosaics*. Stanford: Stanford Universty Press, 1990.

Mossé, Fernand, and André Jolivet. *Manuel de l'anglais du Moyen Âge: des origines au XIVe siècle*. 2 vols. Paris: Éditions Montaigne, 1945.

Muscatine, Charles. *Chaucer and the French Tradition: A Study in Style and Meaning*. Berkeley, Los Angeles: University of California Press, 1957.

Muscatine, Charles. "*The Canterbury Tales*: Style of the Man and Style of the Work." *Chaucer and the Chaucerians: Critical Studies in Middle English Literature*. Edited by D.S. Brewer. London: Thomas Nelson and Sons Ltd., 1966, 88–113.

Nakao, Yoshiyuki. *The Structure of Chaucer's Ambiguity*. Studies in English Medieval Language and Literature 36. Frankfurt am Main: Peter Lang, 2013.

Neuse, Richard. *Chaucer's Dante: Allegory and Epic Theater in The Canterbury Tales*. Berkeley: University of California Press, 1991.

Nolan, Barabar. "The Art of Expropriation: Chaucer's Narrator in *The Book of the Duchess*." *New Perspectives in Chaucer Criticism*. Edited by Donald Rose. Norman, OK: Pilgrim, 1981, 203–22.
Nølke, Henning, Kjersti Fløttum, and Coco Norén. *ScaPoLinE: La théorie scandinave de la polyphonie linguistique*. Paris: Editions Kimé, 2005.
Novikoff, Alex J. *The Medieval Culture of Disputation: Pedagogy, Practice, and Performance*. Philadelphia: University of Pennsylvania Press, 2013.
Payne, Robert. *The Key of Remembrance: A Study of Chaucer's Poetics*. Westport, CT: Archon Press, 1973.
Pearsall, Derek. "The Canterbury Tales II: Comedy." *The Cambridge Chaucer Companion*. Edited by Piero Boitani and Jill Mann. Cambridge: Cambridge University Press, 1988, 125–42.
Pearsall, Derek. *The Life of Geoffrey Chaucer: A Critical Biography*. Oxford: Blackwell, 1992.
Perrin, Laurent. "La notion de polyphonie en linguistique et dans le champ des sciences du langage." *Questions de communication* 6 (2004): 265–82.
Perrin, Laurent. "Polyphonie et autres formes d'hétérogénéité énonciative: Bakhtine, Bally, Ducrot, etc." *Pratiques: linguistique, littérature, didactique* 123–124 (2004): 7–26.
Perrin, Laurent. "Le sens montré n'est pas dit." *L'énonciation dans tous ses états, mélanges offerts à Henning Nølke à l'occasion de ses soixante ans*. Edited by Merete Birkelund, Maj-Britt Mosegaard Hansen, and Coco Norén. Bern: Peter Lang, 2008, 157–87.
Perrin, Laurent. "La voix et le point de vue comme formes polyphoniques externes." *Langue française* 164 (2009): 61–79.
Phillips, Helen. "Morality in the *Canterbury Tales*, Chaucer's Lyrics and the *Legend of Good Women*." *Chaucer and Religion*. Edited by Hellen Phillips. Cambridge: D.S. Brewer, 2010, 156–72.
Pinti, Daniel J. "Dialogism, Heteroglossia, and Late Medieval Translation." *Bakhtin and Medieval Voices*. Edited by Thomas J. Farrel. Gainesville: University of Florida Press, 1996, 109–21.
Polo de Beaulieu, Marie Anne, ed. *Formes dialoguées dans la littérature exemplaire du Moyen Âge*. Paris: Honoré Champion, 2012.
Poplack, Shana. "Sometimes I'll Start a Sentence in Spanish Y TERMINO EN ESPANOL: Toward a Typology of Code-Switching." *Linguistics* (1980): 581–618.
Reiss, Edmund. "Ambiguous Signs and Authorial Deceptions in Fourteenth-Century Fiction." *Sign, Sentence, Discourse: Language in Medieval Thought and Literature*. Edited by Julian N. Wasserman and Lois Roney. New York: Syracuse University Press, 1989, 124–25.
Richter, Michael. *Sprache und Gesellschaft im Mittelalter: Untersuchungen zur mündlichen Kommunikation in England von der Mitte des elften bis zum beginn des vierzehnten Jahrhunderts*. Stuttgart: Hiersemann, 1979.
Rowe, Donald. *Through Nature to Eternity: Chaucer's Legend of Good Women*. Lincoln: University of Nebraska Press, 1988.
Rossiter, W.T. *Chaucer and Petrarch*. Cambridge: D.S. Brewer, 2010.
Sadlek, Gregory M. "Bakhtin, the Novel, and Chaucer's *Troilus and Criseyde*." *The Chaucer Yearbook* 3 (1996): 87–101.
Salter, Elizabeth. "Chaucer and Internationalism." *Studies in the Age of Chaucer* 1 (1980): 71–79.

Saltzstein, Jennifer. "Cleric-Trouvères and the *Jeux-Partis* of Medieval Arras." *Viator* 43 (2012): 147–63.
Sautman, Francesca Canade, et al. *Telling Tales: Medieval Narratives and the Folk Tradition*. New York: Saint Martin's Press, 1998.
Scheler, Manfred. *Der englische Wortschatz*. Berlin: Erich Schmidt Verlag, 1977.
Schendl, Herbert. "Code-Switching in Late Medieval Macaronic Sermons." *Multilingualism and Medieval Britain (c. 1066–1520): Sources and Analysis*. Edited by Judith Jefferson et al. Turnhout: Brepols, 2013, 153–69.
Schultz, James A. *Courtly Love, the Love of Courtliness, and the History of Sexuality*. Chicago: University of Chicago Press, 2006.
Schwebel, Leah. "Livy and Augustine as Negative Models in the *Legend of Lucrece*." *Chaucer Review* 52, no. 1 (2017): 29–45.
Seymour, M.C. *A Catalogue of Chaucer Manuscripts 1: Works Before the Canterbury Tales*. Aldershot: Scolar Press, 1995.
Sharpe, Richard. "Addressing Different Language Groups: Charters from the Eleventh and Twelfth Centuries." *Multilingualism and Medieval Britain (c. 1066–1520): Sources and Analysis*. Edited by Judith Jefferson et al. Turnhout: Brepols, 2013, 1–40.
Shepherd, G.T. "Troilus and Criseyde." *Chaucer and the Chaucerians: Critical Studies in Middle English Literature*. Edited by D.S. Brewer. London: Thomas Nelson and Sons Ltd., 1966, 65–87.
Shippey, Thomas A. "Bilingualism and Betrayal in Chaucer's Summoner's Tale." *Speaking in the Medieval World*. Edited by Jean Godsall-Myers. Leiden, Boston: Brill, 2003, 125–44.
Shutters, Lynn. "The Thought and Feel of Virtuous Wifehood: Recovering Emotion in the *Legend of Good Women*." *Chaucer Review* 52, no. 1 (2017): 85–105.
Simpson, James. "Chaucer as a European Writer." *The Yale Companion to Chaucer*. Edited by S. Lerer. New Haven, London: Yale University Press, 2006, 55–86.
Smith, Jeremy J. "Chaucer and the Invention of English." *Studies in the Age of Chaucer* 24 (2002): 335–46.
Spearing, A.C. "The Canterbury Tales IV: Exemplum and Fable." *The Cambridge Chaucer Companion*. Edited by Piero Boitani and Jill Mann. Cambridge: Cambridge University Press, 1986/1988, 159–78.
Spearing, A.C. *Textual Subjectivity: The Encoding of Subjectivity in Medieval Narratives and Lyrics*. Oxford: Oxford University Press, 2005.
Strohm, Paul. "The Social and Literary Scene in England." *The Cambridge Chaucer Companion*. Edited by Piero Boitani and Jill Mann. Cambridge: Cambridge University Press, 1988, 1–18.
Strohm, Paul. *Social Chaucer*. Cambridge, MA: Harvard University Press, 1989.
Strohm, Paul. *Theory and the Premodern Text*. Minneapolis: University of Minnesota Press, 2000.
Strohm, Paul. *Chaucer's Tale: 1386 and the Road to Canterbury*. New York: Viking Adult, 2014.
Symes, Carol. *A Common Stage: Theater and Public Life in Medieval Arras*. Ithaca: Cornell University Press, 2007.
Taruskin, Richard. *Music from the Earliest Notation to the Sixteenth Century*. Oxford: Oxford University Press, 2005.
Taylor, Karla. *Chaucer Reads "The Divine Comedy."* Stanford: Stanford University Press, 1989.
Thompson, N.S. *Chaucer, Boccaccio, and the Debate of Love: A Comparative Study of the Decameron and the Canterbury Tales*. Oxford: Oxford University Press, 1999.

Todorov, Tzvetan. *Mikhaïl Bakhtine, le principe dialogique*. Paris: Editions du Seuil, 1981.
Tolkien, J.R.R. "Chaucer as a Philologist: The Reeve's Tale." *Transactions of the Philological Society* (1934): 1–70.
Tolkien, J.R.R. "English and Welsh." *The Monsters and the Critics and Other Essays*. Edited by Christopher Tolkien. London: HarperCollins Publishers, 2006, 162–97.
Tolkien, J.R.R. *The Fall of Arthur*. Edited by Christopher Tolkien. London: HarperCollins Publishers, 2013.
Toon, T.E. "The Social and Political Contexts of Language Change in Anglo-Saxon England." *English in its Social Context: Essays in Historical Sociolinguistics*. Edited by T.M. Machan and C.T. Scott. Oxford: Oxford University Press, 1992, 28–46.
Travis, Peter W. "Deconstructing Chaucer's Retraction?" *Exemplaria* 3 (1991): 135–58.
Trevelyan, G.M. *English Social History: A Survey of Six Centuries*. London: Penguin Books, 2000.
Trigg, Stephanie. *Congenial Souls: Reading Chaucer from Medieval to Postmodern*. Minneapolis: University of Minnesota Press, 2002.
Trotter, David A., ed. *Multilingualism in Later Medieval Britain*. Woodbridge: Boydell & Brewer, 2000.
Turner, Marion. *Chaucer: A European Life*. Princeton, Oxford: Princeton University Press, 2019.
Voloshinov, Valentin N. *Marxism and the Philosophy of Language*. Translated by Ladislav Matejka and I.R. Titunik. Cambridge: Harvard University Press, 1973.
Wallace, David. "Chaucer and Boccaccio's Early Writings." *Chaucer and the Italian Trecento*. Edited by Piero Boitani. Cambridge: Cambridge University Press, 1985, 141–62.
Wallace, David. "Chaucer's Continental Inheritance: The Early Poems and *Troilus and Criseyde*." *The Cambridge Chaucer Companion*. Edited by Piero Boitani and Jill Mann. Cambridge: Cambridge University Press, 1988, 19–37.
Walter, Henriette. *Honni soit qui mal y pense: L'incroyable histoire d'amour entre le français et l'anglais*. Paris: Robert Laffont, 2001.
Walter, Philippe. *La mémoire du temps. Fêtes et calendriers de Chrétien de Troyes à La Mort Artu*. Paris: Champion, 1989.
Walter, Philippe. *Chrétien de Troyes*. Paris: PUF, 1997.
Warren, Nancy Bradley. "Chivalric Men and Good(?) Women: Chaucer, Gender, and John Bossewell's *Workes of Armorie*." *Chaucer Review* 52, no. 1 (2017): 143–61.
Wasserman, Julian N. "Both Fixed and Free." *Sign, Sentence, Discourse: Language in Medieval Thought and Literature*. Edited by Julian N. Wasserman and Lois Roney. New York: Syracuse University Press, 1989, 194–222.
Williams, Deanne. "Friar Bacon and Friar Bungay and the Rhetoric of Temporality." *Reading the Medieval in Early Modern England*. Edited by Gordon McMullan and David Matthews. Cambridge: Cambridge University Press, 2007, 31–48.
Wimsatt, James. *Chaucer and the French Love Poets, the Literary Background of the Book of the Duchess*. Chapel Hill: University of North Carolina Press, 1968.
Windeatt, Barry A. "Chaucer and the *Filostrato*." *Chaucer and the Italian Trecento*. Cambridge: Cambridge University Press, 1985, 163–83.
Windeatt, Barry A. "Literary Structures in Chaucer." *The Cambridge Chaucer Companion*. Edited by Piero Boitani and Jill Mann. Cambridge: Cambridge University Press, 1988, 195–212.
Windeatt, Barry A. *Oxford Guides to Chaucer: Troilus and Criseyde*. Oxford: Clarendon Press, 1995.

Windeatt, Barry A. "The 'Troilus' as Translation." *Troilus and Criseyde: "The Book of Troilus" by Geoffrey Chaucer*. Edited by B.A. Windeatt. London, New York: Routledge, 2013, 3–24.

Zink, Michel. "Une mutation de la conscience littéraire: Le langage romanesque à travers des exemples français du XIIe siècle." *Cahiers de civilisation médiévale* 24 (1981): 3–27.

Zumthor, Paul. *Langue et techniques poétiques à l'époque romane: XIe–XIIIe siècles*. Paris: C. Klincksieck, 1963.

Zumthor, Paul. *La poésie et la voix dans la civilisation médiévale*. Paris: Presses Universitaires de France, 1984.

Index

Names and Works

Énide XI, 39–42, 44
Érec XI, 39–42, 44
Érec et Énide XI, 39–42, 44

Achilles 116–117
Advanced Learner's Dictionary 33–34
Adversus Jovinanum 197
Aeneas 38, 44, 77–78, 85, 142–145, 148, 156
Aeneid XI, 44, 74–75, 77–79, 116, 142–143, 155, 182
Al cor gentil 56, 117
Alain de Lille 15
Alceste 127–128, 132, 134, 139
Alfred 26
Alighieri, Dante 35
Allegory, allegorical 37, 45–46, 48, 61
Allegory of Love 37, 45–46, 48, 61, 71, 75, 95, 130, 173
Amleto. *See* Hamlet
Amorosa Visione 55, 62, 74
Anatomy of Criticism 154, 163
Andreas Capellanus 96–98
Anelida and Arcite 88, 181–182
Anglo-Norman 34, 38, 192
Anglo-Saxons 25–26
Apology of Socrates 7
Aquinas, Thomas 120, 171
Argonautica 147
Ariadne 154–159, 182
Aristotle 3, 37, 171
Ars amatoria 98, 153, 160
Arthur (King) 39
Aucouturier, Michel 21
Auerbach, Erich 21, 56–57, 120
Augustine, Saint 78, 153, 204
Austen, Jane 125
Austin, John L. 22
Authier-Revuz, Jacqueline 19, 21–22

Bailly, Harry 174–175, 178–179, 181, 184–185, 199–200

Bakhtin, M. M. XI, 1, 3, 6–7, 10–11, 19–24, 41, 43–44, 48–51, 62, 79, 85, 89, 107, 121, 148, 168–169, 179–180, 184–185, 188–189, 192–193, 203
Bally, Charles 22, 101–102, 106, 110
Barber, Bernard 12, 27
Barberino, Francesco da 35
Bard. *See* Shakespeare, William
Barney, S.A. 95
Barthes, Roland 171, 175
Battle of Maldon 5
Bauchant, Jacques 35
Beatrice 14, 57, 104–105, 107, 116, 124
Beauvais, Vincent de 137
Bede 26
Benson, C.D. 175–176, 178, 191
Benson, L.D. XI, 175, 202
Benveniste, Émile 22
Beowulf 5, 37
Bible 197
Blanche of Lancaster 66
Blois, Peter of 38
Bloom, Harold 58
Bloomfield, M.W. 171
Boccaccio, Giovanni 1–2, 3, 14–15, 55, 57–60, 62, 74, 79, 88, 90, 95–97, 100–101, 105–106, 108, 111–114, 117–119, 122–124, 127, 133, 136–137, 139, 154, 162, 167, 181–185
Boethius 95, 119–120, 183
Boitani, Piero 35, 65, 87, 124–125, 132
Book of the Duchess 1, 14, 50, 61, 66–73, 160
Book of Troilus and Criseyde 2, 4, 15–16, 21, 60, 87–88, 95, 108–109, 120, 125, 127, 132, 134, 137, 149, 165, 167, 170
Bourquin, Guy 68–69
Bres, Jacques 19, 104, 112
Brewer, D.S. 3–4, 66, 86, 90, 203
Butterfield, Ardis 4–5, 27, 30, 32, 36, 59, 62, 83–84

Caesar 138
Candide 41, 115
Canon's Yeoman's Tale 175
Canterbury Tales 6, 16–17, 24, 28, 62, 71, 122, 127–129, 141, 147, 165, 167–204
Cantilupe, Thomas 30–32
Canzoniere 60
Cavalcante de Cavalcanti 105
Celt(s) 25–26, 28, 30, 33–34, 40
Cervantes, Miguel de 62, 168
Chanson de Roland 35
Charles of Anjou 38, 96
Charles V 35
Chaucer, Geoffrey XI, 1–2, 3, 4, 5, 6, 9–17, 19–22, 24–25, 27–37, 48, 50–52, 54–55, 57–61, 63, 65–93, 95–102, 105–115, 118–125, 127–131, 133–134, 136, 138, 141, 144, 146, 151–152, 155–156, 159, 163–165, 167–178, 180–196, 198–204
Chomsky, Noam VII
Cicero 3, 89
Clerk's Tale 176
Cleopatra 117, 128, 130, 136–139, 142, 146
Clifford, James 20
Cligès XI, 44
Coghill, Nevill 196
Collatinus 151, 153
Colonne, Guido delle 147
Complaint to His Lady 88
Confessio amantis 135, 160, 192
Confessions 78, 105
Consolatio Philosophiae 95, 120
Conte du Graal 42, 45
Cook's Tale 192
Criseida 98, 125
Criseyde 2, 4, 15–16, 21, 60, 87–88, 95–98, 106, 108–109, 120–121, 125, 127, 132, 134, 137, 141, 149, 165, 167, 170, 172
Croizy-Naquet, Catherine XI, 39
Curtius, E.R. 1–2, 6, 35, 171

Da Pistoia, Cino 96
Danelaw 26–28
Daniel, Arnaut 56, 58
Dauby, Hélène 195
De Casibus Virorum Illustrium 133

De Civitate Dei 153
De Claris Mulieribus 133, 147
De la Halle, Adam 96
De Miseria condicionis humane 197
De mulieribus claris 79
De Profundis 79
De Ventadour, Bernard 38
Decameron XI, 117, 167, 176, 184–185
Defoe, Daniel 168
Demophon 160–161
Deschamps, Eustache 11, 35, 61, 130–131
Dickens, Charles 52, 101, 113, 168, 172
Dido 77–79, 82, 84, 117–118, 123, 136, 142–147, 157
Dit de la fleur de lis et de la marguerite 130
Dit de la marguerite 130
Dit de Richeut 52
Dittié de la flour de la marguerite 130
Divina Comedia XI, 1, 11, 55, 57, 103
Documenti d'Amore 35
Don Quixote 62
Dor, Juliette 92, 141, 164, 193–194
Dostoevsky, Fiodor XI, 10, 19, 21
Dryden, John 3–5, 170–171
Ducrot, Oswald 22, 102, 104–106, 110

Eclogues 44
Eco, Umberto 9–10, 68
Edward III 60
Eleanor of Aquitaine 38
Eliade, Mircea 86
Eliot, T.S. 65
Enea. *See* Aeneas
Ennius 3
Epistulae morales ad Lucilium 197
Eschenbach, Wolfram von 44
Esthétique et théorie du roman XI, 7, 20–21, 23–24, 41, 44, 50, 62, 79, 121, 168–169, 180, 203

Fables, Ancient and Modern 3–4, 170
Fasti 150, 153
Fielding, Henry 168
Filostrato 2, 15, 57, 62, 95–100, 101–112, 121, 123, 125, 127
First Epistle to the Corinthians 104

Florence 60, 85, 184
Fra Bernabò Reggio 58
Fra Salimbene de Adam 58
Francis of Assisi, Saint 2
Francesca 115–119, 121–124
Frank, R.W.Jr. 131, 133–134, 136, 144, 156, 163, 167
Frederick II 55
Fritz, Jean-Marie XI, 39
Froissart, Jean 14, 30, 66–67, 70, 72, 88, 130
Frye, Northrop 153–154, 163

Galeotto 117–118, 124
Gallehault 117
Ganim, John 6, 172, 176, 204
Garavelli, Bianca XI, 103
Gaunt, John of 66
Geffrey (narrator) 74–75, 77–79, 81–87, 179
Genealogia deorum gentilium 154
General Prologue 28–29, 170–177
General Service List 33
Genette, Gérard 22, 102, 129
Georgics 44
Goethe, Johann Wolfgang von 1, 35
Gospel 201
Gower, John 30, 135, 139, 160, 192, 195
Griselda 184
Guinizelli, Guido 56, 58, 117, 122

Hamlet 1, 125
Henry II 38, 44
Heptarchy 58
Heroides 147
Historia destructionis Troiae 147
Historia regum Britanniae 38
Hoccleve, Thomas 3, 5
Homer 1, 35, 83, 96
Horace 7
House of Fame 1, 14, 62, 73–93, 128, 136, 142, 160, 164, 172, 181, 201–202
Hsy, Jonathan 32
Hypermnestra 17, 162–165, 172
Hypsipyle 147–150, 154, 157, 160

Il Fiore 55, 97
In Johannis evangelium tractatus 78
Inferno 14, 85, 89, 103, 105, 115–116, 118–120, 122, 137
Innocent III 197

James, Henry 176
Jason 147–150, 156, 160
Jeremy 197
Jerome, Saint 197
Jugement dou Roy de Behaigne 67
Jugement dou Roy de Navarre 155

Kittredge, G.L. 176
Knight's Tale 120, 170, 181, 185
Kristeva, Julia 21–22, 193

La Paix aux Anglais 52
La Trahison des images 173
Labov, William 12
Lai de Franchise 131
Lancaster 59, 66
Lancaster, Humphrey of 59
Lancelot (prose) 46, 117
Lancelot ou le Chevalier de la Charrette 42
Larner, John 58–60
Latini, Brunetto 13, 55
Le Conte du Graal 42
Legend of Ariadne 154, 159, 182
Legend of Cleopatra 130, 136, 146
Legend of Dido 142
Legend of Good Women 2, 16, 24, 79, 95, 125, 127–128, 131–134, 136–146, 156, 163, 165, 167, 180
Legend of Hypermnestra 162, 172
Legend of Hypsipyle and Medea 147, 150, 154
Legend of Lucretia 150, 153–154
Legend of Philomela 159
Legend of Phyllis 160
Legend of Thisbe 139, 141
Le Goff, Jacques 2
Leith, Dick 26, 28
Letters to Atticus 7

Lewis, C.S. 2, 37, 45–46, 48, 61, 98–100
Libeaus Desconus 157
Livy 150, 152–154
Lollard 3
Lollius 75, 108, 111, 114
Lorris, Guillaume de 2, 13, 15, 37, 45, 47, 49–50, 53, 97, 130–131, 135
Lucretia 147, 150–154, 163
Lydgate, John 3, 11

Machaut, Guillaume de 8, 14, 30, 66–67, 69–71, 88, 130, 139
Magritte, René 173
Man of Law's Tale 181, 192
Mantova, Sordello of 96
Matthew 1–2, 197
Medea 147–150, 154, 157, 160
Mehl, Dieter 108–109
Merchant's Tale 156
Metamorphoses 44, 139–140, 147, 154–155, 159
Meun, Jean de 13, 47, 49–50, 53, 96, 130
Miller's Prologue 4
Miller's Tale 150, 170, 192
Monk's Tale 57
Monmouth, Geoffrey of 38
Muscatine, Charles 50–51, 52, 71, 92, 97, 112–113, 151, 173

Nakao, Yoshiyuki 10, 69, 100, 106, 108, 119, 146
Nicholas Nickleby 113
Normans 1, 25, 28
Novikoff, Alex 8–9
Nun's Priest's Tale 148

Odyssey 182
Old English 24–27
Orbicciani, Bonagiunta 55
Ovid 44, 69, 72, 77, 79, 98–99, 133, 139–142, 147, 150–156, 162
Ovide moralisé 139, 154–156

Palamon and Arcite 181–182, 184
Pandaro 100, 125

Pandarus 100, 111–115, 119–120, 125, 149, 165, 172, 186
Pangloss 115
Paolo and Francesca 115–118, 121, 123–124
Paradis d'amour 131
Paradiso 85–86
Pardoner's Prologue 181
Pardoner's Tale 196
Parliament of Fowls 1–2, 14, 88, 136
Parson's Prologue 169
Parzifal 44
Patrick, Saint 189
Pearsall, Derek 187–188
Peterborough Chronicles 27
Petrarch, Francesco 1, 14, 55, 58–60, 62, 136
Phaedra 155–158, 160
Philomela 159
Philomena 159
Phyllis 160–161, 163
Physician's Tale 195
Pizan, Christine de 139
Prioress's Tale 178
Privilège aux Bretons 52
Procne 159–160
Purgatorio 75, 77, 82, 124
Pushkin, Alexandre 168
Pyramus 139–141, 150

Rabelais, François 1, 21, 169, 188–189
Reeve's Tale 32, 52, 190–191
Richard II 131
Richter, Michael 30–31
Robert I 58, 96
Roman de Brut 38
Roman de la Rose XI, 13, 35, 37, 45–47, 49–50, 53, 55, 57, 61, 66, 70, 89, 95, 113, 130, 160
Roman de Rou 38
Roman de Troie 38, 142
Roman d'Énéas 142
Rossiter, W.T. 59–60, 88

Salisbury, John of 38
Scheler, Manfred 33–34
Schönau, Elizabeth of 35
Scogan, Henry 3

Scott, Walter 168
Seneca 197
Shakespeare, William 101, 136, 152, 176
Shipman's Tale 176
Shippey, T.A. 28, 30, 33
Shorter English Dictionary 33–34
Sir Gawain and the Green Knight 32, 157
Sir Thopas 178, 200–201
Somnium Scipionis 89
Spearing, A.C. 177, 199
Speculum historiale 137
Spenser, Edmund 3
Statius 116
Stendhal 101
Strohm, Paul 4–5, 92, 129, 168
Strubel, Armand XI, 47, 49, 53
Summoner's Tale 32
Surrey (Henry Howard) 88

Tale of Melibee 178, 200, 202
Tarquinius 150–153, 164
Taruskin, Richard 8
Taylor, Karla 75–76, 79–80, 82, 87, 104–105, 110–111, 114, 122, 169, 202
Tereus 159
Teseida 15, 88, 90, 154, 181–182
Tesoretto 55, 62
Theseus 155–158, 160–161, 182–184
Thisbe 136, 139–142, 146
Tiptoft, John 59
Todorov, Tzvetan 21–22
Tolkien, Christopher 196
Tolkien, J.R.R. 5, 31, 191
Treatise on the Astrolabe 65
Trecento 2, 13, 15, 37, 55, 57–58, 60
Trevelyan, G.M. 1–2
Trigg, Stephanie 4

Trionfi 55
Tristan 39
Troilus 2, 4, 15–16, 21, 60, 87–88, 95–98, 106, 108–109, 120, 125, 127, 132, 134, 137, 149, 165, 167, 170, 172
Troiolo 98–99
Troyes, Chrétien de 2, 12–13, 15, 35, 37, 39–40, 42, 55

Usk, Thomas 3

Valerius Flaccus 147
Verine, Bertrand 104, 112
Vikings 1, 25–26, 28
Virgil 1, 3, 37, 44, 58, 74, 77–80, 84–85, 89–90, 103–104, 107, 115–116, 118, 133, 142–145
Vita Nuova 14, 45–46, 50, 57, 98
Voltaire 41, 115

Wace 38
Wales, Gerald of 38
Wallace, David 55, 60, 85, 96–97
Walter, Philippe 12–13
Wanderer 5
Weinreich, Uriel 11
Wife of Bath's Tale 51
Wilcockson, Colin 71
Wilde, Oscar 79
Woolf, Virginia 125
Wyatt, Thomas 88

Yvain, le Chevalier au lion 42

Zola, Émile 171
Zumthor, Paul 13, 83

Themes and Concepts

Acculturation 12
Actual enunciation 105, 129
Allegory, allegorical 13–14, 37, 45–49, 66, 70–71, 75, 95, 97, 101, 125, 130–131, 173
Ancient 3–4, 6, 11, 13, 28, 38–41, 96, 106, 115, 117–118, 123, 143, 152, 168, 170–171
Antiquity 2, 5, 7, 10, 21, 24, 37, 45, 50, 52, 122, 132, 148, 182
Anxiety of influence 58
Arthurian 13, 35, 38, 45–46, 195
Authentication 2, 15, 87, 106
Authorial responsibility 84
Authorial voice 13, 54, 60
Autodialogism 19, 110

Bilingualism 11, 28, 30, 33
Bivocal narration 14, 54, 79–80, 97, 142
Bivocal prose 6
Bourgeois tradition 13, 50, 52–53, 55, 61, 93, 171

Cacophony 2, 15, 49, 90–91, 136, 173, 184–185, 203
Carnivalesque 2, 6, 13, 15, 21, 62, 72, 85, 89–90, 148, 169–170, 179, 184, 186, 188, 190–191, 194, 197
Characterization 52, 140, 151, 170–177, 182
Chaucerian 1, 3–4, 5, 6, 17, 22, 35, 58, 63, 69, 85, 101, 106, 108, 140, 142, 146, 151, 167, 170–172, 175–176, 179–181, 188, 194, 203–204
Chivalric novel(s) 41, 43–44, 50, 54, 62, 156–158, 168
Chronotope 41–42, 120–122, 168–169
Circumlocution 77

Classics 10, 38, 77, 181–182
Code-switching 31–33
Conjointure 39–40, 129
Comedy 2, 16, 52, 71, 75–76, 79–80, 82, 87, 105, 110–111, 114, 122, 135, 141, 147–154, 160, 167, 169, 188, 191, 202
Continuous present 1
Contrapasso 122

Countrapuntal 8
Courtly code 50, 99–100, 152, 165
Courtly love 1–2, 15–16, 37, 47, 51, 55, 62, 91, 96–97, 99–101, 112–114, 123, 127–128, 130–131, 136–137, 145, 148–149, 173–174, 180–181, 188
Courtly love poetry 11–12, 17, 24, 38, 45, 53, 55–58, 61, 63, 66, 96–97, 117, 130, 133, 135, 165, 167, 172, 180
Cultural assimilation 12

Dantean 57, 62–63, 74–75, 79–82, 84, 108, 115, 121–122, 142
Dialogism, dialogic 1–2, 3, 6–7, 13–15, 17, 19–22, 37, 49, 52–55, 61, 63, 65, 68, 70, 73, 79, 92, 104–105, 107, 109, 111–112, 118, 124, 128, 136, 153, 155–156, 170, 173, 177, 180, 194, 203
Dialogization 19
Diatribe(s) 7
Diegesis 3, 17, 70, 73, 93, 95, 107, 129, 178, 200, 202
Diglossia 25
Discourse 1, 7, 19, 21–24, 31–32, 42–43, 49–50, 52–54, 61–62, 66, 68, 71–73, 84, 101–104, 106, 112, 128–129, 155, 171, 180, 184, 193, 202
Discursive 19, 21, 53, 65–93, 96, 102, 129, 133, 136, 155, 171
Disjointure 40
Disputatio. See Disputation
Disputation 7–9
Dolce Stil Novo 1, 12–13, 37, 55–60, 62
Double enunciation 2, 6, 15, 22, 95–125
Drama, dramatic 8, 24, 52, 54, 106, 111, 148, 156, 163, 170, 173, 175–178, 191, 201, 203

Early Modern 2–3
Enunciation 1–2, 6, 15, 19, 22, 95–125, 129, 160
Enunciative heterogeneity 19
Enunciative lamination 105
Enunciative staging 22, 105
Epistolary novel(s) 23

Exemplum 197–199
Exotopy, exotopic 107, 110, 112
Extradiegetic dialogue 3, 17, 129, 165, 167–204

Fabliau(x) 50, 52, 62, 136, 147, 172, 176, 181, 184–190, 192, 194–195
Fin'amor 1–2, 11–12, 14–17, 37–63, 65–67, 74, 88, 93, 96–100, 112–113, 115–119, 123–125, 130–131, 133, 135, 137, 143, 148, 150–151, 165, 180
Folkloric 50, 52, 169, 184, 188
French XI, 1, 4–5, 6, 12–14, 24, 27–35, 38, 44, 51–52, 55, 58–59, 61–63, 66–67, 70–73, 88, 92, 96–97, 102, 113, 117, 131, 151, 173

Game(s) 2, 21, 82, 87, 100, 151, 164–165, 181
Génies-mères 1
Geste 39
Go-between 113–114, 117–118, 149
Grotesque lowering 179, 186–187
Grotesque realism 50–52, 61, 63, 71, 85, 184–186

Hagiography(ies) 16, 172, 176, 193
Hastings 27–28
Heaven 51, 56, 85–86, 116–118, 121, 132, 169, 183, 188–189
Hell 41, 89–90, 109, 117–118, 121–123, 132, 169, 189, 196
Hermeneutics 8, 65
Heteroglossic 61
Humanism 3, 59
Humanist(s) 3
Hybridization 2–3, 16–17, 127–165, 170

Inamoramento 47, 90, 99, 112, 119, 143
Industrial Revolution 2
Inselgermanisch 33–34
Interdiscursive dialogue 37, 65, 73, 87, 93, 101, 118, 124, 129, 152
Interlocutive dialogue 73
Intertextuality 3, 11, 14–15, 16, 39–40, 46, 95, 129, 159, 194
Intralocutive dialogue 110

Irony, ironic 2, 6, 9, 16, 50, 71–72, 74, 92, 113, 132, 142, 154–165, 169, 196

Kentish 32

Language contact 11, 25, 28, 36
Latin XI, 1–2, 3, 4, 6, 9, 12–13, 24–25, 28–35, 37–39, 44–45, 59, 96–97, 139, 141, 171, 195
Lingua franca 25, 59
Linguistic assimilation 12
Literariness 92, 133
Lowering 52, 85, 89–90, 118, 179, 186–187, 189

Medievalization 99
Memory 10, 66, 69, 82, 108, 117, 121, 124, 204
Metatextuality 129
Middle Ages 1–2, 4, 6–7, 13, 21, 24, 35, 37, 47, 61, 82–83, 139, 142, 159, 171, 189, 197–198
Middle English 1, 3, 12, 29, 32–36, 74, 88, 191
Modal subject 102–104, 106–107, 109–110, 124
Monology, monolgism, monologic 7, 9–10, 128, 155–156
Multiculturalism 14
Multilingual, multilingualism 1, 7, 11–12, 14, 19–36, 49, 58, 60–61, 63, 67, 203

Narrative frame 15, 104, 122, 158, 167, 172, 175, 203
Narrative poetry 1, 24, 130–136, 139, 165
Naturalism 1, 113, 171
Norman invasion 27–36
Novel 1–2, 3, 4, 6–7, 10, 13, 15, 19–21, 23, 39–44, 49–50, 52, 54, 56, 62–63, 83, 101–102, 107, 124–125, 143, 156–158, 168, 180, 183, 203
Novelistic discourse 7, 23
Novelistic genre 37, 44–45, 49, 52, 54–55, 98, 100, 112, 124, 142, 168, 179

Occupatio 143, 181
Old English 12, 27–29
Old Norse 26–27
Ottava rima 88, 182

Paradise. *See* Heaven
Parody, parodic 2, 16, 52, 62, 66, 70, 91–92, 131–132, 154–160, 186, 188, 191, 200
Pathos 2, 16, 102, 147–154, 158, 160, 163, 193
Persona 2, 14, 16–17, 45, 49, 70–71, 84–85, 90, 101, 103–105, 135, 177–180, 187, 192, 200, 203
Pidginization 25–26, 28
Pluristylistic 23, 158
Polyglossic 71
Polyphony, polyphonic 1–2, 3, 5–12, 15–17, 19–36, 62–63, 65, 74, 91–92, 101, 104, 107, 125, 129, 136, 165, 168, 173, 176, 191, 193, 203
Polyvocal 1, 23–24, 61, 66–67, 92, 158
Polyvocality 1–2, 6, 12–16, 23, 39, 42, 49–50, 52, 54, 60–61, 69, 170, 176
Purgatory 56, 76, 80, 116–117, 120–121, 169, 189

Quodlibetical disputations 8

Realism 1, 4, 50–52, 61, 63, 70–71, 85, 170–172, 175, 184–186
Renaissance 1–2, 3, 13, 15, 37, 52, 96–98, 189
Reprocessing 96, 100–101, 112, 115, 118, 123

Rhetoric, rhetorical 3, 7–8, 39, 41, 46, 52–53, 57, 66, 69–70, 77, 87, 98, 115, 139, 141, 160, 164, 167, 176, 181, 194, 197–199, 203
Rhyme royal 88, 182, 201
Roman Empire 39
Romance language(s) 39, 44
Romanesque 39, 41
Rome 25, 44, 137, 151–152, 193, 197

Satire 7, 21, 50, 173, 180, 194
ScaPoLinE 129
Scriba Dei 102, 108, 124
Social stratification 12
Sociolinguistic 6, 12, 32
Speaking subject 19, 101–102, 104, 107, 109–110, 112, 118, 124, 135–136, 138, 176
Stilnovism 55, 57, 63, 65, 93
Stilnovist(s) 37, 57, 59, 62–63, 97, 116
Substratum 34
Superstratum 34
Synaesthesia 76

Terzine 76
Theatrical, theatricality 6, 170, 172, 176–177, 204
Trecento 2, 13, 15, 37, 55, 57–58, 60
Troubadour(s) 13, 35, 37–38, 55–56, 62, 96
Trouvère(s) 9, 13, 35, 37, 44–45, 55–56, 62
Tydynges 81–83

Verisimilitude 46, 120, 151, 171, 173–175
Vernacular(s) 9–12, 25, 31, 35–38, 42, 55–56, 58–60, 62, 65–66, 95, 142
Visibile parlare 76, 78, 142
Visible speech 75–77, 79–82, 84, 87, 142

www.ingramcontent.com/pod-product-compliance
Lightning Source LLC
Chambersburg PA
CBHW070801230426
43665CB00017B/2443